Redating the Teacher of Righteousness

by
B. E. THIERING

AUSTRALIAN AND NEW ZEALAND
STUDIES IN THEOLOGY AND RELIGION

1979

AUSTRALIAN AND NEW ZEALAND
STUDIES IN THEOLOGY AND RELIGION

Number One

Published by

THEOLOGICAL EXPLORATIONS

Box 2197
G.P.O., Sydney
AUSTRALIA

© B. E. THIERING, 1979

Printed by

GLENBURN PTY. LIMITED, Chatswood, Sydney

Typeset and Assembly by

BOYES-SINCLAIR (TYPOGRAPHY) PTY. LIMITED, Brookvale, Sydney

National Library of Australia
ISBN 0 85821 3052

Contents

I.   Introduction   1

PART I

RETRACING SOME STEPS

    II.   Once More the Wicked Priest   8

    III.   The Young Lion Again   22

    IV.   The Palaeographical Dating of 1QS, 4QpIsa^c and 4QD^a 34

    V.   Further Observations Relevant to the Date of the Teacher   50

           The Tenses of the *pesharim*
           The Uses of "Kittim"
           The 390 Years
           The Absence of the Teacher from Contemporary Records
           Was the Teacher in the Roman Period?

PART II

THE TEACHER'S DOCTRINE AND
ITS PLACE IN THE HISTORY

    VI.   The Heavenly Temple   60

    VII.   The Priestly Messiah   75

    VIII.   The Stages of Initiation   90

PART III

THE RECONSTRUCTION

    IX.   Starting-point and Methodology   105

    X.   The Reconstruction   114
       (A separate table of contents for this chapter will be found p.115)

    XI.   The Historical Setting   203

    Abbreviations and Indices   217

CHAPTER ONE

Introduction

It has for some time been apparent that, following the publication of more of the Dead Sea Scrolls, a reconsideration of the history of the Qumran community is necessary, taking into account the new evidence. The Temple Scroll, published only in 1977, supplies sixty-seven columns of new data for a certain stage of the community's outlook. Other fragments have appeared from time to time, and have not yet been absorbed into an historical hypothesis.

The archaeological, palaeographical, historical and literary evidence that was available in the first few years has led to certain agreed conclusions, which form the basis of most historical hypotheses. It will be useful at this point to recall the outlines of the established case.

The Present View of the History

We first hear of the Essenes in Josephus' account of the second half of the second century B.C. He introduces them, together with the Pharisees and Sadducees, in the course of his history of the Maccabean Jonathan (160-142 B.C.).[1] Judas the Essene, who uttered prophecies in the temple, appears in 103 B.C.[2]

Pliny the Elder places a settlement of Essenes on the west side of the Dead Sea, above the town of Engedi.[3] The archaeological evidence shows that Qumran, which answers to this description, was first occupied about the same time as the earliest mention of the Essenes in Josephus, and was expanded 135-104 B.C.[4]

1

The contents of the scrolls link them with the Essenes rather than with any other contemporary group of Jews. 1QS shows that the Qumran community held property in common; so also did the Essenes. They held a regular communal meal of bread and new wine; the Essenes are the only Jews known to have celebrated a daily communal meal. The extreme sobriety and self-discipline of the members is well attested in both sources, as is also their hierarchical approach to organisation and the fact that they had several stages of initiation.[5] The early conclusion, that the Qumran literature is in some way Essene, must certainly stand.

It is admitted that the scrolls contain a great deal more than is known of the Essenes in the contemporary sources. An intense apocalypticism, the expectation of a coming fiery catastrophe and a new messianic era, are nowhere attributed to the Essenes, whom Josephus presents as a peace-loving, highly rational society concerned only with present piety. Neither is there mention of their distinctive doctrine of the New Covenant. But Josephus' tendency to assimilate his subjects to the expectations and sympathies of his Greek readers is well known. Even the fact that he lived among the Essenes as a boy would not outweigh his habit of diplomatic re-interpretation.

In a certain number of the Qumran writings, but not all of them, there are references to the Teacher of Righteousness, *môreh haṣṣedeq,* a leader and revered figure. CD 1:5-11 gives a chronological fact about him: he appeared twenty years after the formation of the "Plant-root", the community which is the subject of CD and 1QS. The Plant-root was itself formed "390 years to the giving *(lĕtitto)* them into the hand of Nebuchadnezzar king of Babylon". If this phrase means "390 years after the fall of Jerusalem", it gives a second century B.C. date for the formation of the community, and a date twenty years later for the appearance of the Teacher. These dates (197 B.C. for the community, 177 B.C. for the Teacher) are too early for the Essenes, but the figure of 390 is taken from Ezek 4:5 and is therefore to be understood loosely, and in any case the exact duration of the Persian period was not known to the writers.

There appears, then, to be reason for putting the Teacher also in the time of Essene origins. There is one immediately obvious fact in the way: the Teacher nowhere appears in the contemporary accounts of the Essenes. This is rather harder to deal with than the lack of mention of their special doctrines. Josephus as a boy might not have heard all their teachings, but he could scarcely have failed to hear about their great founder. In the Roman period, it was held that all the prophecies of scripture led up to him and referred to events in his history (1QpHab). Josephus would surely have heard of him, and have seized the opportunity to present a great spiritual personality to his Greek readers. Nevertheless, this difficulty seems to be overruled by the other evidence.

The main objective evidence for the date of the Teacher is the palaeographical dating of the copies of the writings in which he appears, or which are dependent on him. He could not have lived after the time of their composition.

The system of palaeographical analysis of F. M. Cross[6] has commanded widespread respect because of its emphasis on what are clearly significant indicators of chronological relationship: changes in the method of drawing letters as a result of evolutionary development. For example, a *bet* whose base-line is drawn from left to right, projecting to the right of the downstroke, is later than a *bet* whose base-line continues from the downstroke in a right to left direction. The change of method occurred in order to distinguish *bet* from *kaf,* which was originally a long letter, quite unlike the shorter *bet,* but towards the Herodian period shortened to the same size. Observations of such changes as these, establishing the relationship of one style to another, together with a few absolute dates, have been able to determine the broad periods within which the scripts should be placed: Archaic, Hasmonean or Herodian. Different categories of script have also been isolated: the formal series, professional hands conforming to an accepted method and thus easily able to be set in an evolutionary sequence; cursives; and between them the semiformals and semicursives, mixing the two kinds in different proportions.

The majority of documents dealing with the Teacher of Righteousness are in a Herodian script. However, one fragment of CD is in a script whose date is given as 75-50 B.C. 1QS, which is dependent on the Teacher's doctrine, 4QS^e, one of its fragments, and also one of the *pesharim* (4QpIsa^c) are put in classes of Hasmonean script. If these datings are correct, they prove that the Teacher was in the time of Essene origins, as already suggested by archaeology, history, and CD 1:5-11.

A further support is in the fact that only a few of the writings mention the Kittim, which is certainly a name for the Romans. The Roman power entered Judean history in 63 B.C., after the time of Essene origins. The Kittim are not named in CD and 1QS, but only in parts of 1QM, which does not mention the Teacher, and some of the *pesharim.* This is consistent with an earlier date for the Teacher.

The Teacher, a high priest to his supporters, must have been a member of the expelled Zadokite dynasty, who had been replaced in office by the popularly accepted Hasmonean house. This follows from the fidelity of his party to biblical law: they could not have accepted him as high priest on any other basis. On the assumption of a Hasmonean date, it was then possible to give a plausible interpretation of the Wicked Priest, the object of the hostility of the writers of 1QpHab and 4QpPs[a]. He would have been a Hasmonean high priest, the Teacher's rival. On the occasion when he disturbed the members on the Day of Atonement (1QpHab 11:4-8), he was taking advantage of the fact that they observed a different religious calendar from his own, in order to persecute them as an outlawed sect.

The early conclusions appear to have sufficient support, and to fit together very well. The identity of the writers with Essenes, and the time of the foundation of the Qumran community as a group of Essenes, are soundly established. When to these facts are added: (a) the reading of CD 1:5-11 (on the Teacher of Righteousness) as referring to the origin of the same Essenes; (b) the palaeographical date of scrolls referring to the Teacher; and (c) the absence of Kittim from most writings referring to the Teacher, there seem to be good reasons for treating the history of the Teacher as the same history as that of the early Essenes. It must be noted, however, that these three items are the *only* positive reasons for linking the Teacher with early Essenism. If the literary evidence should be read differently, and the palaeographical datings were successfully challenged on palaeographical grounds, there would be *no* reason for placing the Teacher in the time of Essene origins. The two difficulties mentioned in the course of the summary —the unattested doctrines and the absence of the Teacher from contemporary accounts of the Essenes—would then come into greater prominence as being really significant obstacles.

A further difficulty, apparently minor, for the present opinion may be noted. Col. 1 of the *pesher* (commentary) on Nahum was published very early, but cols. 2-4 not until several years later.[7] On the basis of col. 1 alone, it was concluded by most scholars that this work was of no relevance to the Teacher of Righteousness, as it concerned—they believed—Alexander Jannaeus, who was the "Young Lion of Wrath". Alexander (102-76 B.C.) lived later than the time of Essene origins. But cols. 2-4 deal in detail with "Ephraim" and "Manasseh", who in another of the *pesharim* (4QpPs[a] 2:17) are a particular group of enemies of the Teacher. There is a further possible link between the Nahum *pesher* and the Teacher: the Young Lion of Wrath of 4QpNah 1:5-6 is also named in 4QpHos[b],[8] and this fragment also mentions the "Last Priest", who may be one of the "last priests" who are

4

connected with the Teacher's enemies in 1QpHab 9:4-5. If the "Ephraim" and "Manasseh" of 4QpNah 2-4 were the *same* enemies as those who attacked the Teacher in 4QpPs[a] 2:17, then a substantial revision of the date of the Teacher would have to be made, bringing him into the time of the Young Lion of Wrath.

But these connections have not been given significance by most writers.[9] The Qumran use of symbolic terms, such as "Ephraim" and "Manasseh", has been held to be vague and imprecise. The pesharists are capable of arbitrariness, as, for example, in their assumption that the prophecies of scripture refer to their own times. They have consequently been thought to be capable of considerable verbal inconsistency. The literary analyses of J. Murphy-O'Connor,[10] which have pioneered the observation of changes in organisational terminology as a means of discovering the different historical levels, take the assumption of verbal inconsistency very far, justifying it on such grounds as that "among the Essenes it was not unknown for the same biblical phrase to be interpreted in radically different ways".[11] On this view, it is not difficult to dismiss similar terms in writings which are held for other reasons to be unconnected. Murphy-O'Connor reads the names "Ephraim" and "Manasseh" as "englobing the whole of non-Qumran Judaism".[12]

The Use of the Literary Evidence

The grounds on which the accepted conclusions were drawn are, as stated above, archaeological, palaeographical, historical (the histories of Josephus, Philo, Pliny) and literary. Of these, literary, that is, the internal evidence of the scrolls themselves, comes a bad last. The contents of the writings have been sufficient to supply a positive link between the writers of the scrolls and the Essenes, but their vague, polemical, tendentious style, with the possibility of arbitrariness that has been noted, has led to their being given a low estimate as a source of objective historical evidence. The best that can be done, it is believed, is the observation of clear differences between them, such as the conflicting rules about the control of property in 1QS 5:2-3 and 9:7, and the absence of certain major interests from parts of 1QM. These show different stages of development within the community, but say little or nothing about its place in external history.

The procedure of the present study is to give rather more value to the textual evidence than has yet been done. The text will be assumed to be consistent, until proven inconsistent, rather than the reverse. There is already apparent a habit of consistency that has not been given sufficient weight. Once the pesharists have made their (to us) arbitrary assumption that all the prophecies of scripture refer to their own times, and given

5

particular applications to the scriptural terms, they never change them. The "righteous" of scripture is always interpreted of the Teacher of Righteousness, and named foreign enemies in the OT are always the Kittim.

Their treatment of the general terms of scripture as a source of specific terminology for their movement also gives reason to suppose that they used general terms in a specific fashion themselves. The Teacher of Righteousness is now usually held to be a particular individual, although this is not clearly apparent from his title "he who teaches righteousness". Terms like "House of Truth", "House of the Law" appear to have special meanings in the organisational structure; the former is used in 1QS 5:6 for the house of laity, as opposed to the house of priests. Particular terms constitute useful evidence, which may well be concealed in the apparently general phraseology of the text.

The assumption of consistency and specificity means that many of the original conclusions, which do not make this assumption, must be looked at again.

In Part I of this work, several steps leading to the early conclusions will be retraced. The accepted view of the Wicked Priest (derived from the Hasmonean dating) will be shown to rest on an inadequate understanding of the methodology of the *pesharim* and the meaning of sectarian terms. The accepted interpretation of the Young Lion of Wrath similarly does not take into account the techniques of the *pesharim*. It will be shown also that the few writings whose script is said to give a Hasmonean date are in special categories which further evidence indicates to be later than supposed. The present reading of CD 1:5-11, and the significance of the occurrences of the name "Kittim", will also be challenged on the basis of Qumran usage. As a result of these reconsiderations, the internal evidence for the date of the Teacher must be given greater weight. The tenses of the *pesharim* may show that he was alive in the *Roman* period, not part of early Essenism, but the leader of a later offshoot from the Essene movement, the "Plant-root" of CD 1:5-11. This would account for his absence from the records of the Essenes, and for the unfamiliar doctrines in the writings connected with him.

In Part II, a study of the special doctrines and organisation of the Teacher will be undertaken, necessary for the close analysis of changes in the community structures that will lead to the recovery of the details of the history.

The reconstruction itself will be found in Part III. The successive stages of the history centring round the Teacher will be demonstrated from a very detailed analysis of the writings, making the general assumptions that have been discussed. In the final chapter, the correspondences of this history to events in the time of the Roman occupation of Palestine will be considered, leading finally to an approach to the question of an historical link with the movement that shows so many affinities, doctrinal and organisational, with the Qumran community: the early Christian Church.

We proceed now to a reconsideration of some of the conclusions drawn in the very early days of scrolls research.

NOTES

1. *Ant.* 13§§171-3.
2. *Ant.* 13§§310-13.
3. *Hist. Nat.* 5,15§73.
4. R. de Vaux, *Archaeology and the Dead Sea Scrolls* (OUP, 1973), 3-24.
5. See M. Burrows, *The Dead Sea Scrolls* (London: Secker & Warburg, 1955), 279-294.
6. See ch. IV.
7. Col. 1 was published in *JBL* 75 (1956) 89-95; 2-4 in *JSS* 7 (1962) 304-308. Now in *DJD* V, 37-42. G. Jeremias, in his 1963 study of the Teacher of Righteousness (*Der Lehrer der Gerechtigkeit,* Göttingen: Vandenhoeck & Ruprecht) did not take into account cols. 2-4.
8. Formerly 4QpHos^a (4Q*167*). *DJD* V, 32-36.
9. J. Carmignac, in his reconstruction of the history, used them to identify the Wicked Priest with Alexander Jannaeus (*Les Textes de Qumrân Traduits et Annotés* (Paris: Gabalda, 1961 and 1963, II) 48-60), but this theory has not generally been found acceptable. For details, see ch. II, footnote 9.
10. For details and a critique, see ch. IX, note 14.
11. J. Murphy-O'Connor, "The Essenes and their History", *RB* 81 (1974) 215-244, p.222, n.39. He gives this reason to justify his conclusion that "Damascus" means "Babylon" in one place and "Qumran" in another. The example of different interpretations of the same biblical phrase is drawn from the interpretation in 1QpHab of the biblical text Hab 2:8b and 2:17 (the same words, repeated in the Habakkuk passage). But the two occurrences of the text are dealt with in the *pesher* in related ways: the first is found to concern the Wicked Priest's past punishment; the second his future punishment. On p.52 following a reason for the variation will be suggested.
12. "The Essenes . . .", 241.

part one

Retracing
Some Steps

CHAPTER TWO

Once More the Wicked Priest

It has come to be widely accepted that the Wicked Priest, *hakkôhen harasa'*, of 1QpHab and 4QpPs[a] was a reigning high priest, the official incumbent of the Jerusalem high priesthood, opposed by the community as the representative of the religious establishment.

The identification was made early, on what seemed to be adequate grounds. The Wicked Priest "ruled over Israel" (1QpHab 8:9-10). The Day of Atonement episode (1QpHab 11:4-8), in which the Wicked Priest "pursued after the Teacher of Righteousness to swallow him up" and "caused to stumble" his followers, was easily explained as an attack on the Teacher, who was a schismatic high priest, by his official counterpart in Jerusalem. The occasion was the sect's celebration of a different Day of Atonement according to an unofficial calendar. The deep hostility shown for the Wicked Priest is consistent with the feelings generated by the breach between the Hasidim and the Hasmonean house.

The only difficulty was thought to be his exact identity: which of the usurping high priests of the period of Essene origins fits the data best? G. Jeremias[1] carefully assembles all the known facts about the Wicked Priest, and selects the main fact useful for identification, that he met his death at the hands of Gentiles. For the period in question, this fits only Menelaus (172-162 B.C.) and Jonathan (161-142 B.C.). Menelaus is too early, and could never have been approved at first by the community ("was called by the name of truth when he first arose" (1QpHab 8:9), understood by Jeremias to mean that he had a good reputation with the Essenes at first, but they later changed their minds). Jonathan fits the facts best, in Jeremias' view. He would have been approved by the sectarians until he officially adopted the high priestly office, some years after he became ruler. His character is not known to correspond to the arrogance and greed of

---

* This chapter has appeared, in a slightly different form, in *JBL* 97 (1978), 191-205. Acknowledgement is made to the Editor for permission to reproduce it.

the Wicked Priest (8:2-12), but we must allow for the polemical style. His association with violent men and his robbery of the people (8:11) could reflect an episode when he and his brother attacked members of a wedding to avenge their brother's death.[2] He probably also took temple treasures, like all his successors. His death at the hands of Gentiles is not known to have been painful (cf. 1QpHab 9:1-2, 9-12), but the sources are simply silent on the subject.

Stegemann and Murphy-O'Connor,[3] the more recent writers on Qumran history, agree that the Wicked Priest is Jonathan. The latter follows Jeremias' view of "called by the name of truth": it refers to the "honeymoon" period before Jonathan adopted the high priestly office. His "temporizing character" led him to ally himself with the ruling classes who loved wealth and pleasure; he profited by their depredations. This fits 1QpHab 8:11.

In a book published in 1973, F. M. Cross[4] has re-affirmed his view that 4QTestim 21-30 must be taken into account as evidence for the Wicked Priest. It speaks (he believes) of a "cursed man" and his two sons, who rebuilt Jericho. This and the other data fit Simon Maccabeus (142-135), who with his two sons was murdered by his Idumean son-in-law Ptolemy while on a tour of Jericho. Jeremias[5] dismisses Cross's view, on the grounds that there is no evidence that the document refers to the Wicked Priest, even if it refers to Simon.

It will be observed that the only exact correspondence that Jeremias and those who follow him can find with Jonathan is the fact that he was put to death at the hands of Gentiles. This is not sufficient to make the identification certain. There is no other exact correspondence. The main emphasis of the lines dealing with the Wicked Priest's death is on its painful nature (9:1-2, 9-12); nothing corresponding to this element has been found. If "called by the name of truth when he first arose" means that he was approved by the Essenes before he was proclaimed high priest, it must be demonstrated conclusively that Josephus is wrong when he says that Judas Maccabeus, Jonathan's predecessor, was popularly accepted as high priest,[6] although (as is implied in *Ant.* 20§237) not officially appointed. It must also be established that "called by the name of truth" has the rather vague meaning that Jeremias gives it ("had a good reputation, was acceptable") in writings where both "name" and "truth" have exact and special connotations (see below pp.16-17). And would the sect have called him "the Priest", a titular term, as Stegemann shows,[7] if he was to them illegitimate?

Cross is not wrong in finding that 4QTestim 21-30 is evidence for the Wicked Priest. Both the "cursed man" and the Wicked Priest "shed blood" (4QTestim 29-30, 1QpHab 9:8-9), were associated with violence *(ḥamas)*

(4QTestim 25. 1QpHab 9:8-9, 12:1-2), built a city/house (4QTestim 25-26, 1QpHab 9:12 - 10:1), and committed wicked deeds in Jerusalem (4QTestim 29-30, 1QpHab 12:7-8). The addition of this evidence, especially the reference to two sons,[8] makes the identification with Jonathan more difficult. But it does not point to Simon, whose murderer was his Idumean son-in-law, not Gentiles. (The passage does not make Jericho part of the data for the Wicked Priest. Jericho is not mentioned in the quotation or what follows, and the fact that it was in the scriptural story behind the passage does not mean that it was taken literally: cf. Chaldeans = Kittim in 1QpHab; Nineveh = Jerusalem in 4QpNah.)

Other identifications with reigning high priests have also proved unsatisfactory.[9] Is there any other reason, apart from the paucity of our data, why the Wicked Priest will not comfortably fit into the facts for any reigning high priest?

Parts of 1QpHab, 4QpPs[a], as well as CD and 1QpMic deal with an enemy of the Teacher variously called the Man of a Lie *('îs hakkazab)*, He who Drips Lies *(mattîp hakkazab)*, *Ṣaw,* and the Man of Scoffing *('îs hallaṣôn)*. A few writers[10] have argued that the Wicked Priest is the same as the Man of a Lie, but then assume that he is a Jerusalem high priest. G. Jeremias has established that the Man of a Lie was "the teacher of a larger group wh:ch split off from the Teacher's community and became a formidable danger to that community, because followers of the Teacher went over to it in considerable numbers. The split occurred in the lifetime of the Teacher".[11] It is our purpose to argue that the Wicked Priest and the Man of a Lie are the same, but on the basis of Jeremias' view that the Man of a Lie was the leader of a schismatic party from the Teacher's community. He was not a Jerusalem high priest. The evidence will be (i) the Qumran principles of biblical exegesis; and (ii) the Qumran use of certain terms in a particular, sectarian sense.

The Qumran Principles of Biblical Exegesis

Some questions must be asked about the way the pesharists understood the overall meaning and specific terms of the biblical passages in which they found the Wicked Priest.

The *pesharim* have been characterized as "atomizing" in their approach. Jeremias[12] finds an example of it in the fact that 1QpHab 11:4-8 describes the Day of Atonement episode, while the following passage (11:12-15) makes no further mention of this event. Almost every section of the *pesharim* introduces a new event or theme.

The atomizing, however, is of the contemporary history, not of the biblical subject-matter. The present-day events are necessarily presented in a disjointed fashion because they are found in the text of scripture, whose unity cannot be broken. In order to avoid violating the sequence of topics in the biblical passage, the pesharist breaks up his own history. Respect for the biblical passage as it stands, its unity, integrity, and sequence of ideas, is a basic principle of exegesis.

There is at times an initial appearance of arbitrariness in the treatment of the biblical text, but closer examination shows that it is a first impression only. For example, in Hab 1:13 the subject of *taḥărîś* ("you (s.) are silent") is "God", consistently with the series of verbs in vv. 12-13, whereas in the *pesher* it is "the house of Absalom" (5:9). But the previous verb, *tabbîṭ* ("you (s.) look upon" is a plural in the Qumran text of Hab (5:8), making the change quite consistent.

At first sight also, 1QpMic 8-10 appears to interfere .with the unity of the biblical verse, Mic 1:5. Where the verse by the parallelistic form makes "Jerusalem" a counterpart to "Samaria", each being the sinful centre of their respective territories, the *pesher* interprets Jerusalem favourably of the Teacher of Righteousness and his faithful followers, whereas "Samaria" is interpreted unfavourably of the Man of a Lie, the Teacher's opponent. But the interpretation is in fact consistent with the sense of the whole passage (Mic 1:2-9) and with the exact meaning of its terms. Mic 1:5 reads in MT: "All this is for the transgression of Jacob and for the sins of the house of Israel. What is the transgression of Jacob? Is it not Samaria? And what are the high places of Judah? Are they not Jerusalem?". Jerusalem is not called a "transgression", but "high places" *(bamôt),* which does not have a pejorative sense in the passage, but simply means "heights": cf. v. 3: "the Lord will come down and tread upon the high places *(bamôt)* of the earth". No punishment for Jerusalem is mentioned in the lines following v. 5: they deal with the punishment of Samaria only. In v.9 Jerusalem is used in the sense of a place that is being contaminated by outside influences, but is itself pure. The pesharist found no reason to suppose that Jerusalem was condemned in the passage. The only indication that it was being treated negatively is in the parallelistic form of v.5. But as J. Starcky remarks:[13] "Les scribes de Qumran ne se croyaient pas liés, dans leur exégèse, par la règle du parallélisme".[14] There was good reason for distinguishing the "sins of the house of Israel" from the "high places of Judah". "Israel" was understood as another name for the north, the same as "Jacob", while "Judah" was the south. There is no violation of the unity of the text in this *pesher;* on the contrary, there is a careful observation of its overall meaning and exactitude concerning its use of words.

A second principle of the *pesharim* needs to be observed, following from their recognized habit of giving particular applications to biblical universals. Once the interpretation of a biblical term was fixed, it did not alter. B:blical words like "the righteous", "the wicked" were read as designations of personalities or elements in the sectarian history. They must, then, always refer to the same particular: the meaning of scripture did not vary. In Jeremias' words:[15] "In the study of the Habakkuk commentary, it has often been overlooked how rigorously the commentator sticks to his biblical text *(Vorlage)*. He never voluntarily departs from it. All pronouncements on the Chaldeans he refers uniformly to the Kittim." The "righteous" is always made to refer either to the Teacher or the sectarians.

The biblical passages in which the Wicked Priest is found are Hab 2:5-17 and Ps 37:32. The *pesher* of the Habakkuk passage also introduces the Man of a Lie, and he is found also in the *pesher* of nearby verses of Ps 37.

Hab 2:6b-17 contains a series of four woes: (1) 6b-8; (2) 9-11; (3) 12-14; (4) 15-17. V.6a shows that they are all woes on the Arrogant Man of v.5: "Shall not all these take up a proverb against *him,* and riddling sayings against *him,* saying . . .", followed by the four woes, with no indication of a change of application until v.18 changes the form. Each woe has a thematic link with either the description of the Arrogant Man (2:5) or with another woe: (1) extortion, cf. 5b; (2) greed, exploitation, cf. 5b (3) building on bloodshed, cf. 8b, the blood of men, 10-11, building a house; (4) insatiab:lity, cf. 5b, and v.17b repeats 8b. *Each of the four woes should, then, be interpreted of the Arrogant Man,* whom the pesharist understands to be the Wicked Priest (1QpHab 8:8). The first, second and fourth *are* interpreted of the Wicked Priest (8:7 - 9:12a; 9:12b - 10:5; 11:2 - 12:10a). But the third woe is interpreted of the Man of a Lie (10:5 - 11:1). The Qumran pesharist, observing both the principles of exegesis set out above, would not have disregarded the clear indications that all the woes are on the Arrogant Man. As the Arrogant Man is determined at the outset as the Wicked Priest, the third woe is on the same man. The Wicked Priest and the Man of a Lie are one and the same.

In the same commentary, the word *raša'* ("wicked") is applied to the Wicked Priest frequently and to the Man of a Lie in 5:9, 11. As "righteous" has a cons:stent application to the Teacher and the sectarians, so "the wicked" should refer to the same enemy and his party.

4QpPs[a], a commentary on Ps 37, finds the Man of a Lie in "him who prospers in his way, the man who carries out evil devices" of Ps 37:7 (J·17-18), and the same figure in the "violent *('arîs)* wicked *(raša')* person" of v.35 (4:13-14). It finds the Wicked Priest in the wicked *(raša')* person who "watches for the righteous and seeks to slay him" of v. 32 (4:7-8).

This verse (32) reads: "The wicked man *(raša')* watches for the righteous *(saddîq)* and seeks to slay him: Yahweh will not abandon him in his hand and will not condemn him when he is judged". It is very similar to v.12: "The wicked *(raša')* plots against the righteous *(saddîq)* and gnashes his teeth at him. Yahweh laughs at him for he sees that his day is coming". The meaning of v.12 is found by the pesharist to be "the violent ones *('arîsîm)* of the Covenant in the House of Judah who will plot to destroy those who do the Law in the Council of the Community" (2:12-14). The House of Judah" is a name for part of the sect itself in CD 4:11 and 1QpHab 8:1.[16] 1QpHab 8:1 reads "('the righteous shall live by his faith') refers to all who do the Law *('ôsê hattôrâ,* cf. 4QpPs[a] 2:14 *'osê hattôrâ)* in the House of Judah". The meaning of "the violent ones of the Covenant in the House of Judah" is, then, "those members of the House of Judah (sectarians) who broke the Covenant (that is, the sectarian version of the Covenant) and began to attack those in the Council of the Community who continued to keep the Law". They were apostates from the sect itself, who now turned against their former associates. "Violent" links them with the Man of a Lie, the leader of the apostates, also described as *'aris* (4:13).

If v.12 refers to the apostate followers of the Man of a Lie, v.32, very similar to it in meaning and structure (the wicked against the righteous, Yahweh will defend), might have been taken as referring to the same *kind* of wickedness, apostasy from the sect. The Wicked Priest, found in v.32, would then be one of this group, and as an individual leader most likely the same as the Man of a Lie.

The unitary application of Ps 37, however, is not so certain as that of the woes in Habakkuk, which refer to one man only. The Teacher no doubt had various enemies, all of whom could be included in the body of wicked men whose existence set a theological problem for the writer of Ps 37. It needs to be shown that in every other place where the wicked are mentioned, they are interpreted of the apostate followers of the Man of a Lie, who is found in vv. 7 and 35. It would then be strongly indicated that the pesharist has taken all the wicked of the psalm in a particular sense, as the group of apostates whose activities are shown by CD to have been a major threat to the sect. The sole remaining case, the Wicked Priest of v.32, would then have to be included in this class, in view of the parallels between vv. 12 and 32.

In the present state of research the identity with the apostates of the other examples of wickedness in the *pesher* is not established. Most of them are insufficiently defined to be useful indications (2:3, 22-23; 3:3-4, 7 (but cf. CD 6:6), 11-12 (but cf. CD 3:13· 4:2; 6:2, and the discussion below on "Israel"); 4:1-2, 11, 21). One certainly refers to the apostates: 4:17-19, "the posterity of the wicked shall be cut off" (Ps 37:38) means "be cut off from the midst of the congregation of the Community *('ădat hayyaḥad)"*. The remaining two may be linked with them through CD, the major source of information about the apostates. V.14 of the psalm, "the wicked *(rĕsa'îm)* draw the sword . . . to slay the upright of way" is interpreted of the "wicked *(rĕsa'îm)* of Ephraim and Manasseh who will seek to put forth a hand against the Priest and the men of his Council in the time of trial that is coming upon them". Who are "Ephraim and Manasseh"?

CD 4:19 states that the Wall-builders have followed Ṣaw *(sade-waw)"*. The "Wall-builders" is another name for the apostates, as Jeremias shows.[17] The name Ṣaw is from Hos 5:11: "Ephraim was determined to go after Ṣaw". Ṣaw, whose meaning was unknown, was taken to be a name (it is probably a scr:bal error for *saw')*. The verse must have been chosen as a source for a pseudonym of the leader of the schismatics because it fitted the sectarian events; those who followed the rival leader were already known as "Ephraim", a name used for a particular branch or sub-section of the community. The whole section had gone over to the teachings of the rival leader. CD 7:13 is then understood in the light of these events. It points to the past split between Judah and Ephraim (reading *sar* for *sar)* as a parallel to the present split between Judah, the sect, and its "Ephraim", in order to warn the apostate group of their coming punishment. There is reason, then, for believing that "Ephraim (and Manasseh)" of the present passage means the apostates, and that their attack on the Council is the same as that in the previous passage, by the "ruthless ones of the Covenant in the House of Judah".

2:6-8 interprets the wicked *(rasa')* who will "in a little while" "be no more" and not be "in his place" (Ps 37:10) as "all the wickedness *(kôl hariš'â)* at the end of forty years, when they will be destroyed *(yittammû)* and there will not be found in the land any wicked man *(îs rasa')"*. The destruction of these "wicked" after forty years is clearly part of an accepted scheme, and is not derived from the psalm itself, which says only "in a little while". CD 20:14-15 speaks of the destruction *(tôm)* of all the schismatics after a period of forty years. As 4QpPs[a] is close to CD in its emphasis on the Teacher of Righteousness, the centrality of the schism, and the names "Ephraim and "Judah", there is a strong probability that this passage refers to the same enemies as CD 20:14-15. There was reason for believing that all the apostates would be destroyed at the end of a period of forty years.

14

The pesharist has found the Man of a Lie and his followers in vv. 7, 10, 12, 14, 35 and 38 of Ps 37. The subjects of other verses are not clearly defined, but, as shown above, v. 20 (3:7), and v. 21 (3:11-12) may refer to them. There are no places where a different person or group is clearly intended. This conclusion weighs the evidence in favour of the subjects of vv. 32 and 12 being the same, especially as the two verses are so similar. The Wicked Priest is the same as the Man of a Lie, the leader of the schismatics of v. 12.

The same characteristics are linked with both names in the respective documents. In 1QpHab, both the Wicked Priest and the Man of a Lie "shed blood" (9: 8-9, 10:6-9) and were builders (of a house (9:16 - 10:1) or a city (10: 6-9). In 4QpPs^a the Wicked Priest "watched and sought to slay" the Teacher (4:8), and the followers (Ephraim) set out to slay the Teacher and the men of his Council (2: 16-18).

Jeremias[18] attempts to defend the distinction between the Wicked Priest and the Man of a Lie by saying that in 1QpHab, when the biblical text is dealing with a singular wicked man, it is interpreted of the Wicked Priest, but when a group of wicked persons are in the same context, it is interpreted of the Man of a Lie. There is a plural in each of the three places where the Man of a Lie is found: Hab 1:5, "the traitors" (no singular is present); Hab 1:13b, "traitors" are present with the "wicked man"; Hab 2:12-13, "peoples labour for fire and nations weary themselves". But, apart from the fact that there are only three cases, of which only two contain both a singular and a plural, Jeremias overlooks the fact that in Hab 2:5 the Arrogant Man, who is said to be the Wicked Priest, is associated with "all nations" and "all peoples", who are "gathered" to him. Moreover, the argument is inapplicable to 4QpPs^a, which finds the Man of a Lie in Ps 37:7 and 35-36, where no other persons appear.

There is no reason why a further pseudonym should not be used for the rival leader. Jeremias shows that four other names are used for him (above, p.10). The reason for the variation of names within the same commentary is to be sought either in the biblical text or the immediate context. In 1QpHab 10:9-10, the biblical text uses *rîq*, "empty", a synonym for *kazab*, "lie" in Ps 4:3. In 4QpPs^a 4:8 the Teacher has been called "the Priest" in the immediately preceding context (see below on the meaning of "Wicked Priest").

The Sectarian Terms

Although it is widely recognized that the scrolls use words of general application in a particular, sectarian sense (for example, "righteous" means the Teacher and the sectarians, "traitors" means the apostates),[19] it has not yet become an established methodological principle to look for particular sectarian meanings wherever such words appear. Yet important questions hang on it. For instance, Murphy-O'Connor[20] partly builds his argument that CD 2:14 - 6:1 is a missionary document and separate from the rest of the work on the use of *banîm*, "sons", in 2:14 ("And now, sons, listen to me . . ."). Whereas the previous sections were certainly addressed to members ("all you who enter the Covenant" . . . "who practise righteousness"), he believes that "children" is "a banal term . . . which must be judged entirely neutral in an environment where the communication of knowledge was considered to establish a father-son relationship". He refers to the wisdom literature, regularly using the formula "my son". But it is surely relevant that "sons" forms part of a range of designations for the sectarians (sons of light, sons of heaven) and also that the Hodayot frequently speak of a spiritual father-son relationship between the leader and the members, for example, 7:20-21: "thou hast made me a father to the sons of grace, and a nurse for the men of wonder; they have opened their mouth like sucklings . . ." (see pp.98-9).

The Wicked Priest is said to have been "called by the name of truth when he first arose" *(niqra' 'al šem ha'ēmet bitĕḥillat 'ômĕdô)* (1QpHab 8:9). Jeremias,[21] followed by Murphy-O'Connor,[22] argues that the stress lies not on the word "name" but on the word "truth", and that the phrase simply means that the Wicked Priest had a good reputation when he began his career, but later lost it. He cites Rev 3:1 and Josephus, *J.W.* 2§28 as parallels for "name" used simply in the sense of "reputation". Jeremias thus prefers outside sources to the usage of the scrolls themselves.

"Truth" *('ĕmet)* is a frequently occurring word in the scrolls, appearing more than 120 times in published texts. It is very often used with "righteousness", which appears about the same number of times. Both "righteousness" and "truth" are the *special property of community members.* They are the "sons of truth" (1QS 4:5), are born of truth (1QS 3:19), are the "men of truth" (1QpHab 7:10), "in the service of truth" (1QpHab 7:12), they have been given the spirit of truth in baptism (1QS 4:21). 4QS[e], another copy of the Manual of Discipline, suggests in 8:13 that "the Way of Truth" had been a name for the community. It reads *"lĕpannôt . . . derek ha'ēmet"* ("prepare the way of truth") for 1Qs's *lĕpannôt . . . derek hû'â'* ("prepare the way of Him").[23] (For "Way" used absolutely, see 1QS 9:17-18, CD 1:13.) Those who have "truth" are contrasted with everyone outside the community, who are under the dominion of the spirit of falsehood (1QS 3:18-22). In the light of their appropriation of truth to themselves, it is extremely unlikely that they would speak of an outsider as "called by the name of truth", even temporarily. Anyone who was "called by the name of truth" must be a *member* of the community.

Similarly, "name" has special sectarian associations. It is part of a regular designation of members. They are "men called by a name" (CD 2:11: *qĕrî'ê šem),* "named men" (1QSa 2:2, 8, 11, 13 *'anšê haššem).* At full initiation their names were recorded in a register (1QS 6:22). That the Wicked Priest had been "called by the name of truth when he first arose" means that *he had been given full initiation as a member of the community.* This fits the description of the Man of a Lie, who was an apostate member of the community.

"Priest" is also a sectarian term; when used of the Teacher, it means high priest of the community.

The rival leader's name "he who preaches/drips lies" *(mattîp hakkazab)* has the same play on "teaching/giving water" as that of the Teacher ("he who teaches/rains down righteousness").[24] This suggests that when a large number of the Teacher's followers turned after the rival and formed their own *'edâ* ("congregation", 1QpHab 10:10) they had accepted him as a counterpart to the Teacher, having the same title and role. Their congregation was a "city" (1QpHab 10:10), a symbolic term,[25] as was that of the Teacher, a new Jerusalem (4QpIsa[d]); it also needed a high priest. The rival's title "the Priest" is accounted for by his being also accepted as a sectarian high priest.

The Teacher's claim to the high priesthood undoubtedly rested on Zadokite descent. This is shown both by the fidelity to biblical law on which his organisation was based, and by the stated reason for the separation of the Hasidim from the Hasmonean house. But he also rested it on the doctrine of indwelling by the heavenly high priest, as will be shown pp.81-6. It would not be impossible for a rival to carry this doctrine further and claim possession by the heavenly high priest on the grounds of spiritual qualities alone, thus gaining the support of some of the Teacher's followers. The basis of such a claim will be dealt with further, pp.161-3.

"When he ruled over Israel" *(mašal bĕyisra'el,* 1QpHab 8:9-10) is consistent with his being a sectarian high priest of a new Israel, the community. Although this phrase is used as the main textual evidence for the Wicked Priest's being a Hasmonean high priest, Jeremias[26] points out that *mašal* does not necessarily mean political rule, but is found in the scrolls of the priests' rule over members (1QS 9:7). Although it is used of the rule of Gentiles in 1QpHab 4:5,10, it is used of the rule of Ephraim, the seekers-after-smooth-things, who are false teachers, in 4QpNah 2:4. They "ruled" in Jerusalem, that is, they had made Jerusalem the headquarters of their following.[27]

"Israel" is frequently used of the community (CD 14: 4, 5, etc.). "He ruled over Israel" means "he was (sectarian) high priest of a new Israel".

Although the term "Ephraim" is used for the apostates after their defection, "Israel" is not likely to have been used of the rival "new Israel" in distinction from that of the Teacher. "When he ruled over Israel" must mean that the rival was, for a time, ruler of the Teacher's "new Israel". How is this to be explained? The answer is in the Day of Atonement episode, re-interpreted in the light of the view that the Wicked Priest and the Man of a Lie were one and the same.

The Day of Atonement Episode

IQpHab 11:4-8 on Hab 2:15 reads:

> "Woe to him who gives his neighbour to drink, who pours out his wrath to make him/them drunk in order that he may gaze on their feasts."
> This refers to the Wicked Priest, who pursued after the Teacher of Righteousness to swallow him up in his venomous wrath to his House of Exile.[28] Then, at the Period of the Feast of Rest, the Day of Atonement, he manifested himself *(hôpîaʿ)* to them to swallow them up and to cause them to stumble on the day of fasting, their Sabbath of Rest.

The *pesher* is in two distinct parts, each a complete sentence. In the first, the Teacher is the object of the Wicked Priest's wrath; in the second, it is "them", the Teacher's followers. The notes of time are given only in the second part.

What is the meaning of the Teacher's being "in his House of Exile"? In 1QH 4:8-9 the Teacher himself complains "all my companions and familiars have been banished from me" and "they drive me from my land like a bird from its nest". The cause is the "interpreters of deceit" (4:7), "interpreters of a lie" (4:9-10) *(mĕliṣê rĕmîâ, mĕliṣê kazab)*, that is, the apostates from the sect (cf. 4QpPsᵃ 1:19 "(the followers of the Man of a Lie) did not listen to the interpreter of knowledge *(melîṣ daʿat)*". He goes on to say of them: "They have withheld the drink of knowledge from the thirsty, and for their thirst they have made them drink vinegar, in order to gaze on *(habbît)* their error and to rave at their feasts *(môʿădêhem)* (4:11-12)". As in the present passage, the enemy gives a false drink, causes "drunkenness" (disorderly behaviour) and "gazes" *(habbît* in Hab 2:15) while present at their feasts. Once it is recognized that the subject of the 1QpHab parallel, the Wicked Priest, is also in the party of the apostates, then it becomes highly probable that the exile of which the Teacher complains is the *same* as that in which he was pursued by the Wicked Priest. As on this occasion he was banished from his companions (above), he was not with his community. This fact accounts for the two distinct parts of the *pesher*. There was not one attack by the Wicked Priest, but two. He had launched a two-stage campaign, first against the Teacher in exile, on a date not stated, then against his followers, separated from him, on the Day of Atonement. In each part of the *pesher* "to swallow up" is used; the two uses may be read as successive, and the copula joining the two sentences as "then".

The Wicked Priest was making use of the Teacher's absence to attack his followers and "cause them to stumble" *(kašal)*, a term regularly used for defection from the communal teachings (1QS 2:12, 17, 35; 1QH 4:15-16; 8:36; 9:25).

He chose the Day of Atonement to make them commit doctrinal error. He "manifested himself, shone forth" *(hôpia')* before them. *Yapa'* in the Hiphil is always used in OT of splendid manifestations: of God (Deut 33:2, Pss 50:2, 80:2, 94:1); of the sun (Job 3:4, 10:22)· of lightning (Job 37:15). The noun is used of the splendour of a king (Ezek 28:7, 17). In the scrolls, the verb is used with the subject God (1QH 4:6, 23; 1QM 1:16; CD 20:26); the stars (1QS 10:2); the day (1QM 18:10), truth (1QH 11:26-27); Jerusalem (1QM 12:13); the Teacher shining forth in sevenfold light (1QH 7:24); the speaker's "light" in 1QH 9:26. These uses confirm the meaning "make a splendid appearance". In 1QH 5:32 the verb is used for "revealed after being hidden", with subject "their (evil) heart and inclinations", and in CD 20:3,6 it has the same meaning, with subject "(evil) deeds". These uses are consistent with the meaning of a sudden manifestation of what has previously been hidden.

The use in 1QH 7:24 associates it with the Teacher's high priestly role; the "sevenfold light" refers to the Menorah, the temple lamp. The name "Priest" means that the Wicked Priest was a high priestly rival to the Teacher (above). If he "shone forth" before the Teacher's followers on the Day of Atonement when the Teacher was in exile, it means that *he was offering himself as sectarian high priest in place of the Teacher, in order to fill the vacancy created by the Teacher's absence.* It was absolutely essential that the high priest should be present on the Day of Atonement.[29]

He "shone forth before them . . . to cause them to stumble", that is, to commit doctrinal error (above) by accepting him as high priest. This statement may be taken with "he ruled over (the new) Israel". He had for a time been high priest of the whole community, during the Teacher's absence. This accounts for the title "the Priest" still used for him after the breach widened. He had been accepted as high priest according to sectarian law, and his party continued to accept him as the high priest of their "New Jerusalem". His erroneous teachings caused the Teacher's party to prefix "Wicked" to his title.

The Day of Atonement episode was not, however, the beginning of the schism. The Teacher's exile had been caused by the false teaching of the rival party (above). The rival leader had been the cause of the Teacher's expulsion from his community, his separation from his companions. Almost the whole community, "Israel", had accepted the rival leader on a subsequent Day of Atonement. The writings that continue to condemn the schismatics represent the viewpoint of a small group upholding the Teacher's doctrine and authority even after the loss of most of their fellows.

The conclusion that the Wicked Priest was the same as the Man of a Lie adds a great deal of new data for the study of the schism in the community, and also removes what has been held to be evidence for the appearance of a Hasmonean high priest in the writings concerning the Teacher. Both these results make a considerable difference to the study of the history of the Teacher of Righteousness.

NOTES

1. Jeremias, *Der Lehrer* . . ., ch. 2.
2. *Ant.* 13§§18-21.
3. H. Stegemann, *Die Entstehung der Qumrangemeinde* (Bonn, 1971); J. Murphy-O'Connor, "The Essenes . . .".
4. F. M. Cross, *Canaanite Myth and Hebrew Epic* (Cambridge/London: Harvard University, 1973), 337-40.
5. Jeremias, *Der Lehrer* . . ., 72-73.
6. *Ant.* 12§414; 12§434.
7. Stegemann, *Die Entstehung* . . ., 102.
8. Lls. 24-25 [lihĕ]yot šĕnehemmâ. The subject of *'amad* may be the same as that of *'omed* in 1.24, the "cursed man". A father and two sons are required by the biblical text.
9. J. Carmignac *(Textes de Qumrân,* II, 48-60, "Conjectures sur les écrits de Qumrân", *RevScRel* 2 (1957), 140-168; "Notes sur les pesharim", *RevQ* 3 (1962), 533-38) argues for Alexander Jannaeus as the Wicked Priest. H. Burgmann ("Gerichtsherr und Generalankläger: Jonathan und Simon", *RevQ* 9 (1977), 3-72) gives points refuting Carmignac's case (pp. 34-57); e.g. the lapse of fifty years between the foundation of the community and the appearance of the Teacher; Alexander Jannaeus did not give sufficient reason for the break of the sect with the temple; he did not meet death at the hands of Gentiles. See also M. B. Dagut, "The Habakkuk Scroll and Pompey's Capture of Jerusalem", *Bib* 32 (1951), 542-48.

10. K. Elliger, *Studien zum Habakuk--Kommentar vom Toten Meer* (Tübingen: Mohr, 1953); A. Dupont-Sommer, *Observations sur le Commentaire d'Habacuc découvert près de la Mer Morte* (Paris: Payot, 1953); M. Delcor, "Le Midrash d'Habacuc", *RB* 58 (1951), 521-48.
11. Jeremias, *Der Lehrer* . . ., 126.
12. Jeremias, *Der Lehrer* . . ., 57.
13. J. Starcky, "Les quatre étapes du messianisme à Qumrân", *RB* 70 (1963), 498.
14. The second phrase could be taken as giving additional facts. An example of this is in the famous case in the NT, where both an "ass" and a "colt" were read into Zech 9:9 (Matt 21:2-7). It is illustrated at Qumran in their own use of parallelism (see B. E. Thiering, "The Poetic Forms of the Hodayot", *JSS* 8 (1963), 189-209). In the Hodayot, there is a marked tendency for the parallelistic form to develop into an accretive list of items; e.g., 1QH 9:32-34a, where each of seven successive phrases contains the name of an attribute of God, and 1QH 8:31a-36b, where each successive line of a large number contains the name of a part of the body, giving an anatomical list.
15. Jeremias, *Der Lehrer* . . ., 77.
16. Murphy-O'Connor ("An Essene Missionary Document . . .", 217) defends the "House of Judah" as a name for the sect in CD 4:11 and 1QpHab 8:1, but in "The Essenes . . ." (p.220, n.34) says that the "House of Judah" in 1QpHab 8:1 and 4QpPs^a 2:13 means all Judeans, some of whom are Essenes (1QpHab 8:1) and some are not (4QpPs^a 2:13). This distinction, weakening his own case for CD 4:11, arises from not recognizing that "the violent ones of the Covenant in the House of Judah" in 4QpPs^a 2:13 means apostates from within the sect itself. Jeremias (*Der Lehrer* . . ., 111) agrees that "House of Judah" means the sect in CD 4:11 and 20:27. See pp.175-6 on a more precise meaning for "House of Judah".
17. Jeremias, *Der Lehrer* . . ., 89.
18. Jeremias, *Der Lehrer* . . ., 77.
19. Jeremias, *Der Lehrer* . . ., 89.
20. Murphy-O'Connor, "An Essene Missionary Document . . .", 204.
21. Jeremias, *Der Lehrer* . . ., 38.
22. Murphy-O'Connor, "The Essenes . . .", p.230, n.73.
23. Lohse, *ad loc.*
24. *môreh haṣṣedeq* from Hos 10:12, Joel 2:23. Cf. 1QH 8:16, where the Teacher plays on his name: "(God) has put early rain in my mouth". *Mattip hakkazab* is from Mic 2:6 (*natap*, "to drip", Hiph. "to prophesy"). Jeremias (*Der Lehrer* . . ., 313): the title "is certainly formed in conscious contrast to *môreh haṣṣedeq*".
25. Jeremias, *Der Lehrer* . . ., 87-88.
26. Jeremias, *Der Lehrer* . . ., 40.
27. Burgmann ("Gerichtsherr . . .") puts forward a further argument for Jonathan as the Wicked Priest: that a distinction is made in 1QpHab 8:9-11 between the office (*'omed*) that he legitimately held, and the rule (*mašal*) that he had usurped. "Usurpator war allein Jonathan, alle andern traten nur in seine Fusstapfen" (8). The distinction also fits the holder of a legitimate office in the community, who usurped a high priestly role that was not his.
28. *'abbet* = bĕbet (Mur 42:4).
29. E. Lohse, *The New Testament Environment* (Nashville:Abingdon, 1976), 153.

CHAPTER THREE

The Young Lion Again

*Its interpretation concerns the Young
Lion of Wrath . . . who hangs men
alive.* (4QpNah 1:6-7)

The *kĕpîr heḥarôn*, "Young Lion of Wrath", another of the enemies
of the sect, appears in 4QpNah 1 and the fragment 4QpHos^b. An identification was made in the early days of scrolls research, before all four columns
of 4QpNah were available. It has not, to my knowledge, been reconsidered,
as the first identification was generally acceptable on the prevailing hypothesis
concerning the history.

The passage in which this figure appears is 4QpNah 1:1 - 2:1, a *pesher*
on Nah 2:12-14.

> ["Where is the den of the lions *('arayôt)*, the cave[1] for the young lions
> *(kĕpîrîm)?"* (Nah 2:12a).
> (1) The lions' den is Jerusalem . . . which has become] a dwelling-place
> *(madôr)* for the wicked ones of the Gentiles *(gôyim)*.
> "Whither the lion *('ărî)* went, the lion's cub *(gûr 'ărî)* (tried) to come,[2]
> [and none (2) to defeat *(wĕ'ên maḥărîd)*[3] (Nah 2:12b).
> Its interpretation concerns Deme]trius, king of Yawan, who sought to come
> to Jerusalem on the counsel of the seekers-after-smooth-things *(dôrĕšê haḥălaqôt)*
> (3) [. . .] into the hand of the kings of Yawan from Antiochus to the rise of
> the rulers of the Kittim. And after that, she will be trodden down *(wĕ'aḥar
> terames)* (4) [. . .].
> "The lion *('ărî)* tears sufficient for his cubs *(gûrayw)* (and) strangles for his
> lionesses *(lĕbîyôt)* prey" (Nah 2:13a).
> (5) [Its interpretation] concerns the Young Lion of Wrath *(kĕpîr heḥarôn)*,
> who smites by his great men and the men of his council.
> (6) "[And fills with prey] the cave[4] and his den[5] with torn flesh." (Nah 2:13b).

Its interpretation concerns the Young Lion of Wrath (7) [. . . ven]geance on the seekers-after-smooth-things, who hangs men alive (8) [. . .] in Israel before *(běyiśra'el millěpanîm)*. For of the man hanged *(talûy)* alive on the tree it [re]ads *([yiqqa]re')*:
"Behold, I am against [thee (9) says the Lord of hosts, and I will burn in smoke thine abund]ance,[6] and thy young lions *(kěpîrîm)* the sword will devour, and I will cut [off from the land] the prey and (10) [the voice of thy messengers will no more be heard]" (Nah. 2:14).
[Its inter]pretation: "thine abundance", they are his warrior bands wh[ich are in Jerusal]em, and "his young lions", they are (11) his great men [. . .] and "his prey" is the wealth which was am[assed by the prie]sts of Jerusalem who (12) gave [. . .] Ephraim, and Israel was given [. . .] (2:1) and "his messengers", they are his envoys, whose voice will no more be heard among the Gentiles.

The names "Demetrius" (2) and "Antiochus" (3) are obvious starting-points for an identification, together with the fact that the Young Lion performed crucifixions.

In 88 B.C. a group of Jews, suffering from the tyrannies of their king Alexander Jannaeus (102-76 B.C.) went for help to Demetrius III Eukairos, the Seleucid king. Demetrius came with his army, encamped near Shechem, and was victorious over Jannaeus. But the latter subsequently recovered, after six thousand Jews turned back to him. He then punished the rebels by crucifying eight hundred of them.[7]

There are three points of correspondence between the *pesher* data and the event involving Alexander Jannaeus: the name Demetrius, the crucifixions, and the "seekers-after-smooth-things", both in counsel with Demetrius and being crucified. This has led to an identification of the Young Lion of Wrath as Alexander.[8]

A closer study of the text will show, however, that this conclusion has not taken into account a number of details.

G. Jeremias[9] makes an important methodological point concerning the study of the *pesharim:* no assumption can be made that each segment refers to the same historical period. He endorses Allegro's[10] view: "These commentaries are in no way works of connected history, and the method of the authors does not require any historical connection to be made between the interpretation of one verse and another, or even one word and another." Elliger[11] also speaks of the "atomizing" nature of the *pesharim.* As argued above (pp.10-11), this practice flows from their view of the unity of scripture. The successive elements of the prophetic text are permitted to point to whatever historical events they fit, even if these are widely separated. The above interpretation assumes, without reason, that the section dealing with Antiochus and Demetrius (lls.2-3) is on the same subject as that concerning the Young Lion of Wrath (5-8). There is a link between them, in the "seekers-after-smooth-things" in both sections. But this term covers all Jews who do not hold the rigorous view of the Law adopted by the sect. In Jeremias' words: "Die Schmeicheleisucher sind . . . arglistige Verführer, die den Leuten nach dem Mund reden, d.h. die der Schrift ihren Ernst nehmen und sie so auslegen, wie die Leute es gern hören wollen; *dabei ist der Ausdruck noch nicht prägnant auf eine bestimmte Gruppe beschränkt.*"[12] (italics mine). Both sections simply refer to Jews outside the sect; they are not necessarily the same group in both cases.

The section on Demetrius and Antiochus must be considered independently of what follows, and only linked with it if the interpretations do in fact form part of a single event.

There are three Seleucid kings called Demetrius: Demetrius I (Soter), 162-150 B.C.; Demetrius II (Nicator), 145-139 B.C.; Demetrius III (Eukairos), contemporary with Alexander Jannaeus.

Demetrius "sought to come to Jerusalem on the counsel of the seekers-after-smooth-things" (1.2). There is no evidence that Demetrius III "sought to come to Jerusalem". After defeating Jannaeus in battle at Shechem he "withdrew in alarm", six thousand Jews having left him to join Jannaeus.[13] He went from Judea to Beroea, in Syria, where he engaged in a military encounter with his brother Philip. There he was defeated and held in captivity for the rest of his life.[14] Allegro,[15] followed by Jeremias,[16] recognizes this difficulty, and suggests that the reason why the Jews changed sides to Jannaeus was that Demetrius had decided to take advantage of the opportunity to enter and bring Jerusalem under his control again. But Demetrius was already under threat from Philip,[17] and was fighting for his own survival as king: he was scarcely in a position to do more than try to gain the assistance of Jews, as he had attempted to do through the battle of Shechem, when he tried to help them against Alexander Jannaeus. The change of loyalty of the Jews who went to him is accounted for by Josephus: Jannaeus himself had now made overtures to them, and succeeded in gaining their pity and support in the national cause.[18] His subsequent treachery to them is consistent with his known character.

An additional piece of evidence is to be found in the fact that a parallel exists in the pesharist's mind between a Demetrius and an Antiochus. When he reads: "Whither the lion went, the lion's cub (tried) to come" in the prophetic text, he sees the two kings whom he introduces in the same section. One of them is the "senior" lion who actually "went", the other is the "junior" lion who only "tried to come". The second followed the first in time. The second lion is Demetrius, who "sought to come". Both of them had made an approach to Jerusalem. The first, Antiochus, had succeeded, the second, Demetrius, had tried but not succeeded.

In 167 B.C. Antiochus IV Epiphanes (175-165/4 B.C.) entered the Jerusalem temple and "erected a desolating sacrilege upon the altar of burnt offering" (1 Macc 1:54). The event was the central one of the Maccabean period, the signal for the ensuing war of liberation. Antiochus succeeded in his purpose for three years; the altar was rededicated in 164 B.C.

Demetrius I (162-150 B.C.) was responsible for a parallel attack on the sanctuary to that of Antiochus, but one that did not even temporarily succeed. According to 1 Macc 7:1-7, 26-49, the would-be high priest Alcimus and his hellenizing party (fitting the "seekers-after-smooth-things") came to Demetrius I and asked for his assistance against Judas Maccabeus. Demetrius sent his general Nicanor, who, after a setback by Judas in battle, entered Jerusalem and threatened to destroy the sanctuary unless Judas and his army surrendered to him. Judas defeated him in battle on the 13th Adar, which was subsequently celebrated as a festival, "the day of Nicanor". This festival, which continued to be celebrated (cf. *Megillat Ta'anit,* 13th Adar) reinforced the parallel between Demetrius I and Antiochus IV, as the Feast of Dedication had also been introduced to celebrate the final victory over Antiochus (1 Macc 4:59).

Alcimus and his party were remembered as enemies of the Essenes, not only because of their hellenizing outlook, but because after the Hasidim had trusted Alcimus because of his Aaronite ancestry, he put to death sixty of them (1 Macc 7:12-18). As part of *Essene* history, they fit better the "seekers-after-smooth-things" than do the Jews who went to Demetrius III.

Cross,[19] followed by Jeremias,[20] rejects Rowley's[21] suggestion that Demetrius I is the one in question, on the grounds that Demetrius did not personally involve himself in the campaign in Judea, and that the generals who were sent there by him were effectively in control of the country: "it seems rather unlikely that one would speak of 'an attempt to enter Jerusalem' unless the attempt was against opposition and was not carried out". But this overlooks the attack on the sanctuary, which was strongly opposed, and was not carried out. The fact that Demetrius was represented by his generals makes no difference to his responsibility for the action: a king stood behind all actions carried out in his name.

There is good reason, therefore, for supposing that the pesharist read the prophetic text,concerning the lion and the lion's cub as referring to two parallel attacks on the sanctuary. His basic assumption is that the Nineveh of the Nahum prophecy is Jerusalem, which is under the wrath of God and will soon be destroyed. The "lion's den", a symbol for the city in Nah 2:12-14, is understood by him as the heart of the city, the sanctuary. The lions who tried to come there are the two successive Seleucid kings, whose attacks on the sanctuary were part of popular history, celebrated in annual festivals.

This is supported by the final part of this section. "From Antiochus to the rise of the rulers of the Kittim. And after that, she will be trodden down . . ." is introduced as an interpretation of the last phrase of the lemma: "and none to make tremble".

Harad (Hiph.) (in *we'ên maḥărid*) is used in the sense of "rout in battle, defeat" in Jud 8:12, Ezek 30:9, Zech 2:4. The phrase is ambiguous: it means either "the lions did not defeat" or "no one defeated the lions". Although the latter sense is more natural in the context, the former is possible on the view that *labî' šam* in the first part of the verse means "tried to come there". It has been taken as meaning that the lions tried to defeat the sanctuary, but did not succeed. This is shown by the antithesis in the next sentence: "And after that, she will be trodden down . . .". Neither Antiochus nor Demetrius succeeded in defeating the sanctuary, but after the rise of the Kittim she (the city) was brought under a foreign master, and would be destroyed in the future.

The period in which the city was not defeated is "from Antiochus to the rise of the rulers of the Kittim". The Kittim in this and in all places where the word is used are the Romans.[22] The writer is referring to the change in the fortunes of the city that occurred in 63 B.C. From the time of Pompey's entry (including an intrusion into the sanctuary)[23] the independence of Jerusalem and the nation, which had been maintained against Seleucid encroachments, was lost. The kingship was abolished as the main sign of loss of independence. L.3 will have read: "[She (Jerusalem) did not fall *(lô' natenâ)*] into the hand of the kings of Yawan from Antiochus to the rise of the rulers of the Kittim. But after that, she will be trodden down . . .".

The theme of the first section of the *pesher* is the history of the city of Jerusalem between 167 B.C. and 63 B.C. Antiochus IV temporarily overcame the sanctuary; Demetrius I tried to do so but did not succeed; but the rulers of the Kittim succeeded. The "lions' den" was at last captured. The implication is that the Romans were used by God for the purpose of punishing the city, the main theme of the Nahum prophecies and of the whole *pesher*. Cf. 2:4-5, a detailed prophecy of the destruction of Jerusalem by the Gentiles, bringing upon its inhabitants (the enemies of the sect) the punishment of God.

The next section (5-8) concerns the Young Lion of Wrath. In the lions' den, the lion *('ărî)* "tears sufficient for his cubs, and strangles for his lionesses prey" (Nah 2:13a). This concerns another ruler (lion), but this time the *kĕpîr heḥarôn*. This lion, according to the prophecy, fills his den with torn flesh. The Young Lion's action in performing crucifixions is found to correspond to this. Those whom he crucified were "seekers-after-smooth-things", and, as these are also the enemies of the sect, the following verse in the Nahum passage, "Behold, I am against thee . . ." is applied to "the man hanged".

A further methodological principle of the *pesharim* has been discussed p.12 above. As it was held that the meaning of scripture did not vary, the particular interpretation given to biblical terms was always the same. "The righteous" is always interpreted of the Teacher and the sectarians, and it has been shown, on further grounds, that the "wicked" of 4QpPs[a] are always the same group and their leader (pp.13-15). In 4QpNah 1:1 the pesharist gives his interpretation of the basic terms of Nah 2:12-14. The lions' den, the subject of the passage, is "[Jerusalem . . . which has become] a dwelling-place for the wicked ones of the Gentiles". This establishes that *the lions who occupy the den are Gentiles.* It would be contrary to the principles of the *pesharim* if any of the lions in the Nahum passage were subsequently interpreted as other than Gentiles. The writer remains consistent in the case of the first two lions, the pair formed by the lion and the lion's cub (2:12b); they are Seleucid kings. *The lion who tears flesh, the Young Lion of Wrath, must, therefore, be a Gentile also. He is a Gentile ruler of Jerusalem. He cannot be Alexander Jannaeus, who was a Jewish king.*

The theme of the first section of the *pesher* (above) indicates that he is a *Roman* ruler of Jerusalem. The two Seleucid "lions" had not succeeded in occupying the cave/city. But this lion establishes himself in the cave. He tears flesh for his family there, filling the den with prey. The first section has shown that the Romans successfully occupied the city. He is a representative of the Roman power in Jerusalem.

The reasons why the interpretation in terms of Alexander Jannaeus has been accepted, in the face of the clear statement of 1:1, may be further considered.

The Young Lion crucified Jews, "seekers-after-smooth-things". Jannaeus is the only one in the Hasmonean period known to have crucified Jews, and the event, according to Josephus, was an outstanding one, and would have been retained in public memory.[24]

The principle stated p.23 means, however, that there are no grounds for assuming that the second section of the *pesher* deals with the Hasmonean period, the time of the first section. If a statement of the prophetic passage fitted "exactly" a different stage in the sectarian history, the pesharist accepted it. The mention of the Kittim, together with the Herodian date of the writing (see p.34) means that the work was written in the Roman period. (The *pesharim* are autographs, not copies, as only one example of each was found in the caves.)

L.8, in reference to the crucifixions, continues, after a lacuna with space for some 25 letters, "[. . .] in Israel before". Most writers[25] have accepted the completion: ['ăšer lô' ya'ăśeh] bĕyiśra'el millĕpanîm, "crucifixion did not happen in Israel before". If this means that the crucifixions were the first ever performed in Israel, then it indicates Jannaeus, whose crucifixions were probably the first, and were very notorious. Allegro[26] points to Josephus' strong expressions of emotion at the event: "a thing that was as cruel as could be";[27] "inhuman . . . penalty";[28] "excessive cruelty".[29]

If the reading is "did not happen in Israel", its significance would be, as Jeremias agrees, "was not the custom in Israel", "against Israelite principles", cf. 2 Sam 13:12, Gen 34:7, Gen 29:26. *Millĕpanîm* in the scrolls does not have a simple time sense: it means "in Old Testament times", cf. CD 2:17, *millĕpanîm wĕ'ad hennâ*, "from former times until now" CD 5:17: *kî millĕpanîm 'amad mošeh wĕ'ahăron*, "for in former times Moses and Aaron arose". The whole phrase would mean "crucifixion is against Israelite law, as set down in the Old Testament", and would be a judgement on the legality of the action, not a statement that it was the first time crucifixions had happened. This is not evidence in favour of Jannaeus.

Moreover, new light has recently been thrown on the matter by the Temple Scroll, suggesting that the reading "[did not happen] in Israel" is not correct. Yadin[30] has pointed out that 11QT 64:6-7, in a midrashic interpretation of Deut 21:22-23, reverses the order of verbs in the Deut text, from "if a man . . . is put to death and you hang him on a tree" to "you shall hang him on the tree and he shall die". The same order is found in 10-11 of the passage, on a parallel crime. In Yadin's words: "The fact that the scroll's text has it twice . . . indicates quite clearly that the sect interpreted that such a man should be hanged alive, dying as a result, and not as was maintained by final Pharisaic halakha, that a man should be put to death *prior* to the hanging."[31] The order in l.9 is "put to death and hang", but this reproduces the biblical order. This passage (11QT 64:6-13) actually enjoins crucifixion for the two crimes named: informing against one's people and delivering them up to a foreign nation; and running away into the midst of the Gentiles. Baumgarten's[32] argument that it refers to strangling does not sufficiently take into account the conscious reversal of the biblical order.

28

The seekers-after-smooth-things who were crucified ("hanged up *alive"*, in both 1.7 and 1.8) are only known, in 7-8, to have failed to keep the Law rigorously. But when they are seen to be the subjects of the following section, 1:8b - 2:1, through the link "Behold, I am against thee" (the man hanged (see below p.30)), then they also are seen to be included among the Gentile "lions" who inhabit the city, for they have "young lions" who are their "great men" *(gĕdôlîm)* (10-11), cf. the *gĕdôlîm* of the Young Lion of Wrath (1.5). Yet they are also Jews, as they are expected to keep the Law. The description fits Jews who had become so thoroughly hellenized that they were as good as Gentiles, in the sectarian view. The hellenizing party, the "seekers-after-smooth-things" in the days of the Seleucids are described in the same terms in 1 Macc 1:15: "they joined with the Gentiles and sold themselves to do evil". They therefore have committed the second crime of 11QT 64:6-13, and according to its law crucifixion was a suitable punishment for them. This means that the lacuna at the beginning of 1.8 did not contain a statement condemning crucifixion, as Yadin agrees (revising his own previous opinion).[33] It probably read: "as was done in Israel before *(ka'ăšer ya'ăšeh bĕyiśra'el millĕpanîm)"*, supporting the action on the grounds of an alleged biblical law, that of 11QT. There was no statement in the text that crucifixions had not happened before: the only evidence that could possibly be used for Alexander Jannaeus disappears.

There is reason, then, for seeing that the second section of the *pesher,* 5-8, on the Young Lion of Wrath, deals with the action of a Roman ruler of Jerusalem, who crucified some hellenizing Jews. They were not the same as those in the first section (2-3), but only had in common their hellenizing outlook.

The pesharist has taken Nah 2:12-14, on the successive inhabitants of the lions' den, as referring to a succession of Gentile attackers of Jerusalem. Jerusalem itself has become like the biblical Nineveh, no better than a pagan city. It is under the wrath of God, and will be destroyed. As a sign of this, a succession of "lions", Gentile rulers, have made attacks on the "den", the sanctuary; it is no longer inviolate. The details of the "lions", given by the prophet, fit "exactly" certain well-known events. A pair of lions, senior and junior, had "come" and "tried to come"; this fits the pair Antiochus IV and Demetrius I. Another lion had "torn flesh" in the cave. This fitted the equally well-known action of a Roman ruler of Jerusalem, in the pesharist's own time; he had performed crucifixions. The victims of the crucifixions were themselves on the side of the "lions"; they were Jews who had become like Gentiles. Their predecessors, other "seekers-after-smooth-things", were also on the side of the "lions"; they had been allied with a Seleucid ruler. The ruling "lions" had been used by God to punish

29

the second set, cf. 1.7: "[. . . ven]geance on the seekers-after-smooth-things"; this followed the biblical pattern of God's use of foreign powers to punish sinful Jews.

The distance in time between the first set of events and the second is accounted for by the principle of the *pesharim* stated p.23: the unity was in the biblical passage. As its details "fitted" so well certain outstanding events, all of which were the actions of Gentiles in the city of Jerusalem, the prophet Nahum was understood as having foreseen the whole series of events from the time of the Seleucids to the time of the Romans. All the foreign powers had made encroachments on the sanctuary, and formed a single pattern. The end result would be that the city would be destroyed (1.3), like the biblical Nineveh.

The question of the exact date of the Young Lion of Wrath will be taken up in chs. X and XI.

The third section (1:10 - 2:1) is linked with the second through the use of "Behold I am against thee" of Nah 2:14 to refer both back to the "man hanged" and forward to the rest of the verse, in which the hellenizing Jews are found. The rather clumsy arrangement has led Yadin to separate "Behold I am against thee" from the previous section, finishing it with the verb [*yiqqa*]*re'*, so as to give "the hanged one is called 'alive on the tree' ", a reference to the law of 11QT. Baumgarten[34] also ends the sentence at this point, reading "the Young Lion took 'hanged' (in Deut 21:23) to mean 'alive on a tree' " (that is, he erroneously took it to justify crucifixion). These views do not take into account the fact that "Behold I am against thee" is not interpreted in the following passage, which begins with "thine abundance", in the second phrase of Nah 2:14. The only interpretation given to "Behold I am against thee" is the link with the preceding section. [*Yiqqa*]*re'* introduces it, as Allegro[35] sees; it is a variant of the usual "he says" of the *pesharim*.

A further condemnation of the seekers-after-smooth-things who were crucified is in their equation with the "torn flesh" with which the Young Lion filled his cave. Torn flesh is unclean food (Lev 7:24, 17:15, 22:8). Those crucified are therefore condemned in four ways: (a) they have come under the law of 11QT, for those who desert to Gentiles. God fulfilled this law by causing them to be crucified; (b) they have come under the law of Deut 21:23, "a hanged man is accursed by God")[36] (c) the prophecy "Behold I am against thee" is applied; and (d) they are "unclean food" ("pigs"!). Further information about them is given in the commentary on Nah 2:14 (1:10 - 2:1); this will be discussed p.187.

Cols. 2-4 of this *pesher* give a detailed treatment of "Ephraim and Manasseh", who in 4QpPs^a 2:17 are a particular group of enemies of the Teacher; they there "will seek to put forth a hand against the Priest and the men of his Council in the time of trial that is coming upon them". Despite Murphy-O'Connor's view (p.5 above), that these names cover "the whole of non-Qumran Judaism", the sectarian habit of using biblical terms in a specific sense, and consistently, raises the possibility that they are always the same group. The other signs of a link between 4QpNah and the Teacher — the "Last Priest" of 4QpHos^b, which also contains a reference to the Young Lion of Wrath (p.5) — turn this possibility into a probability. For the writer of 4QpNah, living in the Roman period, the particular group of enemies of the Teacher are a matter of importance (contrary to earlier opinion). This *pesher* must also be taken into account when the data for the Teacher's history are assembled.

NOTES

1. *Mě'arâ* for MT *mir'eh*. Cf. the *pesher, madôr*, "dwelling-place".
2. MT *'ăšer halak 'aryeh labî' šam gûr 'aryeh*. Allegro (DJD V,39) followed by Jeremias *(Der Lehrer ...*, 127) translates "whither the lion, the lioness *(lěbîyâ)* went, the lion's cub". But Strugnell ("Notes en marge ...", 207) points out that "le *yod* apparent (of *labî*) est de la forme épicène qui pourrait être aussi bien un *waw*". The *pesher* on the phrase reads *labô'*. Vermes *(DSSE*, 231) translates "whither the lion goes, there is the lion's cub". The meaning of the phrase as given here is indicated by the *pesher*: Demetrius "sought to come". The pesharist has taken *halak* as the verb for *'aryeh, labô'* as the verb for *gûr 'aryeh*, meaning "tried, intended to come".
3. The lower part of the leg of final *nun* is visible at the end of 1.1, after a space for three letters.
4. Sing., MT plu.
5. Sing., MT plu.
6. *Rôběkâ "abundance"* for MT *rikbâ* "chariots".
7. Ant. 13§§372-383.
8. J. M. Allegro, "Further Light on the History of the Qumran Sect", *JBL* 75 (1956), 89-95; "Thrakidan, the 'Lion of Wrath' and Alexander Jannaeus", *PEQ* 91 (1959), 47-51; A. Dupont-Sommer, "Le Commentaire de Nahum découvert près de la Mer Morte (4QpNah): Traduction et notes", *Semitica* 13 (1963, 201-27; J. Carmignac, "Interprétation de Nahum (4QpNah)" *(Textes de Qumrân.* II, 85-92).

9. G. Jeremias, *Der Lehrer* . . ., 129-30.
10. Allegro, "Further Light . . .", 93.
11. K. Elliger, *Studien zum Habakuk-Kommentar* . . ., 139-142.
12. Jeremias, *Der Lehrer* . . ., 131. See also S. B. Hoenig, *"Dorshe Halakot in the Pesher Nahum Scrolls", JBL* 83 1964), 119-138.
13. *Ant.* 13§379.
14. *Ant.* 13§§384-6.
15. Allegro, "Further Light . . .", 92.
16. Jeremias, *Der Lehrer* . . ., 129.
17. *Ant.* 13§§370-71.
18. *Ant.* 13§§378-9.
19. Cross, *The Ancient Library of Qumran and Modern Biblical Studies* (London: Duckworth, 1958), 93, n. 29.
20. Jeremias, *Der Lehrer* . . ., 129.
21. H. H. Rowley, "4QpNahum and the Teacher of Righteousness", *JBL* 75 (1956), 188-93.
22. Jeremias, *Der Lehrer* . . ., ch. 1.
23. *Ant.* 14§71.
24. According to Josephus, *Ant.* 12§256, and *Ass.Mosis* 8:1, Antiochus IV crucified Jews. Jeremias gives reasons for doubting the statement (*Der Lehrer* . . ., 136). In any case, Antiochus has been interpreted as the lion of 2:12a, and this is a different lion, as shown by the use of *kĕpir*.
25. Jeremias, *Der Lehrer* . . ., 135.
26. Allegro, "Further Light . . .", 92.
27. *Ant.* 13§380.
28. *Ant.* 13§381.
29. *Ant.* 13§383.
30. Y. Yadin, "Pesher Nahum (4QpNahum) Reconsidered", *IEJ* 21 (1971). 1-12.
31. Yadin, "Pesher Nahum . . .", 9.
32. J. A. Baumgarten, "Does *tlh* in the Temple Scroll Refer to Crucifixion?" *JBL* 91 (1972), 472-481.
33. Yadin, "Pesher Nahum . . .", 5.
34. Baumgarten, "Does *tlh* . . .".
35. *DJD* V, 39.
36. See M. Wilcox, "Upon the Tree' — Deut 21:22-23 in the New Testament", *JBL* 96 (1977), 85-99.

CHAPTER FOUR

The Palaeographical Dating of
1QS, 4QpIsaᶜ and 4QDᵃ

The writings which make reference to the Teacher of Righteousness and his contemporaries, or which will be considered in the following pages in connection with the history, are listed below, together with the palaeographical dates that have been given to the copies on the basis of the criteria set out by F. M. Cross in his authoritative work, *The Development of the Jewish Scripts*.[1] The dates of the copies are among the main pieces of evidence to be taken into account in studying the history of the Teacher.

Periods:	Hasmonean	E(arly)	150-100
	(150-30 B.C.)	M(iddle)	100-75
		L(ate)	75-30
	Herodian	E(arly)	30-20 A.D.
	(30 B.C.-70 A.D.)	M(iddle)	20-50
		L(ate)	50-70

11QT(emple) hand A	Herodian, M or L	Yadin, *MM*, I, p.16
„ „ B	Herodian, E	„ „ „
„ fr. Rock. 43.366	Hasmonean, M	„ „ pp.16-18
1QS (1QSa, 1QSb)	Hasmonean semiformal, M	Cross, JS, p.158
4QTestim	„ „ „	„ „ „
4QSᵉ (unpublished)	Hasmonean protocursive, E	Cross, *AL*, p.89, n.17
1QH hand A	Herodian formal	
1QH hand B	Herodian semiformal	Cross, *DJD* III, p.217
1QM	Herodian formal, E	Cross, JS, p.138
CD 4QDᵃ (=ᵇ)	See below pp.45-7	
4QDᵉ	Herodian formal	Milik, MS, p.135
(5 other 4Q copies,	unpublished)	
5Q12	Herodian, E	*DJD* III, p.181
6Q15	Herodian, M or L	*DJD* III, p.129
1QpHab	Herodian	Cross, JS, n.119
4QpIsaᵃ	Herodian semiformal, E	Strugnell, NM p.183, n.17
4QpIsaᵇ	Herodian semiformal, E	„ „ p.186
4QpIsaᶜ	Hasmonean semiformal, M	„ „ p.188
4QpIsaᵈ	Date uncertain	„ „ p.196
4QpIsaᵉ	Herodian formal, E	„ „ p.197
4QpPsᵃ	Herodian semiformal, E	„ „ p.211
4QpPsᵇ	Herodian, E	„ „ p.219
4QpNah	Herodian, E	„ „ p.205
4QpHosᵇ (formerly ᵃ)	Herodian semiformal	„ „ p.201
1QpMic	Herodian	
4Q174	Herodian formal, E	Strugnell, NM pp.220, 177
4Q177	Herodian formal, E	„ „ pp.220, 177
11QMelch	Herodian	„ „ pp.236-7
4QPB	Herodian	

JS. "The Development of the Jewish Scripts."
AL. *The Ancient Library of Qumran.*
MS. "Milkî-ṣedeq et Milkî-rešaʿ."
NM. "Notes en marge du volume V des 'Discoveries in the Judaean Desert of Jordan'."
MM. Mĕgillat-hammiqdaš (see p.111 n.1).

Special consideration may now be given to some of these.

The Archaic and Hasmonean Semiformal Scripts

Cross has isolated a small group of manuscripts which are a subtype of the formal hand, called by him "semiformal". Some members of the group have both archaic and cursive features: they are held to be "formed by the influence of a third-century cursive on the formal character".[2] They are: 4QQoh(elet)^a (= 4QEccles in OMQ),[3] 4QPr(ières liturgiques)^a, 4QPs^a, 4QSy48. Cross dates them in the Archaic or early Hasmonean period (175-125 B.C.). Other semiformals are related to them, but are "influenced at a number of points by the standard Hasmonean style";[4] they are placed in the middle Hasmonean period (100-75 B.C.). They include: 1QS, 4QTestim,[5] 4QSam^c, pM34 recto. J. Strugnell[6] groups with these 4QpIsa^c (4Q163): it is therefore "the oldest of the known copies of the *pesharim*".

A group of dated scripts in Palmyrene are available, together with the Nabatean scripts, for comparison with Qumran hands. They are from 44 B.C. and 33 B.C.[7] The subsequent evolution of Palmyrene, from 9 B.C. to 272 A.D., is set out by Cantineau.[8] The Palmyrene script of the second half of the first century B.C. contains forms which, if they appeared in a Qumran script, would be signs of an early date: for example, the semilooped left leg of *'alef*, the high point of joining of the left leg of *gimel*, the very short left arm of *samekh*, the short-legged *qof*. Certain features have survived in the Palmyrene hands that were not preserved at Qumran.

The late first century B.C. Palmyrene script shows a very marked similarity with 4QQoh^a, the leading example of the group of scripts called by Cross Archaic semiformal. In his words: "(Palmyrene) *'alef, bet, gimel, waw, yod, lamed, mem, 'ayn, shin* and *taw* stem from forms virtually identical with the Archaic semiformal of Qumran".[9] The general appearance is also the same: "both scripts exhibit enlarged, especially broadened forms of letters".[10]

'Alef in both kinds of script (4QQoh^a and Palmyrene) has a semilooped left leg; *bet* "is large, with an angular base at the right, and long baseline",[11] in *gimel* the left arm meets high on the straight right stroke, *waw* is curved, with a curved top, *zayin* is a straight stroke, *yod* is a small semicircle in 4QPr^a and Palmyrene (closer to an inverted "v" in 4QQoh^a), *lamed* slopes right with a rightward-tending base, *'ayn* has a broad top and very short, curved tail, *qof* has a short leg, *shin* is broad, its right arms closer to the horizontal than the vertical, *taw* has the right arm joining low on the left downstroke as a result of the downward direction of the left downstroke (continued into the right arm). *Dalet* and *resh* have the same marked slope to the right, although the head is different.

Palmyrene is much closer to 4QQoh[a] and 4QPr[a] than the related script, Nabatean, although the extant early Nabatean inscriptions (Aslah, c.95 B.C., El-Kutba, 77 B.C. according to Cross, Rabb'el, c.66 B.C.)[12] are given a more complex descent.[13]

On the grounds of the early dating of 4QQoh[a] and 4QPr[a], indicated by their archaic forms, Cross concludes that these scripts represent almost exactly the archetype from which Palmyrene descended. Their date shows the precise point at which Palmyrene began its separate development. The fact that it coincides with the date of the separation of the Palmyrene state (141 B.C.) is taken as confirmation.[14]

There is, however, a problem posed by the closeness of the Palmyrene script of the second half of the first century B.C. to the Qumran hand dated a hundred or more years before. *Cross's conclusion means that Palmyrene scarcely evolved beyond its original forms, during a century of active commercial and political life, with more frequent contacts with other developed countries than occurred at Qumran,*[15] *which evolved rapidly during the same hundred years.* Nabatean, closer in date to the Qumran script, shows a more complex development than Palmyrene.

To this difficulty may be added the fact — not conclusive in itself — that the Hasmonean dating of 4QpIsa[c] is out of step with the dating of the other *pesharim,* all of which come from the Herodian period,[16] and are plausibly assumed to be autographs, as only one copy of each was found in the caves.[17] They are more easily understood as stemming from a single literary impulse at about the same time.[18]

It may also be noted that 4QpIsa[c] includes among its fragments two (2-3) in cursive script, which, as Strugnell[19] agrees, must be by a scribe of the same period. His script includes the ovoid cursive *mem* which is more frequent in literary semicursives after 50 B.C. (4QS135b, 4QEnoch V, Mur26).

The Hasmonean semiformal had a special history. "When it appears at Qumran, (it) is a fully formed style which maintains its integrity and special traits for more than a century, until it disintegrates and can no longer be traced toward the end of the Hasmonean period or slightly later".[20] The script is not fitted into a continuing line of development such as is convincingly traced through the formal hands. Such cases complicate the work of the palaeographer, raising the possibility of a different explanation for forms which, in an evolutionary series, can be used as direct evidence for date. Cross observes such a complication in the case of 4QEx[f]. It has certain very archaic forms, like those of the fourth century scripts, mixed with third century forms. It must be supposed to come from a special locality, presumably Syria-Palestine, where a set of archaic features survived into the third century B.C. In the case of an idiosyncratic hand, the possibility of a regional origin must be taken into consideration along with the forms that indicate date. The possibility is only confirmed, however, if the hand contains forms that are widely separated in date.

Milik[21] supposes a school of scribes, responsible for 4QPs 89, 4QD[a], 4QJub[f], 4QPhyl G-I and others, shown to be non-Judean by their occasional use of *shin* for *samekh*. He suggests an origin in southern Syria or Idumea. The presence of Palmyrene scribes in Jerusalem is shown by inscriptions, one of them dated in the first half of the first century A.D.[22]

The script of 4QQoh[a] and 4QPr[a] contains precisely the archaic forms that are found in Palmyrene: the semilooped left leg of *'alef,* high-joining left leg of *gimel,* straight *zayin,* rightward-tending base of *lamed,* short left arm of *samekh,* short-legged *'ayn* and *qof.* This fact is used by Cross to argue for a descent of Palmyrene from an archetype close to 4QQoh[a] and 4QPr[a]. *But if early Herodian forms were present in the Qumran scripts, then it would be necessary to conclude the opposite: the script of 4QQoh^a, etc., is derived from Palmyrene. Palmyrene scribes of the period of the extant inscriptions (second half of the first century B.C.) have imported into the Qumran scripts regional forms that have retained certain archaic features.* This explanation would remove the difficulty concerning the static nature of the Palmyrene script, and also give 4QpIsa[c] a similar date to the other *pesharim.*

In his first publication of 4QQoh[a], J. Muilenburg[23] did not take into account the similar Palmyrene forms: he simply placed the script midway between the third century Edfu papyri and Hasmonean formal and semiformal hands. The second century B.C. dating was emphasized to give the "coup de grâce" to certain critical views of the late date of composition of Ecclesiastes. Cross, while including the Palmyrene scripts, confirmed Muilenburg's dating, as he does not find reason to doubt that the letter-forms are archaic. Only if early Herodian forms were strongly present would there be reason for supposing a regional origin and later date. Can such evidence be found?

The *'alef* of 4QQoh[a] has a short left leg, projecting outwards to the left, sometimes with a curve downwards. Its right arm is long and vertical rather than short and sloped right to left. The arm begins with a slight left to right curve and is drawn to near the base of the diagonal.

Cross sees the left leg as a less developed form of the semilooped leg found also in 4QPr[a] and in early Nabatean and Palmyrene.[24] The semi-

37

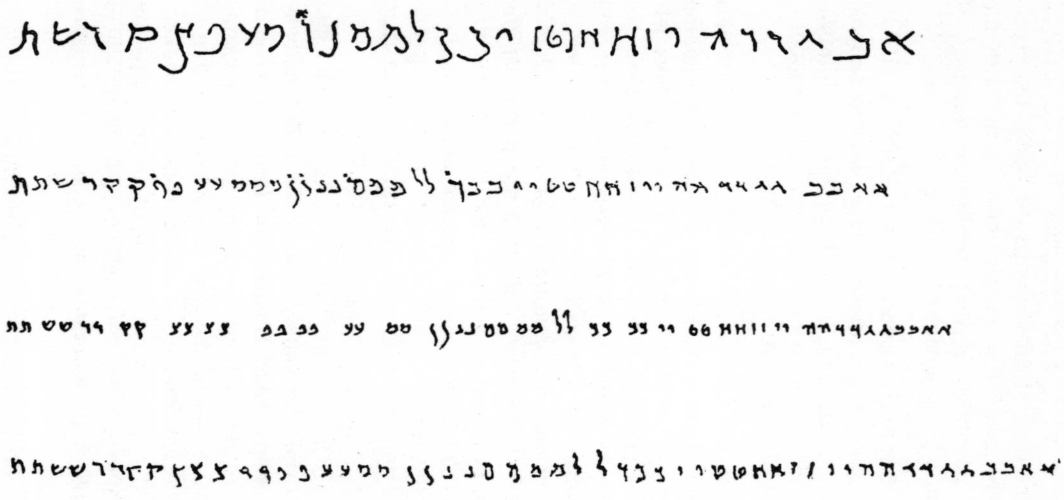

1

2

3

4

Figure 1. Palmyrene, and Qumran Hasmonean Semiformal Scripts

LINE 1   The Palmyrene script of 44 B.C. and 33 B.C. Reproduced from F. M. Cross, *The Development of the Jewish Scripts*, fig. 6, line 2. For details of sources, see Cross, legend to fig. 6, line 2.

LINE 2   The script of 4QQoh[a]. Reproduced from Cross, *Development* . . ., fig. 1, line 6.

LINE 3   The script of 1QS. Reproduced from J. C. Trever, "1QDan[a], the Latest of the Qumran Manuscripts", *RevQ* 7 (1970), 277-286, fig. 1, line 2.

LINE 4   The script of 4QpIsa[c]. Photographed and assembled from Plates VII-VIII, *DJD* V.

looped leg is descended from the crescent-shaped leg of fourth-century cursives, and the form in 4QQohᵃ is like that in some third-century cursives.[25]

The right arm in its curve and vertical stance is like that in the early Nabatean Rabb'el Inscription[26] (Cross states[27] that 4QQohᵃ anticipates the *'alef* of early Nabatean), and the vertical position is found in some early Aramaic cursives. But the connection with the base of the diagonal is not found in the archaic or Nabatean forms. The long, upright right arm of *'alef*, meeting the diagonal at or near the base, is characteristic of the Herodean Rustic (Round) semiformal hand of 4Q*171* (found frequently at Qumran).

The semilooped left leg foreshadowed by 4QQohᵃ and found in 4QPrᵃ is characteristic of Palmyrene throughout its history. The fragment entitled 4QTeharot D,[28] in a Rustic semiformal, has an *'alef* with a distinctly semilooped left leg. Its right arm is vertical. Cf. also the bent or angled left leg of *'alef* in Mur*1* (beginning of second century A.D.). The persistence of this form in the later scripts is to be weighed against the criterion of the reduction of a three stroke to a two stroke *'alef*, held to be the typologically significant criterion.

In 1QS and 4QpIsaᶜ the *'alef* has the inverted-"v" form of the left leg and diagonal, characteristic of the Herodian period. The two strokes are drawn separately, as also in 1QH hand B (Herodian semiformal).

Bet in 4QQohᵃ has an almost equal width of head and base, both being broad. The proportions of head and base, the curved rather than ticked head, the right-slanting downstroke bending sharply into a base-stroke are the same as in early and later Palmyrene *bet*.

Gimel in 4QQohᵃ, 4QPrᵃ and 1QS has the left leg meeting high on the downstroke, as in archaic forms, and also in Palmyrene. It remains high throughout the history of Palmyrene.

This kind of *gimel* is also found in Herodian semiformals: e.g. 4Q*171* and the Vulgar semiformals 4Q*162* (where the left leg kicks up in the same fashion as in 4QQohᵃ and Palmyrene) and 3Q*15* (Copper Document). On the latter, Cross states:[29] "*Gimel* is superficially archaic in form ... It is in fact a style surviving from the early Herodian era in certain late semiformal scripts". As it appears also in second century A.D. cursives (Unid. *134*,[30] Mur*44*), it may rather be seen as an alternative form of the period, possibly influenced by regional hands (it is found also in Nabatean).

Dalet and *resh* in 4QQohᵃ and 4QPrᵃ are not archaic, as Cross agrees. The archaic forms had narrow heads and in the very early period sloped from right to left. These have broad heads and an extreme slope from left to right. The slope is characteristic of the first century B.C. and later

Palmyrene hands, but not to the same extent of Qumran Hasmonean hands. It is found in 11QT, hand A, which has more Herodian forms than hand B. The heads of *dalet* and *resh* in 4QQoh^a and 4QPr^a are ticked, giving them a rectangular form, unlike Palmyrene, but as in the Hasmonean formal. The head in 4QQoh^a is not normally deep, and is paralleled in 4Q*171* and 1QpHab. That in 1QS has the Hasmonean depth.

The *he* in 4QQoh^a is formed with the cursive reversed-"k" horizontal and left leg, added to a crossbar that appears to be drawn from right to left. Palmyrene has a true cursive reversed-"k" form. The first horizontal in 4QQoh^a meets the right arm at the top, and the right arm is short; in archaic cursive *he*'s, the right arm is long and over-arches the left fork. The cursive method may be seen as a sign of early date, or, if other Herodian features are present, as a sign of Palmyrene influence.

Zayin in the semiformals is a straight stroke, as in the archaic and regional scripts.

Het in 4QQoh^a and 4QPr^a has the distinctive treatment of the crossbar — low on both verticals, or meeting the left at the top and the right lower down, producing an N-shape — that links it with third-century cursives, later Qumran cursives, and also with Nabatean and Palmyrene, as Cross notes.[31] 1QS, 4QTestim, 4QpIsa^c have the low crossbar. Palmyrene has a low crossbar in a domed shape. Its slope is to the right in 4QQoh^a, whereas in the archaic period the tendency was to the left.

The *tet* in 4QQoh^a and 4QPr^a is not archaic. Its short left arm and straight base with curled back crossbar are found in Hasmonean and early Herodian hands. Its appearance in an archaic script is surprising, and Cross concludes that the form has appeared "abruptly" at this point.[32] It may be seen as an indication of a later date than has been supposed.

The *tet* of 1QS and 4QTestim has the shape found in the archaic scripts: a long left arm and rounded base, like the figure 6. The shape is also characteristic of early and later Palmyrene *tet*, and could have been re-introduced from a regional source. It is to be observed that in 1QS the *tet*, although in the figure-6 shape, is drawn by the *method* that was only developed in the Herodian period: in two strokes, the left downstroke first, then the right curl drawn downwards and meeting the left downstroke at the base. The join is visible in 3:22:5, 4:20:2, 5:12:9, 5:16:6. The Herodian technique is being used to produce a *tet* that has the appearance of the Palmyrene *tet*.

The inverted-"v" *yod* of 4QQoh^a, a development from the three-stroke *yod* of the archaic style, is said by Cross to be "introduced" at this point.[33] The *yod* in these scripts is easily distinguished from *waw,* an early trait, but found also in Palmyrene and Nabatean.

The *kaf* in 4QQoh^a is quite different from the archaic *kafs:* they are long with a curved base and narrow head, while it is broad in both head and base, and the downstroke is bent into an angle at the base. It may not be linked with the Palmyrene figure-3 *kaf*. Its bowed, rather than ticked head is like that of *bet*.

In the archaic scripts *bet* and *kaf* are quite different shapes: the former broad and short, the latter long. In the Herodian scripts the two letters have come close together in shape, leading to the development of the left-to-right stroke for the base of *bet*. In 4QQoh^a the two letters are much closer in shape than would be expected in an archaic script, the *kaf* being only slightly longer than the *bet*. They are better seen as close to the Herodian period.

Cross finds in 4QPr^a the origin of the straight base of *kaf*,[34] it may also be a sign of later date.

Kaf in 1QS and 4QpIsa^c has the Hasmonean length in proportion to *bet*. The same proportions are found in the Herodian Rustic semiformal hand of 4Q171.

The final form of *kaf*, like that of *pe* and *ṣade*, is not normally used in 1QS and 4QTestim, although final *mem* and *nun* are used. The use of final *mem* and *nun* only is characteristic of the Herodian Rustic semi-formals, e.g. 4Q171.[35] Palmyrene uses final *nun* only. The absence of final forms may be used to link 1QS with the Herodian semiformals.

4QQoh^a uses final *kaf* and *pe* (it has no *ṣade*); if its source is Palmyrene, this may be seen as a Qumran trait.

Lamed in 4QQoh^a has only a slight hook, as in early cursives and early Palmyrene.

Cross holds the medial *mem* of 4QQoh^a to be "idiosyncratic".[36] A semicircle, like the right half of an oval, appears at the beginning of the crossbar. That it was a single stroke added last, rather than the completion of a tick on the crossbar, is shown by the form in col. 1, line 4, word 1 of the main fragment, where a single stroke is added above the crossbar.

The Herodian scripts changed the method of drawing medial *mem*.[37] In the Hasmonean, as in the archaic scripts, the crossbar is drawn first, then the downstroke and base, and the left oblique is added last. In the Herodian scripts, the left oblique is drawn first, continuing into the shoulder of the letter and down into the right downstroke; a short, straight stroke or tick is added last at the top of the oblique.

The intermediate stages in this process may be traced through the *mem* in 1QS. The left oblique is drawn last, in the Hasmonean style. In some cases (6:7:1, 6:15:3, 10:11:4, 11:12:1, 11:19:2) it may be seen that it is drawn by first retracing the tick or curve on the crossbar, then, at the

41

crossbar, the stroke turns left and down. The left oblique thus becomes an angled addition to the crossbar. 11QPs[a] (Herodian) shows the same method, also 4QpIsa[c] and 4QpIsa[b].

In 1QH hand B this method is used, but the lower part of the final angled stroke is on much the same plane as the crossbar. The crossbar thus becomes the left oblique with an added angular stroke. The next step is the loss of the beginning of the crossbar, leaving only the angled final stroke. The final stroke is then either retained as a tick on the crossbar (now become the left oblique), or reduced to a straight stroke.

Figure 2. Evolution of Medial Mem.

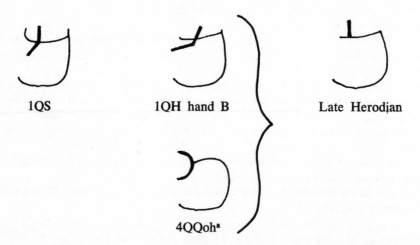

1QS   1QH hand B   Late Herodian

4QQoh[a]

The semicircle at the beginning of the crossbar in 4QQoh[a] may be seen as a version of the angled final stroke, and a sign that the script is transitional between Hasmonean and Herodian forms. The *mem* of 1QS is also seen as transitional, a sign of a somewhat later date.[38]

The final *mem* of 4QQoh[a] is, in the light of the archaic dating, abnormal, as Cross admits.[39] It has a broad head, a straight rather than diagonal left stroke, breaking through at the top, is fully closed at the bottom, and is longer than the other letters, including medial *mem*. It is quite unlike the archaic final *mems,* whose left downstroke is diagonal, which are open at the bottom, and are not differentiated in size from the remaining letters. The projection above the crossbar does not slant to the extent of most late Hasmonean and Herodian forms, but it is the same as that in 11QPs[a]

(Herodian). This letter, like medial *mem*, is an indication of a first century B.C. date.

The final *mem* of 1QS is also out of place in the middle Hasmonean period. It is simplified, with neither an independent tick nor an extension of the oblique above the crossbar. It is found, as Cross says,[40] in the Herodian Vulgar semiformal, and enters the formal script for the first time in the late Herodian period. It is found in 11QT, hand A (Herodian).

Nun in 4QQoh^a and 4QPr^a is short, and has the long base at an angle to the downstroke found in the Hasmonean period, unlike the archaic *nun* which is a long downstroke. Cross finds an antecedent in 4QJer^a,[41] where it is one of the new forms which distinguish this script from the archaic forms. It may also be seen as a sign of a later date.

Final *nun* in 4QQoh^a and 1QS has an angled top, sweeping into a long, curved downstroke, that may be linked with Herodian semiformals, e.g. 4Q*171*.

The *samekh* in 4QQoh^a and 4QPr^a has a short left arm, leaving the letter open at the bottom, and a simplified head, unlike the very complicated head of archaic *samekh*. That in 4QPr^a is both short and drawn downwards. In this feature, it is like the *samekh* of 4QSam^b (Archaic), and also like that of Palmyrene. In Palmyrene, the left arm, drawn downwards, continued to shorten so much that in the later forms it remained entirely above the crossbar. The left arm in 4QQoh^a is drawn upwards, the method found in Hasmonean and Herodian formal scripts; Cross traces it from 4QQoh^a.[42] It may also be seen as the result of Herodian influence on the Palmyrene short arm.

The *samekh* in 4QpIsa^c has the short left arm that may be either archaic or Palmyrene.

'Ayn in 4QQoh^a, 1QS and 4QpIsa^c is broad with a short curved leg. The shortness of leg is archaic, but not the curve. As Cross says,[43] the form is characteristic of Palmyrene.

Pe in 4QQoh^a and 1QS has an angular base, and an angled, rather than curved head; it is paralleled in Hasmonean and Herodian formal hands. In 4QpIsa^c final and medial *pe* have curled heads like those of the Herodian period.

The deeply curved head and curved slope to the right of final *pe* in 4QQoh^a is found in Herodian hands, e.g. 4Q*169*, 1QM. The archaic forms slope to the left and have a shorter head.

There is no *sade* in 4QQoh^a. That in 4QPr^a has the straight lower leg found in 4QSam^b, which can be related to archaic forms, but may also be linked with the final form of *kaf* that is found in the medial position in this script. Its head is the simplified straight stroke found in cursives.

The *sade* in 1QS and 4QpIsa^c has the curved right arm and sharply angled base stroke that is found in both Hasmonean and Herodian hands.

The leg of *qof* in 4QPr^a is short, that in 4QQoh^a is sometimes short, sometimes below the baseline. Cross: "the leg is beginning to lengthen after its extremely short phase."[44] The open-headed *qof* of 4QQoh^a is found in the Nabatean El-Kutba inscription,[45] dated by Cross 77 B.C., and in late cursive hands (Nero Papyrus).

In 1QS and 4QpIsa^c the tail of *qof* is drawn from the tick or curve on the head, as in the late Hasmonean fashion.

The *shin* of 4QQoh^a and 4QPr^a, also 4QpIsa^c, is broad, the two right obliques closer to the horizontal than to the vertical. The Palmyrene *shin* retains this shape throughout its history. The upper right arm in 4QQoh^a and 4QPr^a is very high on the left downstroke, unlike the very early forms where it is low. It is higher in these scripts than in 1QS.

The similarity between the *taw* of 4QQoh^a and 4QPr^a and that of Palmyrene is noted by Cross. The projection at the base of the left leg differentiates them from archaic *taws*.

Strugnell remarks[46] that the Hasmonean semiformal style has not yet been sufficiently studied. It has been suggested above that if Herodian forms were present in 4QQoh^a and its related scripts, then the archaic forms in these scripts should be seen as resulting from Palmyrene influence in the second half of the first century B.C., rather than a sign that they are the archetype of the closely similar Palmyrene forms. The archetype hypothesis results in the difficulty of making Palmyrene all but static for a century, against the historical probability. In the foregoing, the following Herodian characteristics have been observed in 4QQoh^a and 4QPr^a: the right arm of *'alef*, joining the diagonal close to the base; the closeness in shape of *bet* and *kaf*, the slope of *dalet* and *resh*, the *tet*, the medial *mem*, which may be seen as a version of the *mem* transitional between Hasmonean and Herodian, the final *mem*, the final *pe*. It may be suggested, therefore, that these hands are essentially Palmyrene hands, not really at home at Qumran, but influenced by Qumran forms of the late first century B.C. in the use and forms of final letters, the right arm of *'alef*, the formal shape of *he*, the *tet*, *kaf*, medial *mem*, *pe*. Palmyrene, a hand renowned for its calligraphic beauty,[47] preserved archaic forms (semilooped left leg of *'alef*, high-joining *gimel*, "cursive" *he*, curved *waw*, "cursive" *het*, long-armed *tet*, short-armed *samekh*, short-legged *'ayn* and *qof*) as a sign of elegance, and the majority of these have come into the Qumran script indirectly from the regional source, rather than directly from the archaic period.

In 1QS the *gimel*, the shape (but not method) of *tet*, the *'ayn*, the *taw*, apparently early forms, should be balanced against the Herodian *'alef*, the transitional *mem*, the late final *mem*, the method of drawing *tet*, and the non-use of final forms of *kaf*, *pe*, *sade*, to group the script with early Herodian semiformals, as one that has been influenced by Palmyrene in *gimel*, *zayin*, *het*, shape of *tet*, *'ayn*, *taw*.

4QpIsa*c* may be seen as an early Herodian semiformal, sharing with 1QS the Palmyrene influence in *zayin*, *het*, *'ayn*, *taw*, and influenced by it also in *samekh* and *shin*. This conclusion is supported by the hand of fragments 2-3, using the ovoid cursive *mem* more common in the Herodian period. It is also supported by the Herodian date of all the other *pesharim*.

The use of regional, especially Syrian scribes at Qumran may well have complicated the history of the script to an extent that has been difficult to take into account in the first generation of palaeographical analysis. The presence of such scribes is known, through their influence on the orthography and the Palmyrene inscriptions in Jerusalem. In view of the reasons for seeing the Palmyrene script as a prestigious one (its intrinsic beauty, the commercial prominence of Palmyra), the possibility should be considered that they have also imported letter-forms peculiar to their regions. As these forms would be archaic in a native Qumran script, a new hazard for palaeographers results. It is far from impossible that the small group of scripts represented by 4QQoh[a] and 4QPr[a] are a special kind of Herodian hand under strong Palmyrene influence, and that the small group represented by 1QS, 4QTestim and 4QpIsa*c* are a special kind of Herodian semiformal with specific Palmyrene influence in certain letters. The regional source may have re-introduced features which had previously been abandoned, e.g. the shape of *tet* in 1QS, the reason being that the forms were considered more elegant. The scribe of 4QTestim uses a highly embellished script, that may also have permitted stylish regionalisms, and the hand of 1QS is very close to it. The presence of Herodian forms in these scripts raises this new possibility, and should be given consideration before any final date is assigned to them.

The Palaeographical Dating of 4QD[a]

The 4QD fragments are not yet fully published. In his book *Ten Years of Discovery in the Wilderness of Judaea* (1959), Milik states:[48] "As far as the Damascus Document is concerned, the oldest copy we have was written c.75-50 B.C. It is a fairly extensively preserved manuscript, abbreviated provisionally 4QD[b]."

In a 1972 article,[49] he refers to "4QD^a (4Q266) . . . the manuscript which dates from the first third of the first century B.C." In an attached footnote, he says: "cited in my book under the siglum 4QD^b and dated from the years 75-50 B.C."

In a 1966 article,[50] he publishes a piece of 4QD^a. The same information is given concerning the change of siglum (footnote 4, p. 103: "I have several times cited this important manuscript in my previous publications, under the siglum 4QD^b. I have identified remains, sometimes minute, of 33 columns of the scroll, which contained 38"). On p. 103 it is given the number 4Q266, although in the same article it is called 4Q226, presumably a typographical error. That it is the same early piece is shown by Milik's remarks on its inclusion in the work of a school of scribes of three successive generations, beginning 175-125 B.C.[51] Despite the confusion caused by the change of siglum, it is clear that the piece published is from what has been held to be the oldest copy of CD.

It is a *semicursive*, not a formal or semiformal hand. This is shown by its *he* with a reversed-"k" shape, its N-shaped *het,* the round-shouldered *resh,* the *shin* with right arms made in one continuous stroke, the D-shaped *samekh,* and other forms.

Milik's datings are often at variance with those of other palaeographers. However, Cross accepts that "an unpublished copy of CD from 4Q cannot be dated later than the Hasmonean period, and is almost certainly pre-Roman".[52]

The semicursive scripts are the most difficult of all to date, as Cross agrees. In his words: "The semicursive scripts, since they mix cursive and formal typological elements, provide extra, if interwoven and complex, criteria for dating. Since the script has a certain integrity in its tradition, an inner typology can be constructed; this is no simple task, owing, as we have noted, to the variety within the tradition."[53]

The *mem* of 4QD^a is a version of the *mem* of 4QQoh^a described above (p.42). An angular final stroke is added, usually without any crossbar at all. This is a sign of development towards the Herodian *mem*.

Its *tet* is clearly Herodian, with a curled head and right downstroke drawn in a second movement.

The *bet* is drawn left-to-right, with a projection to the right of the downstroke, an essential Herodian feature.

Its high-joining *gimel* is not necessarily an archaic form, as argued p.39. It is found in second-century A.D. cursives.

The *pe* has the angular Herodian head. *Dalet* has the broad head and rightward slope, and *'ayn* the small, narrow top and leftward sloping leg of the Herodian period.

The *taw* is drawn in the same fashion as that of 4QQohᵃ and Palmyrene, the left stroke downwards. Like that of 4QQohᵃ (whose *mem* is also paralleled in this script) it may be seen as a regional rather than archaic form.

These considerations may be brought forward in order to temper the procedure that is sometimes adopted, of using the date of this earliest fragment of CD as an absolute barrier to a consideration of a later than Hasmonean date. Cross himself does not depend on its date alone, but brings in a supporting argument from internal evidence: "An unpublished copy of CD from 4Q cannot be dated later than the Hasmonean period, and is almost certainly pre-Roman. Composition of CD, in any case, must be pushed back into the late second century B.C., or better, perhaps, the early first century B.C. This dating should have been evident already on the basis of internal data. For example, the Kitti'im, normally the Romans in the Qumran scrolls composed late . . . play no role in CD".[54] (See further below pp.53-4 on this argument.)

The date of 4QSᵉ

All that may be known of the date of 4QSᵉ at present is that it is a papyrus copy "in a proto-cursive script which, while more difficult to date, is earlier still (than 1QS)"; it is "early Hasmonean".[55] It is only possible to emphasize that it is in the complex cursive category, and it is "difficult to date".

It has been our purpose here to show that the practice that has grown up among some writers of regarding the palaeographical datings as a fixed starting-point for historical study needs to be accompanied by some hesitation about the more difficult of the scripts. Although the evolutionary stages of the formal and most of the semiformal hands are clear, and useful criteria are able to be laid down, the field is a highly complex one, and it may take yet another generation before the rarer forms are able to be finally classified. This is readily admitted by palaeographers themselves.

In the following reconstruction of the history (ch. X), all the writings listed p.34 except 11QT and 1QM 2-9 will be placed at or after the time of the Teacher of Righteousness. Of these, 1QS, 4QTestim, 4QpIsaᶜ, 4QDᵃ and 4QSᵉ have been dated by palaeographers earler than the Herodian era, and all the rest are Herodian. It has been pointed out above that there is uncertainty about *all* of the non-Herodian scripts. The first three have been put in the rare class of Hasmonean semiformal, which is more convincingly explained as a Herodian script influenced by Palmyrene characteristics. 4QDᵃ is a semicursive, and 4QSᵉ a cursive: both are difficult hands to date. This means that *there is no unshakable palaeographical evidence that the Teacher of Righteousness was in the Hasmonean period.*

NOTES

1. In G. E. Wright (ed.), *The Bible and the Ancient Near East* (London: Routledge & Kegan Paul, 1961). Abbreviated JS.

2. JS, 145.

3. F. M. Cross, "The Oldest Manuscripts from Qumran", *JBL* 74 (1955), 147-72. Abbreviated OMQ.

4. JS, 158, n. 116.

5. Cross states (JS, 158) that 1QS and 4QTestim are by the same scribe. The following letters are drawn differently: *tet* (see p.40); medial *mem* (left oblique joins the top of the right downstroke in 4QTestim, giving a triangular shape); *shin* (left downstroke curved in 1QS, straight in 4QTestim). 4QTestim has more frequent loops and flourishes than 1QS. It may be a different style of the same hand.

6. J. Strugnell "Notes en marge du volume V des 'Discoveries in the Judaean Desert of Jordan'." (*RevQ* 6 (1969-70), 163-276. Abbreviated NM in this chapter.

7. JS fig. 6, 1.2. J. Starcky, "Inscriptions archaiques de Palmyre", *Studi Orientalistici in onore di Giorgio Levi della Vida* II (Rome, 1956).

8. J. Cantineau, *Grammaire du Palmyrénien Epigraphique,* Cairo: Imprimerie de l'Institut Francais d'Archaeologie Orientale, 1935.

9. JS, 165.

10. OMQ, 162.

11. OMQ, 162.

12. JS, figs. 6 and 7.

13. JS, 160-6.

14. JS, 165-6.

15. Palmyra was an important trading centre between Upper Syria and the Euphrates, flourishing, under the name of Tadmor, from an early period; Josephus claimed (*Ant.* 8§154) that Solomon had built it. It became an independent state, separating from the Judean and Nabatean states, after the fall of Seleucia in 141 B.C., and in the first cenutry A.D. was the centre of a trading empire. J. Starcky, *Palmyre,* Paris: Maisonneuve, 1952.

16. 1QpZeph and 1QpPs are also Herodian.

17. Milik, *Ten Years of Discovery in the Wilderness of Judaea* (London: SCM, 1959), 41; Cross, *Ancient Library* . . ., 84.

18. J. Carmignac (*Textes de Qumran* II, 47-8) holds that they are by the same author, but this degree of unity is to be questioned.

19. NM, 189.

20. JS, 158.

21. J. T. Milik, "Fragment d'une source du Psautier (4QPs 89) et fragments des Jubilés, du Document de Damas, d'un Phylactère dans la grotte 4 de Qumran", *RB* 73 (1966), 94-106, p.103.

22. J-B Frey, *Corpus Inscriptionum Iudaicarum,* II (Rome: Pontificio Istituto di Archeologia Cristiana, 1952), No. 1388, cf. also No. 1222.

23. J. Muilenburg, "A Qoheleth Scroll from Qumran, *BASOR* 135 (1954), 20-28.

24. JS, 158.

NOTES

25. S. A. Birnbaum, *The Hebrew Scripts*, I & II (Leiden: Brill, 1971), 123-147, 154-161.
26. JS, fig. 7, 1.2.
27. JS, 158.
28. J. T. Milik, "Milki-ṣedeq et Milki-reša' ", *JJS* 23 (1972) 95-144, p.115.
29. *DJD* III, 219.
30. JS, fig.5, 1.3.
31. JS, 159.
32. JS, 159.
33. JS, 159.
34. JS, 159.
35. NM, 211.
36. JS, 159.
37. JS, 178.
38. A similar *mem* to that of 4QQoh^a is found in Mur*24* (133 A.D.).
39. JS, 159.
40. JS, 178.
41. JS, 159.
42. JS, 186-7.
43. JS, 160.
44. JS, 160.
45. JS, fig.7, 1.1.
46. NM, 250.
47. JS, 160.
48. *Ten Years* . . ., 58.
49. "Milki-ṣedeq . . ." 135.
50. "Fragment d'une source . . ."
51. "Fragment d'une source . . .", 102-3.
52. *Ancient Library*, 59, note 46.
53. JS, 182.
54. *Ancient Library*, 59.
55. *Ancient Library* 89, note 17.

CHAPTER FIVE

Further Observations Relevant to the Date of the Teacher

By going over again the evidences that were thought to give a Hasmonean date for the Teacher of Righteousness, it has been possible to show that they are not so firm as has been supposed. The Teacher was not a contemporary of a Hasmonean high priest; there is no such figure in the scrolls. 4QpNah, which uses the names of opponents of the Teacher, deals with a Roman ruler of Jerusalem. The great majority of the writings concerning the Teacher, and possibly all, are in a Herodian script.

It may now be pointed out that there is some positive evidence that the Teacher was contemporary with the writing of the *pesharim,* which belong in the Roman period.

The Tenses of the Pesharim

The tenses of the *pesharim* have been given particular attention by J. Carmignac,[1] following the observation of Segal, van der Ploeg and Brownlee[2] that in all these works the verbs describing the sins of the enemies of the sect are always in the past (perfect tense), and the verbs describing their punishment are always in the future (imperfect tense). Carmignac establishes that Qumran Hebrew shows a similar development to that of mishnaic Hebrew: the perfect and imperfect tend more and more to represent the purely past in one case, the purely future in the other. In 1QpHab

12:2-6, the transition from a perfect, to express repeated sinful actions in the past, to an imperfect, to refer to a single punishment for the sinful actions, can only be explained if the punishment is in the future (as the imperfect is also capable of being used for repeated actions in the past). In 4QpPs[a] 3:7-8 the same pattern is found.

This observation may be tested on the verbs concerning the Wicked Priest in 1QpHab.

8:13 - 9:12 refers to the fate of the Wicked Priest, as is now generally recognized. 9:1, after a lacuna, begins: "[. . .] *něgô'ô běmišpětê riš'â*, "his chastisement by judgements of wickedness". It follows a quotation of Hab 2:7-8a on the punishment of an enemy by "oppressors" who rise up against him. The "chastisement" is inflicted on the Wicked Priest, the subject of the previous column. The following sentence reads: *wěsa'ărûrîyôt mahălîm ra'îm 'asû bô ûněqamôt bigwîyat běsarô.* In the light of the prophecy concerning the oppressors, this means: "They inflicted on him horrors of evil sicknesses *(mahălîm*, root *halâ*, possibly also a play on *halal*, "defile", as he was a priest), and vengeance on his body of flesh" (9:1-2). The majority of writers agree with this sense.[3] The oppressors have inflicted on the Wicked Priest the punishment that he deserved, a physically painful one. This fact is repeated in the following section: "God delivered him (the Wicked Priest) *(nětanô)* into the hand of his enemies, in order to humble him by a destructive scourge *(nega' lěkalâ)* in bitterness of soul, on account of the evil he did to his Elect One" (9:10-11). The Wicked Priest's sufferings are described in such detail that it follows that they had already occurred, consistently with the perfect tenses.[4] The complication that they were "judgements of wickedness" (9:1), that is, illegally inflicted on him, would not have been introduced if it had been a prophecy. The tenses have a past sense. "God gave him into the hands of his enemies" means that the Wicked Priest is already dead.

This introduces a problem for 12:5, also on the Wicked Priest. "God will condemn him *(yěšôpětennû)* to destruction". (The future sense is strengthened by the following perfect tense "even as he planned *(zamam)* to destroy the Poor".) But 10:3-5 shows that this refers to a final punishment on the Day of Judgement (also referred to in 13:2-3). "He (God) will bring him up from there (the House of Judgement of 10:3a) to judgement and in the midst of them (the nations) he will condemn him and will judge him with fire and brimstone". The Qumran community did not believe in a resurrection, but in a continuation of the present life of the community in the Future Time, as will be shown ch. VI. This is not incompatible with a doctrine of a final judgement, when the wicked, who had died at or before the eschatological climax, would undergo a second death. John 11:23-24 shows that some Jews did not accept an immediate resurrection, but did expect a resurrection at the Last Day. Rev 20:4-6 speaks of a first and second resurrection and a second death for the wicked. The Wicked Priest is here being consigned to a second death. The pesharist has observed that the prophecy "because of the blood of men and the violence done to the land" is repeated in the Habakkuk passage (2:8b and 2:17). At its first occurrence, he refers it to the past death of the Wicked Priest, at its second occurrence, he refers it to his future death.

There are, then, no exceptions to the temporal use of tenses in 1QpHab. The perfect tense refers to the past, the imperfect to the future. The rule that they have a temporal sense may then be applied to 4QpPs^a. In 2:17-18 a persecution of the Teacher by his enemies is described in the future tense: "the wicked ones of Ephraim and Manasseh who will seek *(yĕbaqšû)* to put forth a hand against the Priest (the Teacher) and the men of his Council in the trial that is coming (participle) on them. But God will redeem them *(yipdem)* from their hand". Similarly in 4:8-10: "The Wicked Priest who watches the Righteous [One (the Teacher) and seeks] to slay him . . . But God will not ab[andon him]: *(lô' ya'[zĕbennû])*, and [will not condemn him when] he is judged." *At the time of composition of these passages, the Teacher of Righteousness was still alive,* and it was expected, on the basis of biblical prophecy, that he would be delivered from a trial and judgement that he was about to undergo.

This conclusion may be taken with the evidence concerning the date of composition of the *pesharim*. Only one copy of each was found in the caves, suggesting that they are autographs, as has been widely agreed.[5] Their script, except in the case of 4QpIsa^c, is in the clearly defined Herodian formal or semiformal classes, and this is confirmed by the references to the Kittim, the Romans, in 1QpHab, 4QpIsa^a and 4QpNah. They were written, in their present form, in the Roman period. With the evidence of the tenses, that the Teacher of Righteousness was alive at the time of writing 4QpPs^a, it would follow that the Teacher lived in the Roman period. But this is apparently negated by the accepted view concerning the date of the Teacher.

Cross's solution[6] is that the tradition of applying certain prophecies to the Teacher was worked out in his own time, but not written down until the Herodian period. But this raises a fresh problem. They do not represent verbatim recordings of an earlier tradition, as they deal with the Romans. 1QpHab 9:7 predicts that the Romans will punish certain people in Jerusalem. If the pesharists also composed, why did they retain the exact form of the predictions concerning the punishment of those who had attacked the Teacher (4QpPs^a 2:19, "the wicked ones of Ephraim and Manasseh . . . will be given into the hand of the ruthless Gentiles for judgement"; 4:10, the same fate will befall the Wicked Priest)? As the Wicked Priest did suffer (1QpHab 9:1), why is this fact not stated in 4QpPs^a, as a better support for the truth of scripture (Ps 37) that God would punish the wicked? If the men of Ephraim and Manasseh had not suffered, the prophecy would not have been retained,[7] if they had, the details of the fulfilment would have been given.

On the evidence of the *pesharim alone,* the simplest hypothesis is that the Teacher was in the Roman period.[8] 4QpPs^a was written while he and the Wicked Priest were still alive; 1QpHab was written subsequently, when the Wicked Priest was dead.

The Uses of "Kittim"

Cross supports his palaeographical dating of the earliest copy of CD with the following remark: "This dating should have been evident already on the basis of internal data. For example, the Kitti'im, normally the Romans in the Qumran scrolls composed late (the *pešarîm* and 1QM . . .) play no role in *CD*".[9]

This statement implies that where the name "Kittim" does not appear, the Romans may not be assumed to be present. It may be considered in the light of the uses of the term.

(a) It is used throughout 1QpHab as an interpretation of the Chaldeans of the prophecy of Habakkuk. The same enemy are also called "Gentiles" *(gôyîm)*·in 5:3.

(b) In 4QpIsa^a (frs. 8-10) it interprets the Assyrians of Isa 10:33-34.

(c) In 1QM 11:11-12, it interprets the Assyrians of Isa 31:8.

(d) In 4QpNah 1:3 it interprets the Assyrians of Nahum, whose home or "den" is Nineveh. Cf. 1:1, "Jerusalem (=Nineveh) has become a dwelling-place for the Gentiles (Kittim). (In frs. 1-2:3, a word beg:nning with the definite article, with no further letters extant, interprets "the sea". The following sentence reads: " . . . to execute against them judgement and to exterminate them from the face of the earth with their rulers *(môšelehem)* whose dominion *(memšelet)* will be brought to an end". Allegro supplies "the Kittim" after the definite article.[10] But in 2:4 of the same work "Ephraim" (the seekers-after-smooth-things, 2:2) exercise "rule" *(memšelet)* in Jerusalem, and "Manasseh", their associates, are "surrounded by sea and waters" in 3:10. A word referring to this group is to be supplied.)

(e) In 1QpPs frs. 9-10:4 it interprets the Egyptians and Ethiopians of Ps 68:30-32.

(f) In 1QM 1, 15-19 (framework and battle narratives),[11] it is used throughout. Col. 1 is partly editorial, binding together 15-19 with the earlier part of the work. The first use, in 1:2, names "the Kittim of Assyria".

(g) It appears in 4Q247, in a fragmentary context which Milik[12] believes to refer to the building and destruction of the first temple.

In *all* cases, the word is used when the inhabitants of OT Assyria, Babylon, Egypt and Ethiopia are in the background. It reflects a pesher convention: as all named biblical foreign powers mean the contemporary foreign power, the same name is used for all of them. "Chaldeans", "Assyrians", "Egyptians" and "Ethiopians" are but disguised names for Romans, and "Kittim" is used to bring out this fact. But it is *only* used when the OT foreign powers are in the mind of the writer. Itself a biblical name, used for convenience to cover all the powers, it refers always to the OT. When contemporary foreign powers are being dealt with apart from a biblical context, another name has to be used. They are called "the Gentiles", or "Yawan" (see below).

In 4QpNah 2:5 there is a prediction that Gentiles *(gôyîm)* will attack the city of Jerusalem. This confirms the above. Col. 1:3 of the same work has called the *inhabitants* of the city, the "lions" who dwell there, the Kittim; its point is that as Nineveh is the city of the Assyrians, so Jerusalem has become a foreign city, the dwelling-place of the Kittim (thoroughly hellenized) (cf. pp.25-9). The writer cannot, therefore, call the Roman attackers of the city Kittim; he must call them Gentiles.

CD 8:11 speaks of the kings of Yawan, who will come to punish the enemies of the sect. In the sense of "Greece", found in the second century B.C., this appears to be support for an early date. But the word *hellen,* at first "Greek", subsequently came to be used for all Gentiles, including Romans (e.g. Rom 2:10). It meant "all persons who came under the influence of Greek, i.e. pagan culture".[13] 4QpNah 1:3, in the interpretation given above (p.26) includes the Kittim in "Yawan": "the kings of Yawan from Antiochus until the appearance of the rulers of the Kittim". All were Gentiles who attacked the sanctuary; the prophet Nahum was held to make no distinction between them.

The absence of Kittim from a Qumran writing is not, then, a valid criterion of dating. It simply means that the writer was not thinking of a biblical foreign power.

The 390 Years

The Qumran principles of biblical interpretation may also be seen to lie behind CD 1:5-11, an important passage for the date of the Teacher.

In the Period of Wrath *(qeṣ ḥarôn)*, 390 years for the giving them (lit.; *lĕtîttô 'ôtam)*into the hand of Nebuchadnezzar king of Babylon, he (God) visited them and caused to shoot from Israel and from Aaron a Plant-root *(šôreš matta'at)* to inherit the land and to grow fat in the goodness of his soil. They understood their wrongdoing and knew that they were guilty men. But they were like blind men, groping for the way, for twenty years. God then observed their works, that they sought him whole-heartedly, and he raised up for them a Teacher of Righteousness to guide them in the way of his heart.

Lĕtîttô has been taken as meaning "after he gave", and the date of Nebuchadnezzar's attack on Jerusalem (587 B.C.) then gives a starting-point for the 390 years. But I. Rabinowitz[14] has pointed out that *lĕ* "never occurs in Hebrew in the temporal meaning 'after', 'from the time that' ", and it never has this meaning in the scrolls. *"Lĕtîttô* quite clearly means 'at (the time of) His giving' or 'to (the time of) His giving' or 'as of His giving' ".

If it were established that the Teacher was in the Roman period, there would be no difficulty in accounting for "Nebuchadnezzar king of Babylon" as a *symbol for the ruler of Rome,* derived from the custom of the *pesharim* of using biblical names for contemporary figures. It is known that the biblical Babylonians, as well as the Assyrians and Egyptians, were interpreted as Romans. In the NT "Babylon" is used as a symbol of Rome (1 Pet 5:13). The sentence would then be read: "In the Period of Wrath, the 390 years for his giving them into the hand of 'Nebuchadnezzar king of Babylon' (that is, the ruler of Rome), he visited them . . ." (and established the Plant-root). It would mean that there was a historical period, the Period of Wrath, characterised by subjection to Rome; during this period the community of CD (also that of 1QS, cf. "the Plantation", 1QS 8:5) was founded. *Harôn,* "wrath", is associated with the Romans in 1QpHab 3:12, and, as shown p.27, the Young Lion of Wrath was a Roman.

The figure of 390 years would then be seen as a *prophecy* of the duration of the time of subjection to Rome, drawn from Ezek 4:4-5. Ezekiel had been commanded to lie on his left side for 390 days, as a sign of a coming punishment for Israel lasting 390 years. At the time he wrote, the punishment was said to be inflicted by Nebuchadnezzar. But the basic assumption of the Qumran *pesharim* is that all biblical prophecy refers in a disguised form to events in the time of the community. The prophetic Babylonians are the Romans. With other evidences of a Roman date for the Teacher, the CD passage would be seen as drawing upon this assumption of the *pesharim,* stating in symbolic form that the Plant-root was founded in the Roman period, whose duration is known from OT prophecy, although it is still the time of the writer. (There would be two resulting problems if this were the meaning: why are the conventions of the *pesharim* not usually drawn upon in CD, which employs a distinctive allegorical method

(6:4); and why is such a long period of subjection to Rome accepted, when elsewhere there is the expectation of an imminent eschatological climax? An answer to these questions will be supplied by the reconstruction, p.194 below.)

When this passage is understood in the terms of the *pesharim*, it gives positive evidence that a community called the "Plant-root" was established in the Roman period, and that the Teacher came twenty years later.

The Absence of the Teacher of Righteousness from Contemporary Records

As indicated in the Introduction (pp.2-3), the complete absence of the Teacher from the accounts of Josephus, Philo, Pliny, and the writings dependent on them, is an immediately obvious fact in the way of placing the Teacher at the foundation of the Essene movement. He was an outstanding personality, who was believed by his followers to be the subject of scriptural prophecy. As will be shown (pp.65-71), he was responsible for the doctrine of the superiority of the spiritual to the fleshly, a doctrine which, according to Josephus, attracted many Gentiles to the Essenes.[15] Josephus loses no opportunity to recommend a saintly Jewish personality, and he had spent part of his youth among the Essenes.[16] All of this makes it quite extraordinary that the Teacher never appears in the contemporary records. The Essenes were well known prior to the discovery of the scrolls, but the existence of their leader was never suspected. It is surely necessary to find a place for this fact in a reconstruction of the history.

Was the Teacher in the Roman Period?

We are in a position now to make a survey of what has so far been discovered, as it promises to point to at least a tentative conclusion. As stated at the beginning of this chapter, the evidences for a Hasmonean date for the Teacher are not so solid as has been supposed. There are no objective reasons why he should be put in that era, once it is admitted that there is uncertainty about the script of the few apparently early writings.

It now appears that there are some positive reasons why he should be placed in the Roman period, which began 63 B.C. The future tenses of 4QpPs[a], when the temporal sense of Qumran verbs is taken into account, mean that the Teacher was still alive at the time of writing, and this work, with the other *pesharim*, is from the time when the Romans were present. "Yawan" in 4QpNah 1:3 includes the Romans, supporting this meaning in CD 8:11, for contemporaries of the Teacher's enemies. The conventions of the *pesharim* are in widespread use, even in works that are not in *pesher* form, leading to the use even in 1QM of the biblical term Kittim as a disguised name for Romans. This gives a reason for seeing "Nebuchadnezzar king of Babylon" as a symbol for the ruler of Rome, giving a Roman date for the Plant-root and the Teacher.

If this were the case, then the last-mentioned problem, concerning the absence of the Teacher from contemporary records, would be solved. The Essenes had been founded in Hasmonean times, but somewhat later, under the Romans, a related but different community, the Plant-root, was formed. The Teacher appeared as leader of *this* community, and so was not classed with the Essenes by contemporary writers.

Keeping in mind this tentative conclusion, we now proceed to as thorough an analysis as possible of the writings connected with the Teacher, in order to discover what stages of development they went through. Those writings which show no sign of his presence must also be considered, in order to account for their differences from those of the Teacher. The new evidence of the Temple Scroll will also be brought into the discussion. Our purpose is to learn whether the history that is revealed from the writings themselves is able to be matched in any way with the events of the well-documented period of the Roman occupation of Palestine.

NOTES

1. J. Carmignac, "Interprétations de Prophètes et de Psaumes" in *Textes de Qumrân* II, 43-126; "Conjectures sur les écrits de Qumrân"; "Notes sur les Pesharim"; Review of Stegemann, *Die Entstehung . . .* , *RevQ* 8 (1973) 277-281; Review of Cross, *Ancient Library . . .* , *RevQ* 1 (1959), 440-443.
2. M. H. Segal, "The Habakkuk 'Commentary' and the Damascus Fragments", *JBL* 70 (1951), 131-147; J. van der Ploeg "L'usage du parfait et de l'imparfait comme moyen de datation dans le Commentaire d'Habacuc", in *Les Manuscrits de la Mer Morte*, Colloque de Strasbourg (1957); W. H. Brownlee, "The Historical Allusions of the Dead Sea Habakkuk Midrash", *BASOR* 126 (1952), 10-20.
3. Carmignac translates (*Textes de Qumrân*, II, 108); "evil diseases have inflicted horrors on him and vengeance on his body of flesh", as he interprets it in terms of the illness, not the death, of the Wicked Priest. But see H. Burgmann, "Gerichtsherr und Generalankläger . . ." , 47-48.
4. Carmignac, inconsistently with his own case concerning the tenses, draws upon biblical usage to argue that *nĕtano* is a prophetic perfect, as he holds that the Wicked Priest was still alive at the time of writing 1QpHab, and 12:5 refers to his first death.
5. Cross, *Ancient Library . . .* , 84. Milik, *Ten Years . . .* , 41.
6. Cross, *Ancient Library . . .* , 85.
7. Cf. Burgmann, "Gerichtsherr . . .", 52, who points out that the sect could not afford failed prophecies, even among their own members.

57

8. Carmignac *(Textes de Qumrân,* II, 8-60), sees the necessity of combining the important indication of the tenses with the presence of the Romans, and holds that the *pesharim* were written shortly after the first warnings of the coming of the Romans, at the time of Sylla's campaign against Mithridates in 85-84 B.C. But this does not do justice to the indications of 1QpHab that the Romans are actually present in the land. It also either disregards the palaeographical evidence, or assumes that the *pesharim* are not autographs.

9. Cross, *Ancient Library* . . ., 59, note 46.

10. DJD V. Strugnell ("Notes en marge . . .", 207) does not comment.

11. See p.106.

12. J. T. Milik, *The Books of Enoch* . . ., 256.

13. Arndt and Gingrich, *A Greek-English Lexicon of the New Testament,* ad loc.

14. I. Rabinowitz, "A Reconsideration of 'Damascus' and '390 Years' in the 'Damascus' ('Zadokite') Fragments", *JBL* 73 (1954), 11-35, note 8b, p.14.

15. *J.W.* 2§158.

16. *Life,* §§10-11.

part
two

The Teacher's Doctrine
and its
Place in the History

CHAPTER VI

The Heavenly Temple

In this part of the project, it will be necessary to proceed more slowly. In order to discover the history, a close analysis of the texts will be undertaken, looking for changes and developments in doctrine and organisation. At certain points, a special examination of the meaning of some central doctrines is required, not only for purposes of comparison with other stages, but because they are naturally related to the history; for example, the future expectation, which has determined the sect's orientation to its present circumstances.

There is in some of the writings a doctrine of the future that may be called eschatological, although it will be pointed out that there are important differences from Christian eschatology. It is not the same as other forms of future expectation found elsewhere in the Qumran literature. It is associated with the terms *'aḥărît hayyamîm* (here translated "Future Time"), *qes 'aḥărôn,* "Last Period", and *pěquddâ,* "Visitation". These are found in 1QS, 1QSa, 1QH, CD, the *pesharim* and other fragments. But they are not found in the Temple Scroll, nor in 1QM. The meaning of the doctrine, and the reason why it is confined to some works only, should be given careful consideration.

As will be seen, a specific point of relevance to the history emerges: the central thrust of the doctrine is *the restoration of the Zadokite high priesthood in the recovered Jerusalem temple.*

The Partnership with the Heavenly Temple[1]
The fellowship between members of the community and the members of heaven, who are thought of as continually worshipping God in a heavenly temple, is illustrated in several of the sources.

1QS 11:7-8, speaking of the privileges of the members of the Community: "God . . . has caused them to inherit the lot of the holy ones, and with the sons of heaven he has joined *(hibber)* their company *(sôd)* as a Council of the Community and the foundation of a holy building for an eternal plantation". *Hibber* is found in the context of building or physical joining in Ex 26:11, 39:4, Ps 122:3, also of alliance between two parties (2 Chr 20:36, Ps 94:20). The passage means that there are two communities, one in heaven ("the lot of the holy ones", "the sons of heaven"), one on earth, the Qumran members. The two are allied or joined with one another. Consequently, membership of the earthly community entitles one also to membership of the heavenly, "to inherit the lot of the holy ones". A. R. C. Leaney[2] remarks on this passage: "The members of the sect are to share the life of angels, and they are united with them in one community". P. Guilbert:[3] "Le culte de la Communauté, qui respecte le calendrier cosmique, est rendu à Dieu en union et en synchronisme avec celui des anges; d'où l'union qui existe entre l'assemblée céleste et l'assemblée terrestre".

The same view is found in 1QH, both in the hymns of the Teacher[4] and those not written by him. In 1QH 3:21-23, again in a context of election, the writer praises God for making him stand "with the host of the holy ones, and to come into community *(yahad)* with the congregation *('edâ)* of the sons of heaven. Men, the sectarians, are in an "eternal lot with the spirits of knowledge to praise thy name in communal rejoicing". The inhabitants of heaven form a community and congregation, exactly as the earthly members do, and the latter have membership in the heavenly *yahad*. Cf. also 1QH 6:13 (by the Teacher): "in the lot of the community *(yahad)* with the angels of the presence"; 1QH 11:11-12: "to bring him into a community with the sons of thy truth and in a lot with thy holy ones . . . to stand in the office (of worship, *ma'ămad)* before thee with the eternal host and the spirits of [. . .]".

In 4Q181 fr. 1: 3-6[5] "God has brought near some of the sons of the world to be reckoned with him in the [council of the go]ds as a holy congregation in the office (of worship) for those who have eternal life and in the lot with his holy ones".[6]

H. W. Kuhn[7] holds that these passages mean that the members are now in heaven; H. Hübner[8] that they are predestined for heaven, and will belong to it in the future. Carmignac[9] is uncertain whether it means that men after death will participate in the life of angels, or whether angels participate now in the earthly life of the community.

It is difficult for the modern mind to take into account the extent to which heaven was conceived structurally and spatially in Qumran thought. The heavenly temple and the earthly community are understood as two different structures, both existing at present in two different places, far away from one another. The Qumran members on earth have been divinely brought into an alliance, a legal bond, with the heavenly community. They are, as it were, constituted as a distant branch of the heavenly headquarters. To join their community is to receive membership of heaven. They cannot be in heaven now (against Kuhn): that is physically impossible. But they do not have to wait for the future to have their membership of heaven (against Hübner): they have it now. Dequeker[10] correctly observes: "The Qumran community is a holy community, because it is taken into partnership with the heavenly community of angels".

In his preliminary publication of 4QŠirŠabb, Strugnell[11] shows that the work is based on "the idea of the heavenly temple and therefore its cult as a model of the earthly one". He notes that the names for the different groups of those being blessed, although they seem to be angels, are sometimes human, e.g., "walking uprightly", "perfect of way", "eager for his will", "waiting on him". The angelic titles often include "priest". In the second fragment (formerly 4QS1 40), the 'Elôhîm may throughout be understood as the inhabitants of heaven, "godly ones" rather than God, including 1.6.[12] "In all the camps of the 'Elôhîm appears in 8b; "camps" is an organisational term for part of the earthly community. The liturgy is one to be performed on earth, among the sectarians. As Strugnell recognizes:[13] "This is no angelic liturgy, no visionary work where a seer hears the praise of the angels, but a *Maskil's* composition for an earthly liturgy in which the presence of the angels is in a sense invoked and in which . . . the heavenly temple is portrayed on the model of the earthly one and in some way its service is considered the pattern of what is being done below". Yet the community members are named as angels and godly ones.

Although 1QM does not contain the future terms listed above, 1QM 12:1-5, in a section of the work that has been linked with the developed Qumran theology,[14] contains a clear statement of the doctrine of partnership with heaven. "For thou hast a multitude of holy ones in heaven, and hosts of angels in thy holy habitation, praising thy name. Thou hast placed the elect ones of the holy people in [. . .][15] book of the names of all their host is with thee in thy holy abode". F. Nötscher[16] believes that although the text is not certain, it may be brought together with the evidences of a written register of members (CD 19:35, 4:5, 13:12, 1QS 6:22, 1QSa 1:21) and the fact of the parallel communities to show that there was held to be a parallel book in heaven, in which the names of the sectarians were written. When their names were entered in the earthly register, they were at the same time recorded in the heavenly book, as a means of ensuring that they belonged to the higher community also.

What are the implications of the belief that members of the community are in partnership with the members of heaven?

The Separated Temple

It is recognized that some of the writings contain the concept of the community members themselves forming a "temple"· e.g. 1QS 8:4-6: "When these (men) are in Israel, the Council of the Community is established in truth, as an eternal plantation, a Holy House for Israel, and a foundation ·(sôd) of the Holy of Holies for Aaron". Cf. also 1QS 5:4-7, 9:3-6, CD 3:19. This doctrine, unique in contemporary Judaism and found elsewhere only in the NT, has been studied by B. Gärtner,[17] and, with more attention to textual detail, by G. Klinzing.[18]

The doctrine is logically continuous with the belief that the sectarians have co-membership with the angels in a heavenly temple. The Qumran priests and the angelic priests are operating in two separate locations of the temple: the latter in its heavenly headquarters, the former in an earthly outpost. They do not possess the sacred site in Jerusalem, prescribed in the Law as the place of the earthly temple. But their adherence to the Law requires them still to hold Jerusalem as the site of the earthly temple. The emphasis on their partnership with heaven is accounted for as a means of affirming the legitimacy of their priesthood. Its authority is denied by the Jerusalem establishment, but to their members they are able to claim that they have a higher authorisation, that of heaven itself.

Both doctrines, the community as a temple and the partnership with heaven, were therefore developed to deal with the separation of the Qumran priesthood from the Jerusalem temple priesthood. It is usually held[19] that the Essenes are to be connected with the Hasidim, who according to 1 Macc 7:13-14 separated from the Hasmonean house on the grounds of its illegal adoption of the high priesthood. As upholders of the Zadokite line (cf. the importance of the Zadokite priests in 1QS and 1QSa), the Essenes no longer had a place in the temple. The doctrines enabled them to continue to hold the Jerusalem site as sacred; but, while the true priesthood was not operating there, it could rely on the invisible authorisation of heaven. By admitting that Jerusalem was the true place of the earthly temple, they implied also that the present situation was only temporary. The doctrines have an inseparable future dimension, concerning the restoration of the Jerusalem site to the Qumran and Zadokite priesthood. As the heavenly temple is also

63

involved, there is an eschatological dimension, in the sense of a divinely initiated event in the future. This point has not been developed by Gärtner, and has been denied by Klinzing, who holds that the community temple ideal is in antithesis with the ideal of an eschatological temple; it meant that the eschatological temple was fulfilled already. It may be argued that Klinzing's view fails to take into account the structural, spatial and temporal nature of the Qumran view of heaven and earth.

11QMelch,[20] dealing with the *'aḥarît hayyamîm* (1.4), quotes in 1.10 Ps 82:1: "*'Elôhîm* stands in the congregation of God; in the midst of the *'Elôhîm* he judges". The quotation is introduced by "that is the time of the acceptable year of Melchizedek . . . as it is written concerning him . . . " (1.9). Van der Woude and de Jonge,[21] followed by J. A. Fitzmyer,[22] agree that the author here means that Melchizedek is the first *'Elôhîm,* the godly one or heavenly being. As heavenly high priest[23] he presides over the congregation in heaven. The *'Elôhîm* in the midst of whom he judges have been conjectured to be an angelic court[24] or condemned angels.[25] In 1.8, the "men of the lot of Melchizedek" are the "sons of light", a name for the community members. Fitzmyer[26] has pointed to other terms in the fragment denoting the community: "captives" in 1.4, "the heritage of Melchizedek in 1.5 ("it may be that the priests of the Qumran community are thus envisaged"). As the members of the present community also have membership in heaven, does not this fragment mean that in the *'aḥarît hayyamîm,* the Future Time, the present members will be the *'Elôhîm* in the heavenly temple, presided over by the heavenly high priest? They will then no longer be separated from their heavenly headquarters, but be back home in the heavenly temple, reunited with their fellow-priests, the angels. 4QŠirŠabb speaks of the same persons as angels and sectarians either because it refers to this period, or because the community members are potential angels.

1QSa, also referring to the Future Time (1:1), shows that members will age normally (1:8), marry (1:9-10), be capable of mental and physical infirmity (1:19-20, 2:5-7), eat and drink (2:17). Yet, according to 1QH 3:25-36 there will be a violent conflagration over the whole world, in which the bases of the mountains will burn, the rocks will melt, and the world will be covered by torrents of pitch. The two expectations are apparently opposed: one foresees natural, one supernatural conditions. This has led to opposing views on Qumran eschatology. Carmignac[27] argues that there is no eschatology at Qumran; the fire of 1QH 3:25-36 is metaphorical. Starcky[28] and Jeremias[29] accept an eschatological outlook, and assume that it means a belief similar to the Christian view of a radical alteration of present material conditions.

The two interpretations are reconciled by an understanding of the Qumran doctrine of the flesh and its survival at the Visitation, found also in the eschatological writings.

The Qumran Doctrine of Flesh and Spirit[30]

Two passages of 1QS, both accepted as coming from the developed stage of the theology,[31] may be compared with one another to elucidate the doctrine of flesh and spirit and the future of the flesh. They are 3:6-9, dealing with initiation into the community in the present time, and 4:18-22, dealing with the Visitation.

> 3:6-9:
> (A) For by the spirit of the true counsel[32] of God[33] the ways of a man will be atoned for, all his iniquities. He will behold the light of life. In the Spirit of holiness[34] (which is given) to the community[35] in its truth he will be purified from all his iniquities. By a spirit of uprightness and humility his sin will be atoned for.
> (B) When his soul is humbled before all the decrees of God, his flesh will be purified. He will be sprinkled with the waters of purification and sanctified with the waters of washing.

The passage deals with two different *objects* of cleansing and with two corresponding *instruments* of cleansing. (A) concerns the cleansing of "ways", (B) concerns the cleansing of the flesh. Sinful behaviour is differentiated from impure flesh. Sin is only named in (A); (B) deals with the cleansing of the flesh as *following* inward penitence. "When his soul is humbled . . . his flesh will be purified". Sin is, according to this distinction, located in the mind and will. It is in the inward parts, of which the flesh is only the outer expression. The flesh does not carry the real guilt, but is defiled as a result of the inner sin. The flesh is only secondarily impure; the real guilt is inward. The distinction in the locations of sin, and their relative importance, is like that of Matt 5:21-22 and 27: murder and adultery are performed in the heart, in the intention; the fleshly action is not the essential guilty action. Cf. also Mark 7:20-23: "What comes out of a man is what defiles a man". The same distinction and order are found in Josephus' account of the baptism of John: "They must not use it (baptismal ablution) to gain pardon for whatever sins they had committed, but as a sanctification of the body, the soul being already cleansed by righteousness".[36] Cf. also Heb 10:22 for a distinction between two locations of sin and two actions of purification: "with our hearts sprinkled clean from an evil conscience and our bodies washed with pure water".

There are, then, two locations of sin, one primary and one secondary. The inner man is the primary location, the outer man, the flesh, the secondary.

There are also, according to the passage, two corresponding *instruments* of cleansing. The inner man is cleansed by *Spirit* (the Spirit of holiness, the spirit of the true counsel of God, the spirit of uprightness and humility); the outer man by *water*. Water is not mentioned in (A), spirit is not mentioned in (B). Water cleansing is only appropriate to the outer man. The inner man, who is spirit, can only be cleansed by spirit.

1QS 3:4 also refers to two kinds of sin and two means of purification: "he (the man who refuses to join the community) will not be made clean by atonements *(kippûrîm)* and not purified by the waters of purification. "Atone" is used for the moral restoration in (A) in 3:6-9.

The distinction between an inner purification, not by water, and a purification of the flesh by water, rests on the OT distinction between sin and ritual impurity. Sacrifice was the means of removing sin, water ablutions the means of removing ritual impurity.[37] At Qumran, the inner virtue (spirit of uprightness, etc.) takes the place of sacrifice, on the authority of such texts as 1 Sam 15:22 (obedience is better than sacrifice). The washing does not take the place of sacrifice, as J. A. T. Robinson[38] supposes: it remains an ablution for the removal of ritual impurity. What is new is that the inward sin is held to defile the flesh, that is, make it ritually impure. Scobie[29] sees that "in the scrolls . . . moral offences render a man ritually unclean and therefore require rites of ablution". Leaney:[40] "The sect is the first group within Judaism of whom we know who believed that moral failure . . . incurred ritual defilement". But the OT distinction between moral sin and ritual impurity is not blurred, as is sometimes assumed. The difference was maintained, as shown in the present passage, by distinguishing inner and outer sin, removed by two different instruments.

The inner purification is associated with entry into the community. "In the Spirit of holiness (which is given) to the community in its truth, he will be cleansed from all his iniquities". The penitent had received an inner atonement, by the intangible virtues that had operated in his heart (the spirit of the true counsel of God, the spirit of uprightness and humility). He is given also a cleansing by the Spirit of holiness, which was available to him in the community. Virtue could more easily be practised within the society where the same sort of spirit resided as had operated in the individual's heart. The penitent's continuation in holiness is ensured by his membership of the community.

We turn now to 1QS 4:18-22, dealing with the future Visitation.

> God, in the mysteries of his insight and in his glorious wisdom, has set an end-time for the existence of evil *(qeṣ liḥĕyot 'awĕlâ)*. At the season of the Visitation he will destroy it for ever. Then there will go forth for ever the truth of the world. For it pollutes itself in evil ways under the dominion of iniquity until the season

of the appointed judgement. Then God wll cleanse by his truth all the works of a man *(geber)*[41] and will purify some for himself from among the sons of men. He will destroy every spirit of iniquity from the defilement[42] of his flesh. He will purify him by the Spirit of holiness from all evil deeds. He will sprinkle upon him a spirit of truth like waters of purification from every lying abomination and from being polluted in a spirit of impurity. He will cause the upright to understand the knowledge of the Most High and the wisdom of the sons of heaven, and cause the perfect of way to have insight.

This passage does not contain the same distinction between inner and outer sin as does 1QS 3:6-9. There is sinful behaviour ("the works of a man", "evil deeds"), but it is located in the flesh. There is a similar change with regard to the two instruments of cleansing, the Spirit and water, differentiated in 1QS 3:6-9. The evil deeds are still cleansed by the Spirit of holiness and by a spirit of truth. But spirit is "like waters of purification". Water now stands for spirit: there is no marked difference between them. Leaney:[43] "(In this passage) moral or ceremonial defilement . . . contaminates the physical body, and . . . God's spirit must cleanse the body as well as the spirit of man (the two being integrated)". Wernberg-Møller:[44] "That the text alludes to spiritual baptism seems clear".

But these facts do not negate the observations drawn from 1QS 3:6-9. They add, rather, a significant dimension to the understanding of the Qumran view of the present and the future time.

The expectation concerning the Future Time centres above all on the *abolition of sin*. The key phrase is in the above passage: "an end-time for the existence of evil". Sin is understood as an external pollution, extrinsic to matter, as in the OT. The flesh will be, not destroyed, but cleansed. The community members will be, not transformed, but purified. "Then God will cleanse by his truth all the works of a man and will purify some for himself from among the sons of men. He will destroy every spirit of iniquity from . . . his flesh."

The means of doing this is shown in the phrase "he will sprinkle upon him a spirit of truth like waters of purification". This brings together water and Spirit in a way that is not found in 3:6-9. At the present time, water cleansing and Spirit purification are kept carefully apart, because flesh and spirit are the outer and inner parts of man, different from one another. The fact that moral sin can ritually defile the flesh means, however, that the two cannot be wholly separated. The spirit cannot survive without the flesh. This entity will continue to exist in the Future Time, just as both Spirit and water will be found in the Future Time. But the bringing together of Spirit and water means that there will be a new relationship between the human soul and flesh. The barrier between flesh and soul will have been overcome: there will no longer be a difference between inward and outward. The difference and conflict between the flesh and the spirit are felt to be impediments to holiness at the present time. But in the future, the differ-- ence, with the conflict, will have been removed. The reunion of inward and outward will be unlike anything known at the present time — in this respect, it will be a supernatural change — but it will be a change within the physical order, not a change from a physical to a spiritual order.

The present distance between flesh and spirit corresponds to the distance between the earthly and heavenly priesthoods. There is a great space between the spiritual or heavenly, and the fleshly or earthly places. In the future, the two places and orders will have come together; the separation will have been overcome. The myth of the primeval separation of heaven and earth has recently been shown by P. D. Hanson[45] to be an important element in 1 Enoch 6-11. The two were originally united, but were cut asunder with a giant cleaver. The Qumran eschatological doctrine evidently expected that heaven and earth would come together at the Visitation, and when this occurred, sin would be destroyed. When heaven and earth come together, the human soul and flesh would come together. The great distance between heaven and earth at present is the means whereby the flesh becomes polluted. It is the heavy part, whereas the soul is light. The flesh sinks down towards the Pit, *šahat*. Sinners are called sons of the Pit (1QS 9:16, 10:19). The soul is drawn upwards, and the virtuous are closest to heaven, climbing up the ladder of the stages of initiation (cf. pp.91-6). Their souls are "weighed" (root *šaqal)* to determine promotion (1QS 9:14).

It has been held, however, that 1QH teaches that the flesh is intrinsically evil, so that it would have to be destroyed in the future (W. D. Davies, K. G. Kuhn, E. Brandenburger[46], in different forms). The sinful flesh is contrasted with the soul, in the many passages of 1QH in which the writer calls himself by terms denoting flesh ("creature of clay", "edifice of sin") describing it as evil. It is to be observed, however, that in these passages the contrast is always between the unworthiness of the sectarian and the great gifts bestowed on him by the divine Spirit, e.g. 4:27-32, 15:21. "Flesh" is used in contrast with the *divine* Spirit, but not with the soul of the sectarian himself. Both his flesh and his soul are capable of sin, as 1QS 3:6-9 shows, and as is shown by the many 1QH and 1QS passages referring to his soul as "perverted" (1QH 1:22, 3:21, 5:36, 11:12; 1QS 2:14, 7: 18, 23, 10:18). "Flesh" includes both the human body and soul; the term is used to emphasize the present separation from the spiritual realms.

The view that there is not an ontological difference between the flesh and the spirit in 1QH receives support from H. Hübner,[47] who attacks

E. Brandenburger's view, directed, like that of W. D. Davies and K. G. Kuhn, to the Pauline antithesis of flesh and spirit. Hübner studies the passages dealing with the salvation of the elect, showing that when he is saved, he does not cease to be the "dust", "creature of clay" that he defines himself to be. When he enters the community (where he receives salvation) he is delivered from the power of death and receives new life. This consists in a cleansing of his perverted self. But he does not receive a new self (ein neues Sein). He is given a new orientation (eine neue Ausrichtung seines Seins); henceforward he goes in the right direction. His self is altered, but not renewed: "Nicht ein neues Sein des Gerechtfertigten wird behauptet, sondern eine qualitative Änderung seines Seins".[48] There is no sign of a gnostic view of the loss of the old fleshly self and the survival of a purely spiritual self.[49]

When the Spirit of holiness is poured out at the Visitation, the elect will be "plunged" (*hitgôlel*, 1QS 4:21) in it, their outer flesh rejoicing for the first time in contact with the Spirit. The spirit of truth will give them an increased endowment of divine wisdom and understanding, beyond that which they are given at present at their election. They will receive "the wisdom of the sons of heaven", the full knowledge of the angels (1QS 4:21-22). Cf. 1 Cor 13:9-12: "For our knowledge is imperfect and our prophecy is imperfect; but when the perfect comes, the imperfect will pass away . . . Now I know in part; then I shall understand fully".

This understanding enables the two apparently contradictory descriptions of the Future Time, one natural (1QSa) one supernatural (1QH 3:25-36) to be reconciled. The equation between the supernatural and the abolition of matter is influenced by Christian conceptions. The Qumran expectation is of a supernatural order in the sense of an order different from the present one, one that will unite the material and spiritual in a new way. Its emphasis is on the restoration of matter, which has become polluted by sin. Once the extrinsic evil is purged off, material forms will remain the same. The community members, now cleansed by the outpouring of spirit, will continue their manner of life as it is now, eating, living in houses, meeting together. There will have been a violent conflagration, as described in 1QH 3:25-36, but it will be for the purpose of destruction of falsehood, cf. also 1QS 4:11-14. The righteous will emerge from ˙it unscathed to continue their material existence. This is shown by 1QH 17:13-14; " . . . foundations of the mountains, and fire . . . in Sheol beneath it . . . for thy servants in faithfulness [to b]e their seed before thee [. . .] thou hast raised . . . ". The Zoroastrian belief[50] in an ordeal by molten metal, which the righteous would feel only as warm milk, is a probable influence. They would continue to live on earth (cf. 1QpHab 13:3-4: "all wickedness will be destroyed from the earth") newly joined to heaven. Heaven will come down to earth, rather than earth going up to heaven.

The Future Temple

In the present time, the community members belong to the heavenly community of angels, but they are parted from them by the distance between heaven and earth, absent from their true home (p.62). With the removal of the separation and the descent of the heavenly temple to earth, the Qumran priests will officiate in it with their fellow-priests, the angels, as described in 11QMelch, 4QŠirŠabb, and possibly also 1QSb, cf. 4:23-26, "as an angel of the presence in the holy habitation", 3:25-26: "(the priests will be) as a splendid jewel in the midst of the holy ones."

F. F. Bruce's remark:[51] "the recognition of their community as a spiritual temple did not prevent the men of Qumran from expecting to worship one day in a material sanctuary" depends on a Christian material-spiritual antithesis. The men of Qumran never held a spiritual temple, in the sense of a non-material temple. They held a heavenly temple, which was at present separated into two parts. The community was the part of it that was now visible; the remainder (and also the perfect, sinless form) was invisible. The future would bring full visibility and reunion of the two parts.

There is no antithesis between the idea of an eschatological temple and a present "temple" of community members, as Klinzing holds. The eschatological temple cannot be fulfilled in the present: realized eschatology is a Christian concept. The present community, far from fulfilling the future temple, is a proof that it exists, and will one day come, as the other half of what is now visible. 1QH 6:24-35 gives the Teacher's view of his present community, in terms which, as Jeremias[52] shows, have influenced 1QS 8:1-15a. "I was like one who comes to a fortified city . . . thou wilt set its foundation on a rock, a basis by the measuring-cord of justice, and by the plumb-line of truth thou wilt lay the tried stones . . ." It speaks of a "Jerusalem" already present in the community. Klinzing[53] uses this fact in support of his view. But the passage speaks of security in the "city" *"until the escape* ('ad palet, 6:25)". There are still limitations in the present, but the guarantee of salvation given by the present New Jerusalem will be taken up in the freedom of the Jerusalem to come.

The last passage puts it beyond doubt that the eschatological doctrine described in this chapter is that of the Teacher of Righteousness. He was himself accepted as the high priest of the community, as shown by his title "the Priest" (4QpPs[a] 2:18, 3:15)[54]. He had every reason to support his and his fellow priests' authority with his doctrine of the heavenly temple, whose coming would in the Future Time vindicate their position. Those major works which do not contain this doctrine may not be connected with him.

NOTES

1. The literature includes: F. Nötscher, *Zur Theologischen Terminologie der Qumran-Texte,* (Bonn, 1956); "Heiligkeit in den Qumranschriften" *RevQ* 2 1960), 163-181, *RevQ* 2 (1960) 315-344; "Geist und Geister in den Texten von Qumran, *Mélanges bibliques rédigés en l'honneur d'André Robert* (Paris: Bloud et Gay, 1957) 305-315; Himmlische Bücher und Schicksalglaube in Qumran", *RevQ* 1 (1959), 405-411; H. W. Kuhn, *Enderwartung und gegenwartiges Heil: Untersuchungen zu den Gemeindeliedern von Qumran* (Göttingen, 1957, Exkurs 4: "Der Ausdruck *die Heiligen* in den Qumrantexten und im sonstigen Spätjudentum", 90-93; M. Mansoor, *The Thanksgiving Hymns* (Leiden: Brill, 1961), 77-84; M. Noth, "Die Heiligen des Höchsten", *NorTT* 56 (1955), 146-161; C. H. W. Brekelmans, "The Saints of the Most High and their Kingdom", *OTS* 14 (1965), 305-329; S. Lamberigts, "Le sens de *Qdwšym* dans les textes de Qumran", *ETL* 46 (1970), 24-39; R. Hanhart, "Die Heiligen des Höchsten", *VT* Sup 16 (Leiden, 1967), 90-101; L. Dequeker, "The 'Saints of the Most High' in Qumran and Daniel", *OTS* 18 (1973), 108-187; D. Barthélemy, "La Sainteté selon la communauté de Qumrân et selon l'Evangile" *RechBib* 4 (1959), 203-210; R. E. Brown, "Pre-Christian Semitic Concepts of 'Mystery' ", *CBQ* 20 (1958), 417-424, J. Maier, "Zum Begriff *yḥd* in den Texten von Qumran", *ZAW* 72 (1960), 148-166.

2. A. R. C. Leaney, *The Rule of Qumran and Its Meaning,* (London: SCM, 1966), 253.

3. P. Guilbert, "La Règle de la Communauté", in J. Carmignac, *Les Textes de Qumrân,* I, p.77, n.137.

4. G. Jeremias *(Der Lehrer . . .,* ch.6) has established, on the basis of vocabulary, style, and ideas, that certain of the hymns are by the Teacher of Righteousness. They are: 2:1-19; 2:31-39; 3:1-18, 4:5-5:4, 5:5-19, 5:20-7:5, 7:6-25, 8:4-40.

5. J. Milik holds ("Milki-ṣedeq et Milki-reša' ", 109-112) that *4Q180,* *4Q181,* 11QMelch form parts of a single work coming from the time of the Teacher.

6. Brekelmans ("The Saints . . .", p. 322) suggests that it may be "people *('am)* of the holy ones".

7. H. W. Kuhn, *Enderwartung . . .,* 55.

8. H. Hübner, "Anthropologischer Dualismus in den Hodayoth?" *NTS* 18 (1972), 268-284.

9. J. Carmignac, *Les Textes de Qumrân,* I, p.200, n.10.

10. L. Dequeker, "The Saints . . .", 141.
11. J. Strugnell, "The Angelic Liturgy at Qumran — 4Q Serek Širot 'Olat Haššabbat'," VTSup 7 (Leiden, 1959), 318-345, p.335.
12. Carmignac (Textes de Qumrân, II, 311-320) translates "God" in all cases; Strugnell "godly ones", except in 1.6.
13. "Angelic Liturgy", 320.
14. P. R. Davies, 1QM. The War Scroll from Qumran. Its Structure and History (Rome: Biblical Institute Press, 1977); "Dualism and Eschatology in the Qumran War Scroll", VT 28 (1978), 28-36. P. von der Osten-Sacken, Gott und Belial (Göttingen: Vandenhoeck & Ruprecht, 1969).
15. Yadin (The War of the Sons of Light against the Sons of Darkness (OUP). 1962 , p.314) reads bĕ(yaḥad), "in a community", but the letter after bet does not appear to be yod.
16. Nötscher, "Himmlische Bücher . . .", 409.
17. B. Gärtner, The Temple and the Community in Qumran and the New Testament (CUP), 1965 .
18. G. Klinzing, Die Umdeutung des Kultus in der Qumrangemeinde und im NT (Göttingen: Vandenhoeck & Ruprecht, 1971).
19. But see the recent article by P. R. Davies, "Hasidim in the Maccabean Period", JJS 28 (1977), 127-140.
20. Milik ("Milki-ṣedeq . . .") shows that the main published section of 11QMelch is 3 II. Original publications: A. S. van der Woude, "Melchisedek als himmlische Erlösergestalt in den neugefundenen eschatologischen Midraschim aus Qumran Höhle XI", OTS 14 (Leiden, 1965), 354-373. See also: M. de Jonge and A. S. van der Woude, "11QMelchizedek and the New Testament", NTS 12 (1966), 301-326.
21. See Note 20.
22. J. A. Fitzmyer, "Further Light on Melchizedek from Qumran Cave 11", in Essays on the Semitic Background of the New Testament (London: Chapman, 1971).
23. See the discussion on Melchizedek as heavenly high priest in de Jonge and van der Woude, "11QMelchizedek . . .".
24. Fitzmyer, "Further Light . . .", 262.
25. De Jonge and van der Woude, "11QMelchizedek . . .", 304.
26. Fitzmyer, "Further Light . . .", 257-8.
27. J. Carmignac, "Les Dangers de l'Eschatologie", NTS 17 (1971,), 365-90; "Notes sur les Pesharim", RevQ 3 (1962), 505-38; "Conjectures sur les Ecrits de Qumran"; Review of Stegemann, Die Entstehung . . ., Textes de Qumrân I, p.201, n.27; p.202, n.39.
28. J. Starcky, "Les quatre étapes du messianisme à Qumrân", RB 70 (1963, 481-505, p.486.
29. Jeremias, Der Lehrer . . ., 268.
30. Parts of this section have appeared in my "Inner and Outer Cleansing at Qumran as a Background to N.T. Baptism", NTS 25, 3 (1979).
31. J. Murphy-O'Connor ("La Genèse Littéraire de la Règle de la Communauté", RB 76 (1969), 528-549), sees 3:6-9 as from the developed theology. Milik ("Milki-ṣedeq . . .", 135) foreshadows a study of 1QS showing, from Cave 4 copies, that 1:16-3:12 belongs to a revision of the work.
32. 'esâ Wernberg-Møller chooses the sense "council" (= community). Lohse, Brownlee, Vermes, Guilbert, Leaney, translate "counsel". 'Eṣâ without Yaḥad has this sense in 1QS 6:4, 9, 8:18, 11:17,22.

Translations and commentaries of 1QS: E. Lohse, *Die Texte aus Qumran, Hebräisch und Deutsch* (Munich, 1964); P. Wernberg-Møller, *The Manual of Discipline* (Leiden: Brill, 1957); A. R. C. Leaney, *The Rule of Qumran* . . .; P. Guilbert, "La Règle de la Communauté", in *Textes de Qumran;* G. Vermes, *The Dead Sea Scrolls in English* (London: Pelican, 1962-8); W. H. Brownlee, *The Dead Sea Manual of Discipline, BASOR* Sup 10-12 (1951); J. T. Milik, "Manuale Disciplinae", *Verbum Domini* 29 (1951), 129-58.

33. Guilbert, Vermes, Leaney take *'el* as a preposition linking "true counsel" with "ways". Lohse, Wernberg-Møller, Brownlee, read "God". The "truth of God" (cf. "his truth", 1QS 1:11, 15, 19; 2:26; 3:7, 24; 4:20; 5:10) is the special doctrine given by God to the community.

34. "Spirit of holiness" rather than "Holy Spirit" is used throughout, following Vermes, *DSSE*, as it does not have the characteristic of personality at Qumran.

35. *Běruah qědošâ layyaḥad ba'amitto.* MS 1 from Cave 4 reads *běruah qodšo.* Cf. CD 2:12, *ruah qodšo.* Lohse translates: "durch den heiligen Geist (der) der Gemeinschaft in seiner Wahreit (gegeben ist)". Wernberg-Møller "by the holy spirit of the community in His truth". Guilbert (accepting *qědošâ*) "par l'esprit sanctifié dans une fidélité commune, littéralement par l'esprit sanctifié à la Communauté par sa fidélité". Leaney, Brownlee, Milik do not take *yaḥad* as "the community". But it is the most commonly used name for the community in 1QS, and could not have been used without this meaning.

36. *Ant.* 18§117.

37. D. Flusser, "The Baptism of John and the Dead Sea Sect", in C. Rabin and Y. Yadin (eds.) *Essays on the Dead Sea Scrolls in Memory of E. L. Sukenik* (Jerusalem, 1961 (Hebrew)).

38. J. A. T. Robinson, "The Baptism of John and the Qumran Community", in *Twelve New Testament Studies* (London: SCM, 1962), p.16. See also K. G. Kuhn ("The Lord's Supper and the Communal Meal at Qumran", in K. Stendahl (ed.), *The Scrolls and the New Testament* (London: SCM, 1957), 65-93, who says that the bath of immersion mediated the divine forgiveness of sins. M. Black (*The Scrolls and Christian Origins* (London: Nelson, 1961, p.98, n.1) calls this statement a "capital error".

39. C. H. H. Scobie, "John the Baptist", in M. Black (ed.) *The Scrolls and Christianity* (London, SPCK, 1969), p.64. See also his *John the Baptist* (London, 1964).

40. Leaney, *The Rule of Qumran* . . ., 139.

41. Opinions are divided on whether *geber* is a collective, referring to all the sectarians (Leaney, p.157, Wernberg-Møller pp.85-6) or an individual, a Messiah (Robinson, p.23, Brownlee, "The Servant of the Lord in the Qumran Scrolls. II", *BASOR* 135 (1954), 33-8. It may be seen as referring to fully initiated members (p.85). It does not refer to mankind in general, as Leaney sees (*Rule of Qumran* . . ., 158, the purification of all mankind "is a doctrine to which the scrolls are everywhere else completely opposed"). The wicked will have been destroyed by fire (1QS 2:8, 4:13; 1QH 3:29-36, 6:18, 1QpHab 2:11-13, CD 2:5-6).

42. Wernberg-Møller, following Brownlee, reads "destroy . . . from them", Lohse agrees with Yadin in reading *mittakme.* Yadin ("A Note on DSD 4:20", *JBL* 174 (1955), 40-43) connects it with Arabic "suffer from indigestion", translating "the inward parts of his flesh"; Guilbert "entrails".

It is possible that the form results by metathesis from m-k-t-m-y and means "from the defilements of his flesh" (k-t-m, "stain"). Our argument depends, not on this word, but on "flesh".

43. Leaney, *The Rule of Qumran* . . ., 158.
44. Wernberg-Møller, *The Manual of Discipline*, 86-7.
45. P. D. Hanson, "Rebellion in Heaven, Azazel and Euhemeristic Heroes in I Enoch 6-11", *JBL* 96 (1977), 195-233.
46. W. D. Davies, "Paul and the Dead Sea Scrolls: Flesh and Spirit" in K. Stendahl (ed.), *The Scrolls and the New Testament;* K. G. Kuhn, "New Light on Temptation, Sin and Flesh in the New Testament," in Stendahl; E. Brandenburger, "Fleisch und Geist, Paulus und die dualistische Weisheit", *WMANT* 29, Neukirchen, 1968.
47. Hübner, "Anthropologischer Dualismus . . .".
48. Hübner, "Anthropologischer Dualismus . . .", 281.
49. See also J. Pryke, " 'Spirit' and 'Flesh' in the Qumran Documents and some New Testament Texts", *RevQ* 5 (1965), 345-360; H. Wildberger, "Der Dualismus in den Qumranschriften", Asiatische Studien, Bern, 1954, 163-177.
50. See D. Winston, "The Iranian Component in the Bible, Apocrypha, and Qumran. A Review of the Evidence", *HR* 5 (1966), 183-216.
51. F. F. Bruce, " 'To the Hebrews' or 'To the Essenes'?", *NTS* 9 (1963), 217-232, p.228.
52. Jeremias, *Der Lehrer* . . ., 245-248.
53. Klinzing, *Umdeutung* . . ., 90.
54. H. Stegemann, *Die Entstehung der Qumrangemeinde*, 102, nn. 328, 329; G. W. Buchanan, "The Priestly Teacher of Righteousness", *RevQ* 6 (1969), 553-8.

CHAPTER VII

The Priestly Messiah

> Then shall the Lord raise up a new priest . . .
> And he shall open the gates of paradise
> And shall remove the threatening sword against Adam
> And he shall give to the saints to eat from the tree of life
> And the spirit of holiness shall be on them.
>
> Test. Levi 18:2, 10-11 (Charles)

If the community members, under the Teacher's doctrine, expected that in the coming Future Time they would themselves be priests in the heavenly temple come to earth, what of the high priest himself? The implication of the doctrine — that the high priest would become the priestly Messiah of the eschatological period — is illustrated in a body of literature related to the scrolls, and is also found in some passages of the scrolls.

Elijah and the Priestly Messiah in the Karaite Literature

It is generally agreed that the Karaite literature, found in the Cairo Genizah, is related to CD and the Qumran sect. S. Schechter,[1] who first published CD, believed that its rules belong to the group of laws which Samaritans and Karaites upheld in fierce controversy against the Pharisees (rabbinic Judaism).

Fitzmyer[2] also points to "the obvious intrinsic similarity of tenets and practices that were represented in the two groups . . . The medieval Karaites were somehow tributary to the group of Jews who produced the Damascus Document".

N. Wieder[3] has published extracts from several Karaite writers, showing that they expected two Messiahs, one called *měŝîaḥ kĕhunnâ*, "the priestly Messiah, or simply "the Priest", the other *maŝîaḥ ben dawîd,* "Messiah ben David", or simply "the Messiah". The same distinction between the two Messiahs is found in the scrolls,[4] and also the same shortened forms of their titles in 1QSa 2: 12, 19.[5]

In several of the authors quoted, the priestly Messiah is equated with Elijah. David ben Abraham al-Fasi:

(a) (In Zech 4:14, on the two sons of oil) " . . . two anointed ones *(měŝuḥîm)* are meant, they are Elijah, let him be remembered for good, and the Messiah ben David."

(b) (on the same text) " . . . two anointed ones, they are Elijah, let him be remembered for good, *who is the priestly Messiah (měŝîaḥ kĕhunnâ)* and the Messiah ben David, the expected one . . . as it is said concerning the priest: 'My covenant was with him of life and peace' (Mal 2:5), that is, Elijah. And with regard to the Messiah . . .".

Wieder concludes that "two anointed ones" here has the technical connotation of "two Messiahs".

Another Karaite author[6] finds that the "horn" and "lamp" of Ps 132:17 are the davidic Messiah and the messianic high priest, respectively. The high priest will be a ruler, with the king: "the two of them will be in the temple, as it is written: 'And he shall sit and rule upon his throne and there shall be a priest upon his throne' (Zech 6:13)". The writer goes on to equate the high priest with Elijah of Mal 3:23-24: "he will be like a lamp to the Messiah and his people, to teach them the way of the Lord and his Torah, 'and he will turn the heart of the fathers to their children, and the heart of the children to their fathers' ".

Judah Hadassi equates the messianic high priest with the messenger of the Lord in Mal 2:7, who, Hadassi says in another place, is identical with Elijah. He also, in another passage, equates Elijah with Aaron.

Wieder suggests, further, that a passage from the Karaite Prayer Book[7] should be emended by the omission of a *waw* to read: "Let us behold the face of thy Messiah, namely Elijah thy prophet, and hasten to us the Branch, the son of David thy servant".

A. S. van der Woude,[8] followed by Jeremias,[9] accepts Wieder's evidence as explanatory of certain points of CD messianic expectation. But R. B. Laurin[10] denies that Elijah is equated with the priestly Messiah in these sources. "Elijah . . . who is *měŝîaḥ kĕhunnâ*" simply means that Elijah is anointed of priesthood. He holds that the context in the latter part of the David al-Fasi passage (b) distinguishes Elijah from the Messiah, showing that Elijah is not a Messiah. On this point, he does not take into account the use of "the Messiah" to refer to the davidic Messiah as opposed to the priestly Messiah, found in another passage of al-Fasi cited in the article (" . . . the oil is the one with which *the Messiah and the Priest* will be anointed in the future"). The passage (b) is on the "two sons of oil", that is, the two figures are parallel: they are both Messiahs. Laurin also cites David al-Fasi in *Mishnah Horayot* 3:4, where he says that *hakkôhen hammas̄iaḥ* in Lev 4:3 is not a king, he is "Elijah the high priest". This must mean, Laurin thinks, that the high priest is not messianic (= a king). But the unnamed Karaite author quoted by Wieder says that the high priest and the king will both be rulers in the temple. Moreover, Lev 4:3 is, as K. G. Kuhn[11] has pointed out, one of the sources for the use of the term "the Priest" to refer to the priestly Messiah (the beginning of each section (4: 3, 5, 16) uses the full title, *hakkôhen hammas̄iaḥ,* and the continuation of each uses only "the Priest" (6, 7, 10, 17)).

J. Gnilka[12] brings forward a more formidable objection to the equation of Elijah with the priestly Messiah: not all the Karaite authors make the identification. Yefet ben Ali, commenting on Mal 3:23, appears to distinguish them. "When the time of the 'End' comes, he will send him (Elijah) to teach the people and to remove the disagreement. Israel will enter with him the land of Israel from the 'wilderness of the peoples' *(midbar ha'ammîm),* he will conquer the country for them, take Jerusalem, and rebuild the altar. It will be he *who will anoint the high priest* and the king Messiah and make known the genealogies". Wieder[13] agrees that the two figures, Elijah and the high priest, are here distinguished. Van der Woude[14] meets the problem by suggesting Rabbanite influence: the Rabbanites, against the Zadokites, expected a single, royal Messiah only, and made Elijah a mere forerunner.

But there is reason for believing that Elijah is not here distinguished from the priestly Messiah; that, as in the other Karaite texts, he is the same person, who in his role of forerunner will anoint himself as high priest. 1QM 1:3 gives to the future high (chief) priest the same place as is given to Elijah by Yefet ben Ali: he will appear in the "wilderness of the peoples" *(midbar ha'ammîm),* and lead the people into Jerusalem. In the first stage of 1QM (see below p.106) the temple cult is set up as the first achievement of the war (2:1-6). Cf. 15:4, 16:13-14 for the leadership of the high (chief) priest in the battle, and the Chief Priest of 2:1.

The identity of the roles of forerunner and high priest in the one person is claimed for Jesus in Heb 6:20: "(into the inner shrine . . .) where Jesus has gone as a forerunner on our behalf, having become a high priest for ever after the order of Melchizedek". In contemporary hellenistic Judaism, a view of the high priest compatible with this definition was held. In Philo's exalted view[15] the high priest was entirely self-contained: "who alone, and by himself, and without any other, is capable of considering and executing all things". If he were anointed by another, his authority would be derived from another: if anointed by himself, his authority would be underived and therefore absolute.

There is a strong suggestion, then, that in the Karaite messianic doctrine the eschatological high priest, the priestly Messiah, will first appear as Elijah, the forerunner, and then, having re-established the true temple cult, will, after the Day (Mal 3:23), himself become the priestly ruler, along with Messiah ben David, the royal ruler. The priestly Messiah was called "Elijah" because of his status before the Day.

The Mebasser and Melchizedek in 11QMelch

11QMelch[16] deals with Melchizedek and a *mĕbaśśer*, "herald of good tidings". Melchizedek is both heavenly high priest, as he was in later Jewish tradition,[17] based on Gen 14:18 and Ps 110, and also, as van der Woude[18] argues, Michael, who is a heavenly high priest in the Babylonian Talmud.[19] De Jonge and van der Woude[20] point to a passage from Ass. Mosis (10:1-2) in which an archangel, described with a technical term denoting the installation of a high priest, is a warrior. The eschatological high priest who led the priests controlling the battle in 1QM had a predominantly warrior role.

Because of the fragmentary state of the text, it is not at first sight clear whether Melchizedek is the same as the *mĕbaśśer* who in lls. 15-24 announces to Zion: "Your *'Elôhîm* is king". Lls. 5-6 read: " . . . *malkî ṣedeq*, who will restore them to them and will proclaim to them liberty *(qara' . . . dĕrôr)* to set them free and [(to) make atonement] for their sins". De Jonge and van der Woude[21] show that the subject of the series of verbs in l.6 is the *mĕbaśśer*, a figure whom the writer of the fragment finds in a combination of Isa 61:1-2 and Isa 52:7.[22] In Isa 61:1 the *mĕbaśśer* "proclaims liberty" *(liqrô' . . . dĕrôr)*. If in l.6 *l-k-p-r* is read before "for their sins", the subject announces the atonement, if *k-p-r,* he brings it himself, and is high priest.[23] This would mean that he is also Melchizedek, whose name is to be restored before "who", and may, or may not be its antecedent.

Fitzmyer[24] is inclined to believe that the two are the same: a parallel is in the attribution of both roles, *mĕbaśśer* and Melchizedek, to Jesus (Luke 4:18-21, Heb 6:20), Sabugal[25] holds that they are the same.

As, in the Karaite sources, Elijah prepares for his own coming as high priest, so, in 11QMelch, the *mĕbaśśer* is heralding his own manifestation as heavenly high priest. He brings tidings of the "year of acceptance" (Isa 61:2 and l.9), the year of jubilee, which begins with the Day of Atonement (Lev 25:9 - 10:22). In the second temple, the high priest not only made atonement on the Day of Atonement, but read the biblical passages announcing its institution.[26]

The *mĕbaśśer* is called *mĕśîaḥ harûaḥ,* "anointed with the spirit" (1.18).[27] Sabugal[28] holds that *maśîaḥ* here has its technical sense, meaning Messiah (although, as he holds that there was only one Messiah at Qumran, he believes that the term makes Melchizedek a davidic Messiah). Fitzmyer[29] uses the term to support his view that the figure in this line is the "anointed prince" *(mĕśîaḥ nagîd)* of Dan 9:25. But he assumes that the anointed prince is a kingly Messiah, whereas Melchizedek would be a priestly Messiah. His assumption that the priestly Messiah has no ruling function is negated by the evidence of 1QSa, in which the priestly Messiah is superior to the davidic Messiah, and by the Karaite source on the rule of two in the new temple (p.76). *Test. Reuben* 6:10-11 speaks of the high priest as king: "And draw near to Levi in humbleness of heart . . . because the Lord has chosen him to be king over all the nation".

The use of *maśîaḥ* for the *mĕbaśśer* here indicates the way in which the two senses of the word were made use of in the eschatological doctrine. In the meaning "anointed one" it applied to all prophets. It has this sense in 1QM 11:8: "by the hand of thine anointed ones *(mĕśîḥîm)* the seers of the testimonies, thou hast revealed to us the periods of the wars". But the fact that it also means "priest" and "king" is used to support the concept that the present forerunner, a prophet, will become priestly Messiah after the Day.

This throws light on two passages of CD in which the word *maśîaḥ* appears. CD 2:11-12: "He raised for himself men called by a name, in order that a remnant might be left to the land, and to fill the face of the world with their seed. And he made them know, by the hand of *m-ś-y-ḥ-w,* his Spirit of holiness."

Schechter[30] and Lagrange[31] took it without change as *mĕśîḥô,* "his Messiah", referring to a past Messiah or founder of the sect. R. H. Charles[32] made the sentence a prophecy, reading the verb as a iussive. The majority of writers since the discovery of the scrolls correct the clear *waw* of the MS to *yod,* or insert *yod,* making it "those anointed with his Spirit of holiness" or "by the hand of his anointed ones". K. G. Kuhn[33] justifies the alteration: the medieval scribe has changed an original plural to a singular, just as he has changed the plural in CD 12:23, 14:19, 19:10 to a singular, through his belief that there was only one Messiah. Kuhn (who accepts the verb in 2:12 "he made them know", as a past tense) implies that the scribe did not make a difference between a past Messiah and a future Messiah, but made all into a singular. The basis of the argument was removed when the caves fragments of CD were found: one fragment contains 14:19, "the Messiah of Aaron and Israel" in the singular.[34] This passage calls a past leader of the community, who "made them know his Spirit of holiness", the Anointed One. As it was the Teacher who gave this doctrine (pp.65-71), he is here being called the Anointed One.

CD 5:21 - 6:1 uses the same term in a similar context, that of the history of the sect. "And in the Period of the Desolation of the Land, there arose removers of the bound (that is, the apostates from the sect, p.149) and they led Israel astray, and they made waste the land, for they spoke rebellion against the commandments of God by the hand of Moses and also by *m-š-y-ḥ-w haqqôdeš*, and they prophesied falsehood . . . ".

In the medieval copy, the word was originally written *m-š-y-ḥ-w*, then the *w* was obliterated. It has been restored in modern editions because the caves fragment which contains the same line (6Q15, fr.3) contains either *yod* or *waw* in the same spot (although there is a hole in the crucial space, the editors state that the trace of one of the two letters is visible).[35] As Kuhn points out,[36] the phrase with *w* (if it means "his holy Messiah"), violates the basic rules of syntax: a genitive cannot be attached to a noun with suffix. This suggests a reason why the medieval scribe has obliterated the *waw*. Kuhn suggests that the word originally ended with *yod* ("by the holy anointed ones"), then was changed to a *waw* to make a singular Messiah. But this does not take into account the obliteration of the *waw*. The problem is met if it is recognized that the phrase originally included the *waw*, and meant "his Messiah, the Holy One". A determined noun may be followed by a word in apposition, e.g. Zech 4:10, *ha'eben habbĕdîl*, cf. also Ezek 39:17, 2 Kgs 16:14, Jer 32:12.[37] The phrase distinguishes the Teacher as both the Anointed One (Messiah) and the Holy One. Cf. his title the Righteous One in 4QpPs[a] 4:8.

In 11QMelch Melchizedek, who is also the *mĕbasśer* (above), is called *'Elôhîm*. Lls. 9-10: "That is the time of the acceptable year of Melchizedek . . . as it is written concerning him . . . 'The *'Elôhîm* stands (sing.) in the congregation of God; in the midst of the *'Elôhîm* he judges' ". Van der Woude[38] rules out the possibility that the author here means "God", and Fitzmyer[39] accepts his argument (see p.64). Similarly, in l.16, " . . . who says to Zion: 'Your *'Elôhîm* is king' ". De Jonge and van der Woude[40] state: "if the author had meant to refer to God, an explanation of this expression (in 25ff.) would hardly have been necessary . . . it seems certain that *'ĕlôhayik* in the quotation of Isa 52:7 was explained as referring to the heavenly Melchizedek". Note also the substitution of the name Melchizedek for "the Lord" in the quotation of Isa 61:2 in l.9: "the acceptable year of Melchizedek".

Philo's description of the high priest throws general light on the identification:[41] "(the high priest is) a being whose nature is midway between man and God, less than God, superior to man. 'For when the high priest enters the Holy of Holies he shall not be a man' (Lev 16:17). Who then, if he is not a man? A God? I will not say so, for this name is a prerogative, assigned to the chief prophet, Moses, while he was still in Egypt, where he is entitled the God of Pharaoh (Ex 7:1). Yet not a man either, but one contiguous with both extremes, which form, as it were, one his head, the other his feet". For many Jews of the period, the high priest was a mediator between heaven and earth, a semi-divine being.

As *'Elôhîm,* he judges in the midst of the *'Elôhîm.* In ch. VI the future expectation for the community members has been discussed: they are the separated members of the heavenly temple now, and will become "godly ones" *('Elôhîm)* in the future. 11QMelch contains a statement of the future doctrine for both the high priest and the members of the Teacher's community. In the Future Time (cf. *[aḥ]arît hayyamîm,* 1.4) they will find themselves in a heavenly court, in a council with the angels, ruled over by their own high priest, who will then be Melchizedek, the priestly Messiah. He is in the present time a *měbaśśer,* a preacher of the good tidings concerning the coming liberation on the Day of Atonement in the year of jubilee (Lev 25:8-10, the jubilee year begins on the Day of Atonement). When it comes, he will as heavenly high priest bring the atonement.

1QSb 4:20-28 includes a blessing on the high priest in a series of blessings on community members.[47] He will be "like an angel of the presence in the holy habitation . . . causing the lot to fall with the angels of the presence, and a Council of the Community [with the holy ones] . . . ". This is further support for the doctrine of 11QMelch.

In 1QH 18:14 the writer uses the verb *baśar* (Piel) of himself; but this is not a hymn of the Teacher.

The way in which the high priest and the members of the community may be ordinary human beings now, but *'Elôhîm* in the future, may be explored through a study of the words for "man" in the scrolls.

The Initiation Doctrine: From Adam to Adam

The words for "man" found in the scrolls are: *'adam, 'ěnôš, geber,'îš, zakar. Zakar* is found only for "male"; *'îš, 'ǎnašîm* are used for the different classes of men within mankind; *běnê 'îš* for "mankind", without the moral and hierarchical associations that are found for the first three words. It is these three that are used in special senses.

I. *'adam*

1. Mankind *(ha) 'adam, ben (ha) 'adam, běnê (ha)'adam.*

   (a) as opposed to divine beings, weak and sinful.
        1QH 1:27: "for the sons of men is the service of iniquity".
        1QH 4:30: "perfection of way is not for a son of man".
        1QS 11:10, 1QH 4:38, 10:3, CD 10:8, CD 12:4.[43]

   (b) the human origin and nature of the sectarians.
        1QS 11:16: "thou hast accepted the elect ones of mankind".
        1QH 4:32: "to perfect the way of the sons of men".
        1QS 11:9: "and I belong to sinful mankind".

   (c) unsaved men as against the sectarians.
        1QS 11:6: "skill (hidden) from the sons of men."
        1QS 11:15: "thou hast cleansed me . . . from the sinfulness of the sons of men".
        1QH 2:25: "thou hast made me strong before the sons of men".
        CD 9:1 (b,c),[44] CD 19:25, 1QH 5:11, 15; 6:11, 11:6.

   (d) as against other species.
        1QM 10:14: "animals . . . birds and the frame of mankind."
        CD 11:16, cf. 13-14.

   (a) as against the inhabitants of above and below.
        1QH 1:15: "the spirit of mankind which thou hast created in the world."

   (f) the body, in relation to uncleanness
        1QSa 2:4, CD 12:16.

2. A/the man *((ha)'adam),* the sectarian.
        CD 3:16: " . . . the ways of his truth and the desires of his will which a/the man *(ha'adam)* shall do and live."
        CD 14:11: "every matter which a man *(ha'adam)* shall have to say, let him say it to the *měbaqqer."*
        CD 9:1 (a)[45].
        1QH 17:27: "I will look on every covenant of man."
        4Q*174* (4QFlor) 1:6: "to build for himself a sanctuary of man (also meaning "human", see p.182).

3. Adam.
        1QS 4:23: "(at the Visitation, the members will be finally purified, receive the wisdom of the sons of heaven, and . . .) theirs (will be) all the glory of Adam."
        CD 3:20: "those who cleave to it (the 'sure house', the sectarian 'temple') will have eternal life and all the glory of Adam will be theirs."

1QH 17:15: "to cause them (the elect) to inherit all the glory of Adam."

4QpPs^a 3:2: "the Returnees of the wilderness (the sectarians, cf. 2:2-3 and p.176) who will live a thousand generations in uprightness, and theirs will be all the inheritance of Adam, and for their seed for ever."

(1QS 5:17, 1QM 11:12 are biblical quotations.)

It is recognized that the phrases "the glory of Adam", "the inheritance of Adam" (3 above) refer to the future state in the messianic era. M. Black:[46] "The world is to be restored to its "paradisiacal" state before the Fall; the glory which Adam lost at the Fall is to be restored to the renewed mankind ... Thus Adam is to be restored to his state before the Fall and lives for ever in his new Paradise". Wernberg-Møller:[47] "the glory in store for the pious is identical with, or of similar grandeur to, the glory of Paradise before the Fall". Leaney:[48] it refers to "God's new act of creation".

The varying uses of *'adam* should be considered in the light of the Qumran doctrine of flesh and spirit (pp.65-70). All men are both flesh and spirit. One group of men is distinguished from others by being members of the sect. They are rising towards heaven, while others who are not members are "sons of the Pit". But, until the Future Time, the flesh and the soul of man are separate: they will not come together until the Visitation. The sectarians continue to share in the humanity of all men, being dragged down towards the earth by their fleshly component. There are thus three states of mankind, corresponding to the three uses of *'adam:*

1. Mere sinful humans, all mankind, the fallen Adam.
2. Members of the sect, on their way to heaven.
3. Full participation in heaven and the redemption of Adam.

The second use is to be seen against the background of the many passages in 1QH where the writer calls himself a "creature of clay, dust". Adam was made from dust, by the entry of the divine Spirit (Gen 2:7). The use of the word for the sectarian, as opposed to other humans, means that it was held that he had become an Adam, and started the journey to heaven, by the entry of the Spirit of holiness at initiation (p.66). He had been given "life" by this means. Cf. 1QS 3:7, in the passage on initiation: "to behold the light of life" (see further below pp.98-9). The entry of the Spirit at initiation gave him a "manhood" that others did not possess (a common understanding of initiation). This is supported by a hymn of the Teacher (1QH 4:27-32):

> For thou hast made me know thy marvellous mysteries, and through thy wondrous secret thou hast dealt mightily with me, to act marvellously before the many for the sake of thy glory, and to make known to all the living ones thy

strength. What is *flesh* (to be worthy of) this? And what is a creature of clay to exalt thy wonders? For it is in iniquity from the womb, and until old age it is in guilty sinfulness. And I know that righteousness is not for a human, and perfection of way is not for a son of man *(ben 'adam); of God most high are all the works of righteousness, and the human way is only made secure by the Spirit which God created for himself to perfect the ways of the sons of men (běne 'adam).*

Cf. also 1QH 15:21:

And what then is *flesh,* that it should have insight? How can dust secure its steps? *Thou hast created a spirit* and determined its deeds . . . and from thee is the way of all the living ones.

The sectarian, after initiation, is not like other men, because he has received the additional component of the divine Spirit. Whereas others are flesh and soul, he is flesh, soul, and has also the Spirit of holiness. This is the reason why the members will be *'Elôhîm,* "godly ones", in the future. They already possess the heavenly spirits, and at the Future Time these will be manifested in them. Although their outer form is at present that of ordinary men, their inner glory will, at the eschatological climax, be revealed.

There is, then, a concept of the first and second Adams, although these terms are not found. At initiation, the sectarian becomes a second Adam by the gift of life, and proceeds through the stages of perfection until the glory of Adam is revealed in him in the Future Time.

These observations are supported by the uses of *'enôs* and *geber.*

II. *'enôs.*

    1. Mankind (no art).

        (a)   as opposed to divine beings, weak and sinful
            1QS 11:10, 1QH 1:25, 1QH 4:30, 31; 11:20; 15:13.

        (b)   unsaved men as against the sectarians
            1QS 11:6, 11:15, 1QH 1:34.

        (c)   all mankind
            1QS 3:17

        (d)   the body, in relation to uncleanness
            CD 3:17

    2. The sectarian

            1QH 1:32: "thou hast strengthened the spirit of a man."
            1QH 11:10: "thou hast cleansed a man from sin."
            Probably also 1QH 9:15.

'Enôs is used in the same senses as *'adam.* Unlike *'adam,* it does not lend itself to use as a name.

III. *geber*

    1. All members of sinful mankind

            1QS 4:23: "up till now the spirits of truth and falsehood contend in the heart of a *geber"*. Cf. the parallel in 1QS

3:17, using *'enôš*.
1QH 11:20: "I know the inclinations of a *geber* and the return of *'enôš* (to the dust)."

2. (a) The sectarian
1QS 4:20: "(at the Visitation) God will cleanse with his truth all the works of a *geber*."
1QS 10:18: "with good I *(the maskil)* will pursue a *geber*."
Probably also 1QH 9:15.

(b) The Teacher, the high priest
1QH 2:17: "they turned to the grave the life of the *geber*, in whose mouth thou hast established and taught him thine understanding (himself, the Teacher)."
4QpPs^a 3:14-15: " 'by Yahweh are the steps of a *geber* secured' (Ps 37:23). Its interpretation concerns the Priest, the Teacher of Righteousness."

3. A rival high priest
1QpHab 8:3: " 'the arrogant *geber* (Hab 2:5) . . .' Its interpretation concerns the Wicked Priest."

4. A Messiah
1QH 3:9, 10.

Geber, like *'adam* and *ënôš*, refers to all mankind, but like *'adam* it also has a titular use. In two places, where it occurs in a biblical passage, the pesharist recognizes in it a high priest or an anti-high priest. *Gabar* means "to be strong", and E. Lohmeyer[49] has pointed out that in the NT "the Strong One" refers to divine or anti-divine powers. As the high priest is to become priestly Messiah, he is the Strong One, the supreme Man.

All sectarians are made "men" at initiation, and the Teacher, the high priest, is the Man. Having received the heavenly spirits when they become "men", they will be able to be *'Elôhîm* in the future. To have *become* a man is also to have become, potentially, a "god". The term "the son of man" *(ben (ha)'adam*, found with the article in 1QS 11:20-21, is therefore suitable to express the Teacher's (and the members') double identity. Its OT uses give it the sense of "prophet" (Ezekiel *passim*, Dan 8:17). A prophet is a human being through whom the Spirit of God speaks; he is the vessel of a spirit who is not himself. There is evidence that the Teacher likened himself to Elijah,[50] Ezekiel,[51] Daniel,[52] Jeremiah,[53] and other prophets.[54] The term expresses their inner power, but at the same time it serves to distinguish them from their inner spirit. The Teacher calls himself "son of man" as a sinful mortal, using the first sense of "Adam" (1QH 4:30). In this way he emphasizes that he has not yet attained his glory. He will not be a "god" until his soul and flesh have come together at the Future Time.

G. Jeremias[55] has pointed to the Teacher's great emphasis on his lowliness as a mere mortal in order to dispute the implication of some texts that he was expected to become the priestly Messiah. These passages mean, he holds, that the Teacher was not "beyond human bounds". A closer study of the messianic doctrine shows the difference between actuality and potentiality in Qumran thought. By the play on "son of man", the Teacher is able to say that although he is a lowly, suffering person at present, dragged down by sin towards the dust, his reception of the divine spirit has also made him a "son of man", a prophet, who contains within himself the spirit which will eventually make him priestly Messiah. As the anointed one he will become the Anointed One, the Messiah who presides over the heavenly co''ncil of angels and community members.

The references to the Suffering Servant of Deutero-Isaiah are in accordance with this concept. The Servant allusions isolated by Carmignac[56] are in 1QH 4:8, 4:23, 5:31, 7:10, 7:32, 8:36. 1QH 8:10-11, *lô' neḥsab,* is surely to be added: Jeremias argues against it[57] on the grounds of the general use of *ḥasab,* in the affirmative, elsewhere, but *lô' neḥsab,* "not esteemed" (Isa 53:3) is an unmistakable Servant allusion. The image is only used, as is usually agreed (Ringgren, R. E. Brown, van der Woude)[58] to express the present lowliness and suffering of members (1QS 8:4, 1QpHab 8:2, 1QM 17:1-9, show the expectation of suffering). It may be related to the messianic theory, in that the members at present concealed heavenly beings in themselves, but were not recognized by other men for what they were, "not esteemed". Cf. the image of the Shoot, hidden in the secret garden among the trees of life, "not esteemed", and concealed from outsiders (1QH 2:4-15). Their present suffering as prophets, rejected by men, was a preparation for their future greatness.

Their sufferings were those resulting from human existence and their present separation from the temple: temptations of the flesh, and persecutions by enemies. It is important to recognize that an implication of the Teacher's eschatological doctrine is that *the suffering did not include death.* The flesh would survive in the Future Time: the members would continue in their present form. It was presumably promised for their own lifetime. But the concept of the indwelling divine spirit meant that there could be a succession of persons into whom the spirit entered. If one priest or high priest died, his son would take his place (as the priesthood was hereditary). Into him, at initiation, the heavenly spirit would enter, in preparation for the Future Time. After the Future Time, the nature of time would change, so that members would live "for a thousand generations" (4QpPs^a 3:1) or have "eternal life" (1QS 4:7). But the privileges of the new era were not inherited through death; this is a Christian conception only.

Summary

The findings of this chapter are in accord with the doctrine of the heavenly temple. As the Qumran priests were now members of heaven, and would shortly take up their liturgical office in that temple come to earth, so the high priestly leader of the community would become the head of the future hierarchy of angelic priests. Both he and they at present were made of two elements: sinful humanity; and the indwelling heavenly spirit, the *'elôhîm*. As both sinners, and prophets who contained the heavenly spirit, they were "sons of men" and as sufferers from human weakness who were also God's chosen ones, they were "suffering servants". At the removal of the separation between heaven and earth, the difference would be overcome, and they would be manifested as *'elôhîm* or angels. The high priest, the "anointed one" *(maśîaḥ)* would become the priestly Messiah *(maśîaḥ)*, revealing himself as Melchizedek, the heavenly high priest who held the supreme rank in heaven. He was now a *mĕbaśśer* ("preacher of good tidings", NT *euangelizōn),* preparing for his own coming as *'Elôhîm*. He was also Elijah preparing for the coming of the Day, when he would anoint himself as high priest. Both he, the Zadokite heir, and his followers, the legitimate priests, were able to endure their present rejection from the Jerusalem temple because they believed that it would be only a short time before their hidden glory was unveiled and they would take up their true office in a purified world.

NOTES

1. S. Schechter, *Documents of Jewish Sectaries. Vol. I. Fragments of a Zadokite Work.* Prolegomenon by J. A. Fitzmyer, S. J., New York, 1970. P.50.
2. In Schechter, *Documents . . .* , 13-14.
3. N. Wieder, "The Doctrine of the Two Messiahs among the Karaites", *JJS* 6 (1955), 14-25.
4. 1QS 9:11; 1QSa 2:11-22, 1QSb 3:1-21, 5:20-29, 4QTestim 1-20; CD 7:18-21; 4Q174 1:11; 4QPB 3; 4QpIsaª frs. 8-10:17.
5. On the two Messiahs in this passage, see further pp.127-8.
6. For a discussion of his identity, see Wieder, "The Doctrine . . ." n. 17. He concludes: "it may be taken for certain that (he) belonged to the Karaite settlers in Jerusalem . . . in the tenth or eleventh century".
7. *Karaite Prayer Book* I (Wilna, 1868), p. 34.
8. A. S. van der Woude, *Die messianische Vorstellungen der Gemeinde von Qumran* (Assen, 1957).
9. Jeremias, *Der Lehrer . . .*, 279.
10. R. B. Laurin, "The Problem of the Two Messiahs in the Qumran Scrolls", *RevQ* 4 (1963), 39-52.

11. K. G. Kuhn, "The Two Messiahs of Aaron and Israel", in Stendahl, *The Scrolls and the New Testament*.
12. J. Gnilka, "Die Erwartung des messianischen Hohenpriesters in den Schriften von Qumran und im Neuen Testament", *RevQ* 2(1959-60), 395-426.
13. Wieder, "The Doctrine . . .", n. 8.
14. Van der Woude, *Vorstellungen* . . . 60ff.
15. *De Somniis* 2§187.
16. See ch. VI, note 20.
17. *Aboth de Rabbi Nathan* 34, *Pesiqta* 51a. Cf. Strack-Billerbeck *(Kommentar zum Neuen Testament)* IV, 464. Cf. also *Targum Neofiti* I, fol.23v., lls.14ff, in J. A. Fitzmyer, "Now This Melchizedek" in *Essays on the Semitic Background* . . .
18. Van der Woude, "Melchisedek als . . ." 369-372.
19. *Hagigah* 12b, *Menachot* 110a, *Jebachim* 62a. See Fitzmyer, "Further Light . . .", 255 for some reservations about the identification.
20. De Jonge and van der Woude, "11Q Melchizedek . . .", 306. In this context, it is stated that "11QMelch gives no certain references to a (high)-priesthood of Melchizedek. He is so much God's warrior that his priestly activities remain completely in the shadow". The combination of high priest and leader of battle is familiar in 1QM, and Gen 14:18 and Ps 110 fix the high priestly identification.
21. De Jonge and van der Woude, "11QMelchizedek . . .", 306. See also van der Woude, "Melchizedek als . . .", 363.
22. See also M. P. Miller, "The Function of Isa 61:1-2 in 11QMelchizedek". *JBL* 88(1969), 467-9.
23. Milik ("Milkî-ṣedeq . . .", 98 reads m-ś-', "lifting up".
24. Fitzmyer, "Further Light . . .' 253-4, 266.
25. S. Sabugal, "1Q regla de la Comunidad IX 11: dos Ungidos, un Mesias", *RevQ* 8(1974), 417-23.
26. *Yoma* 7:1-10.
27. Y. Yadin ("A Note on Melchizedek and Qumran", *IEJ* 15 (1965, 152-4) suggested this reading rather than van der Woude's first conjecture, *h-m-ś-y-ḥ h-w-'-h*.
28. Sabugal, "1Q Regla . . .", 4-18.
29. Fitzmyer, "Further Light . . .", 265-6.
30. Schechter, *Documents* . . ., 65.
31. M. J. Lagrange, "La secte juive de la Nouvelle Alliance," *RB* 21 (N.S.9, 1912), 212-40, 321-60.
32. R. H. Charles, *Apocrypha and Pseudepigrapha of the Old Testament*, Oxford, Vol. II, ·p.804.
33. K. G. Kuhn, "The Two Messiahs . . .", 59.
34. Milik, *Ten Years* . . ., 125.
35. Baillet, *DJD* III. Photographs of medieval copy in S. Zeitlin, *The Zadokite Fragments* (JQR Monograph Series 1, Philadelphia, 1952).
36. Kuhn, "The Two Messiahs . . .", 59.
37. Gesenius-Kautzsch-Cowley, *Hebrew Grammar*, Oxford, §127,f,g,h.
38. Van der Woude, "Melchisedek als . . .", 367-8, also de Jonge and van der Woude, "11QMelchizedek . . .", 304.
39. Fitzmyer, "Further Light . . .", 255.

40. De Jonge and van der Woude, "11QMelchizedek . . .", 305.
41. *De Somniis* 2§188.
42. See ch. X, note 12.
43. CD 12:2-4 may be interpreted: "Every man who is in the power of the spirits of Belial so as to speak rebellion, shall be judged according to the law for a medium or a wizard (i.e., put to death, Lev 20:27). But everyone who errs so as to profane the sabbath and the feasts shall not be put to death (against Ex 35:2, Num 15:32-36), for it is for the sons of men to keep it (*šamar* with "the sabbath", CD 6:18) (i.e., to break it comes from human weakness). And if he is healed of his error, and they keep watch over him for seven years, after that he will be admitted into the assembly". The passage distinguishes between different kinds of sin. Breaking the sabbath is "human", therefore not so serious as apostasy. See ch. X note 25 for a discussion of "put to death".
44. CD 9:1. I. Rabinowitz ("The Meaning and Date of 'Damascus' Document IX,1" (*RevQ* 6 (1968), 433-5) shows the meaning of this verse: "any man who devotes-and-destroys a man 'of mankind' (Lev 27:28-29) because of the 'customs of the nations' (Lev 20:23) is himself to be put to death". Members of the sect (the first "man", *'adam*) were attempting to exterminate apostatizing Jews outside the sect (the second and third *'adam*) by using Gentile laws against them.
45. See n. 44. The first *'adam* refers to members of the sect.
46. M. Black, *The Scrolls and Christian Origins*, 139.
47. P. Wernberg-Møller, *The Manual of Discipline*, p. 87, n. 80.
48. Leaney, *The Rule . . .*, 160.
49. E. Lohmeyer, *Das Evangelium des Markus* (Göttingen: Vandenhoeck & Ruprecht, 1963), 18.
50. In 1QH 8:16-25 the Teacher gives rain/teaching (play on *yârâ*, meaning both "teach" and "rain") to his followers, and they become fertile; when he withdraws his hand, they become barren. 4Q ar P (see Starcky, "Quatre Etapes . . . 497-8) shows that Elijah was part of the future expectation; it paraphrases Mal 3:23 and relates Elijah to an "Elect".
51. 1QH 7:7, 4:22, 4:36, he is filled with God's Spirit and made to stand (cf. Ezek 2:2, 3:24, 11:5); his tongue cleaves to the roof of his mouth (1QH 5:31, cf. Ezek 3:26) and he is dumb (1QH 7:1, cf. Ezek 3:26); he suffers an exile (1QH 4:9, cf. Ezek 12:3-6).
52. 1QH 5:7,10, he is thrown to the lions, whose mouths are shut by God (cf. Dan. 6:16, 22).
53. 1QH 5:31a, cf. Jer 4:19, 48:36; 1QH 3:7, cf. Jer 4:31; 1QH 4:15, cf. Jer 7:24.
54. Jonah, 1QH 6:23, cf. Jon 2:4, 5:37-39, cf. Jon 2:6-7, 1QH 7:4, cf. Jon 4:8.
55. Jeremias, *Der Lehrer . . .*, ch. 7.
56. J. Carmignac, "Les citations de l'Ancien Testament, et spécialement des Poèmes du Serviteur, dans les Hymnes de Qumrân", *RevQ* 7 (1960), 337-394.
57. Jeremias, *Der Lehrer . . .*, 303-4.
58. H. Ringgren, *The Faith of Qumran* (Philadelphia: Fortress, 1963), 196-8; R. E. Brown, "The Messianism of Qumran", CBQ 19 (1957), 54-66; A. S. van der Woude, "Vorstellungen . . . See also W. H. Brownlee, "The Servant of the Lord . . .

CHAPTER EIGHT

The Stages of Initiation

An understanding of the initiation practice is necessary for the close analysis of the organisation, to be undertaken in ch. X.

There was a rite of entry into the community, practised once a year. 1QS 2:19, in the section of 1QS dealing with initiation (1:1 - 3:12), reads: "thus shall they do, year by year, all the days of the dominion of Belial." The caves fragments of CD[1] contain a passage[2] establishing that it was on the Day of Pentecost: "Those who dwell in camps will form a *qahal* in the third month and will curse him who stretches out his right hand [or his left hand from the L]aw." As Milik shows,[3] this and the related passages have close verbal links with 1QS 1:16 - 3:12, and the festival of the third month could only be on the fifteenth, the Day of Pentecost, in the Qumran calendar.[4]

The study of 1QS 3:6-9 and the meaning of initiation (pp.65-6) has shown that the community was the location of the Spirit of holiness, and initiates received the Spirit. The rite of full initiation into the community was also the rite of purification with the Spirit of holiness. It would have been the highest point of the ceremony, a matter of mystery, and no description would be included in 1QS 1:1 - 3:12, which contains the liturgy only. But cf. 1Q34[bis]2:6:[5] "thou hast renewed thy Covenant with them with the appearance of glory and the words of thy Spirit of holiness (given) through the works of thy hands".

It has also been shown (pp.65-6) that there was a secondary purification, the washing of the flesh by water, as a ritual cleansing only. Water-washings are referred to in the initiation passage, 3:4-12. As flesh and soul were separated at the present time (pp.67-70) there must have been two rites, one for the washing of the flesh by water, one for the reception of the Spirit. The Spirit-washing was the superior rite, as spirit was superior to flesh.

We turn now to a study of the process of initiation set out in 1QS 6:13-23.[6] It is possible to relate it to the Qumran doctrine of flesh and spirit so as to discover more about the community hierarchy, essential to an understanding of the organisation. The passage describes four steps:

(a) (13) Every man from Israel who volunteers (14) to be added[7] to the Council of the Community shall be questioned by the *paqîd* at the head of the Many concerning his insight and his works. If he is capable of discipline *('im yaśśîg mûsar*[8]*)* he shall bring him (15) into the Covenant to turn to truth and to depart from all evil. He shall instruct him in all the laws of the Community.

(b) Then afterwards, when he brings him to stand before the Many, they shall all test (16) his case *(wĕniśālû hakkôl 'al dĕbarayw).* According to the way the decision (lot) goes according to the counsel of the Many, he shall be either brought near or sent away. If he is brought near to the Council of the Community, he shall not touch the Purity *(tohorâ* (17) of the Many until he has been examined[9] concerning his spirit and works on the completion of another full year. Also he shall not mingle[10] his property with that of the Many.

(c) (18) When he has completed a year in the midst of the Community, the Many shall examine[11] his case concerning his insight and his works in the Torah. If the decision is made (19) to bring him near to the *sôd*[12] of the Community under the authority of the priests and the multitude of the men of their covenant, his wealth and his income will be brought near and put into the hands of (20) the *mĕbaqqer* over the income of the Many. It shall be inscribed by him in the record, but he shall not spend it on behalf of the Many.

(d) He shall not touch the Drink of the Many until (21) he has completed a second year in the midst of the men of the Community. At the completion of the second year he shall be examined under the authority of the Many. If the decision is made (22) to admit him to the Community, he shall be inscribed in the order of his ranking in the midst of his brothers, for law, judgement, the Purity, and the mingling of his wealth, and his council and (23) judgement will be for the Community.

Each of the four steps may be further examined with the aid of related texts.

(a) "Every man from Israel" is allowed to proceed to full initiation. Cf. also 1QSa 1:6,[13] on the stages leading to participation in government: "every man born in Israel". A man who is born a Jew comes first to the *paqîd,* who makes the initial decision concerning his suitability and degree of amenability to the discipline of the sect. He then administers to him the *preliminary vow,* which "brings him into the Covenant". The phrase indicates a ceremony. The novice promises to turn to the truth (that is, the community teachings) and depart from all evil.

Further information concerning the preliminary vow is found in CD 15: 7-15,[14] on the duties of the *mĕbaqqer* for the Many who, as is widely agreed,[15] is the same as the *paqîd* at the head of the Many; cf. 1QS 6:12, the *mĕbaqqer* over the Many. This passage confirms that the preliminary vow is a ceremony: " . . . every man who repents of his corrupted way. On the day when he speaks with the *mĕbaqqer* for the Many, they shall enrol *(paqad)* him with the oath of the Covenant which Moses made with Israel, the Covenant to return/repent to the Law of Moses with all his heart and soul . . . the *mĕbaqqer* . . . for a full year". The last phrase probably indicates that the period between the preliminary vow and the next stage of membership is a full year, although the fragmentary state of the text makes this not quite certain. Cf. Josephus on Essene initiations:[16] "For one year, during which he remains outside the fraternity . . . this probationary period". This would mean that the ceremony occurred at Pentecost, as the next stage was at Pentecost (below). The *mĕbaqqer,* as in the 1QS 6 passage, is the only community member who is in contact with the novice during this period. He has no teaching from other members and is not yet a member. Cf. 10-11: "No man shall make known to him the decrees until he has stood before the *mĕbaqqer".*

The preliminary vow is followed by a period of instruction by the *paqîd* in the special doctrines of the community (1QS 6:15a, CD 15:11).

(b) The *paqîd* then brings him to stand before the Many, who make the decision concerning his acceptance or rejection. If he is "brought near", a word used also for the final step (l.22), he must still spend two more years before he attains all the privileges of membership, during which time he may leave, as is shown by the fact that his property is not mingled with that of the community until the final step (20, 22). He is, however, at this stage a member; cf. the introduction to the next stage: "when he has completed a year in the midst of the community" (18). This step is therefore that of *provisional membership.* As the next two steps each take a full year, and as final initiation takes place at Pentecost, the admission to provisional membership also takes place at Pentecost.

(c) A full year later he takes a further step. But it is still only a partial membership.[17] His property is received, but not spent; he is still able to leave altogether and take his property with him. As there was a preliminary step before provisional membership, so this is a *preliminary step before full membership.*

At this stage he may touch the Purity of the Many (17), but not the Drink of the Many (20), which is confined to full members.

Some writers (Wernberg-Møller, Liebermann)[18] consider that the Purity, which clearly refers to something palpable (cf. "touch the Purity" l.16), means certain ritually clean articles, or (Leaney)[19] objects not capable of transmitting uncleanness. But this is difficult to accept in view of the fact that exclusion from the Purity is the most regular punishment for offenders against the community's code (1QS 6:25, 7:3, 16, CD 9:21, 23) and that the Purity consistently appears as the main privilege of membership (1QS

8:17, 6:16, 22, 8:24, 7:25). There is no evidence whatever that membership centred round the touching of certain objects. There is evidence, however, that membership was expressed by participation in a communal meal of bread and new wine, held wherever there was a group of ten members (1QS 6:2-7, 1QSa 2:11-22). It was an expression of community solidarity. 1QS 6:3: "In community they shall eat, in community they shall bless, in community they shall take counsel". It was something that members "touched", at which they sat (1QS 7:20, those who touched the Purity but not the Drink *sat* below the full members), from which they could be excluded in an obvious manner, and which was suitable as the highest privilege of membership. Vermes'[20] view that it is to be translated "the pure Meal" is therefore to be accepted. He holds[21] that the name is due to the fact that it was prepared in accordance with special ritual purity. It seems more likely, however, that it was understood as a location of the purity of the community itself, whose members, on initiation, were "made pure" *(taher,* 1QS 3:4, 5, 7, 8; 4:21, cf. *tohorâ* "Purity"). Their meeting together made a pure place, consistently with their image of a temple (1QS 8:5-6, 9:5-6). In 1QS 5:13, lapsed members are not admitted to it because they are not "pure" *(lô' yittahărû).*

When, then, was the difference between the Purity, taken at preliminary full membership, and the Drink,[22] taken at full membership (1.22)?

The Meal consisted of bread and new wine. 1QSa 2:19-21 shows that in the Future Time (reproducing for community members the conditions for the present time (pp.62-4)), the Messiah of Israel blesses only the bread, whereas the Priest, the priestly Messiah, blesses both the bread and the new wine. "For he (the Priest) blesses the firstfruits of (both) the bread and the new wine. He stretches out his hand over the bread first. After this, the Messiah of Israel stretches out his hand over the bread." The Messiah of Israel is subordinate to the priestly Messiah: he takes his place after him (2:14) and blesses the bread after him (2:20-21). The Priest blesses the bread before the wine: the order is emphasized. These facts indicate a hierarchy in the elements of the Meal. The bread is the subordinate element, the new wine the higher element, reserved for the blessing of the Priest. This distinction is consistent with the hierarchy of flesh and spirit (pp.65-70): the wine, as the less substantial element, is the higher.

There is a Qumran terminological usage, the recognition of which facilitates the solution of a number of problems concerning the meaning of terms. It is: *When two different members of a hierarchy are placed in ranked order, the subordinate is described by a term general to the two, the superior*

93

by the term special to him. When they are not paired, or not placed in hierarchical order, a lower rank term may be used for a higher rank. Examples are: When the two Messiahs are placed in order, the subordinate one is called the Messiah (1QSa 2:12), the superior one the Priest (1QSa 2:19), although both are Messiahs (1QS 9:11) (not ranked in this text). All members are an "Israel", but when laity are paired with and distinguished from priests and levites, they are called Israel and the ministry called priests and levites (CD 14:4, 5). All members are law-interpreters (1QS 8:15),[23] but when the lower minister at the Meal is paired with the priest, the lower one is called the law-interpreter (1QS 6:6). The usage derives from the pyramidal nature of the community, built on the principle that the outer is the lower, drawn from the hierarchy of flesh and spirit. All higher ranks incorporate the functions of the lower ranks, and so may be called by any name that applies to the lower ranks. But each higher rank has a special function not shared by the rank below, so may be distinguished from the rank below by that term.

The Purity, the Meal, consisted of the bread, the subordinate element, and the new wine, the superior element. It follows from the above that the name that applies to both elements, the Purity, would be used for the lower element, the bread, when it was necessary to distinguish the two. The higher element would be called by its special term, the Drink. 1QS 6:16, 20 means that preliminary full members are allowed to partake in the bread at the Meal, but not the wine, and at full membership the full Meal, with both elements, is taken. When the two stages are not paired, the Purity is used for the whole Meal (1QS 6:22, 25, 7:3, 16, CD 9: 21, 23, 1QS 8:17, 7:5).

The wording of 1QS 6:4-6 supports the conclusion that some members took the bread only: l.4 reads: "to eat *or* to drink".

(d) A year later full membership is given, with participation in the full Meal, and in government (22-23: "his counsel and judgement will be for the community"). The member's property is now fully mingled and he can no longer leave.[24] It is at this point that he makes his decisive break with the world.

The passage just studied, 1QS 6:13-23, deals with the laws concerning the stages of initiation, especially as concerns the discipline appropriate to each. It takes for granted the underlying doctrines which determine the nature of membership. But the basic doctrine of 1QS 3:6-9, concerning the two rites of initiation, is to be linked with this passage. It may be seen to account for the essential features of the scheme. There are, as has been shown, four steps. taken at four successive Pentecosts (on the time of the

first, see further below p.97). The period occupied is three years. Two
of the steps, (a) and (c), are defined as preliminary to the succeeding stage,
so that there are only two main kinds of membership; provisional and final,
steps (b) and (d). The provisional member is in a very different state from
the full member. He has not handed over his property, so that he is free
to leave if he chooses; and he does not take part in the expression of communal solidarity, the Meal. The full member is bound so that he cannot
leave, and the privileges of membership are reserved for him.

Membership of the community is conceived, as Gärtner[25] has suggested,
in spatial terms: "rings of holiness widening and diminishing according to
their proximity to the 'Holy of Holies' of the inner group". The inferior
members are the *outer* members, the superior ones are *within,* at the holy
centre of the community.

The two grades, provisional and lower, and final and higher, accord
with the doctrine of flesh and spirit. The flesh is outer and inferior; the
spirit inner and superior. Provisional members may be seen as *fleshly*
members, having given their bodies only to the community activities, whereas
full members are *spiritual* members, having committed their whole life; if
they left they would not survive, as they had no property. Josephus[26] describes
the plight of expelled Essenes who are dependent on the charity of others.

It would follow that at provisional membership a rite of water-washing
was administered, to mark the cleansing of the flesh from ritual defilement,
and at the final stage the Spirit of holiness was given, as the decisive
purification of the soul and the highest privilege of membership of the
community in which the Spirit of holiness dwelt. 1QS 3:7: "In the Spirit
of holiness (which is given) to the Community in its truth he will be purified
from all his iniquities".[27]

The water-washing was a repeated action, as has often been emphasized,[28] and accompanied every celebration of the Meal. 1QS 5:13: "he
(the lapsed member) shall not enter the waters to touch the Purity". The
flesh repeatedly became ritually defiled. But a special water-washing would
be associated with the first act of entry into the community, the fleshly membership, giving this washing the character of an initiation rite. According
to Hunzinger,[29] a papyrus has been found concerning a rite of baptism or
purification by water.[30]

Summarizing:

THE QUMRAN SCHEME OF INITIATION

Rite I	*Rite II*
Outer, fleshly, provisional membership by water.	Inner, spiritual, final membership by Spirit.
(a) Pentecost 1 Preliminary vow, followed by contact with the *paqîd* only.	*(c)* Pentecost 3 · Preliminary full membership. Property received, but not spent. Participation in the bread only.
(b) Pentecost 2 The water-washing for fleshly, provisional membership. No participation in the Meal, no giving up of property.	*(d)* Pentecost 4 Participation in both the bread and new wine. Property given up.

This analysis is found to correspond without difficulty to the stages of Essene initiation described by Josephus, whose account has been thought[31] to be erroneous on different interpretations of 1QS 6:13-23. In *J.W.*2§150 he speaks of four grades, with such a difference between two kinds, "seniors" and "juniors" that they are aliens to one another. In *J.W.*2§§137-142, he describes the phases of entry, with the associated discipline, in a way that is easily reconciled with the above:

(i) One year's probationary period outside the fraternity, but following the rule of life (137). This corresponds to step *(a)*.

(ii) Next "he is brought into closer touch with the rule and allowed to share the purer kind of holy water, but is not yet received into the meetings *(symbiōseis)*" (138). The "purer kind of holy water" reflects the initiatory water-washing of step *(b)*. Josephus' phrase means that it is more significant than the ordinary ablutions of the sect, not, as Leaney[32] holds, washings purer than those of Israel outside the sect. "Not received into the *symbiōseis"* means exclusion from the communal Meal, the rule for provisional members who have been baptized only.

iii) "After this exhibition of endurance, his character is tested for two years more, and only then, if found worthy, is he enrolled in the society. But, before he may take the common food *(hē koinē trophē)* he is made to swear tremendous oaths . . . (including the keeping of community secrets)" (138-142). As Rabin sees,[33] Josephus makes no division in the final two years. The "common food" is the full Meal. Steps *(c)* and *(d)* are put together.

Josephus' information is sufficiently accurate to enable the acceptance of his note concerning the duration of the probationary period, one year, as completing the lacuna of CD 15:15.

As the two rites were hierarchically graded, and as the lower one was a ritual washing while the higher one corresponded to a sacrifice for the removal of sin, there can be no doubt that the higher one was a priestly rite, the lower a levitical. Cf. the task of ritual cleansing given to the sons of Levi in 1QSa 1:25: they purify the congregation for three days before an assembly. At the stage before baptism, the novice has contact only with the *paqîd,* who is also called a *mèbaqqer* (pp.91-2); reasons will be given (pp.137-9) for seeing all *mèbaqqèrîm* as members of the levitical class.

Further information concerning provisional membership is to be found. 1QSa 2:4-11: "Any man who is afflicted with these (following things) shall not be confirmed in his standing in the midst of the congregation. Any man who is afflicted in his flesh, crippled in hands or feet, limps, is blind, deaf or dumb or has a visible fleshly blemish, an old, tottery[34] man, shall not be confirmed in the midst of the congregation. These shall not come to stand in the midst of the congregation of the men of a name, for the holy angels are in their midst. If any of these wishes to say a word to the Holy Council, he shall be questioned, but that man shall not come into the midst of the congregation, for he is afflicted."

CD 15:15ff[35] adds *petî,* "simple, foolish", to a list of persons with similar afflictions, and states that they may not "enter into the midst of the community", for the same reason concerning the holy angels. 1QSa 1:19-22 deals separately with the *petî* (spelt *pôtey)* stating that he must not take part in "decisions or judgement" or "lift up a burden", that is, take part in government, the privilege of the fully initiated member (1QS 6:22-3), or hold office in the war against the Gentiles, only be inscribed in the "order of the host" *(serek hassaba')* and be given some service to do.

1QpHab 12:4 names the "simple of Judah" *(peta'ê yehûdâ)* with the Council of the Community as two major sections of the congregation, interpreting "Lebanon" of Hab 2:17 as the latter, and the "beasts" *(behemôt)* of the same verse as the former. It is not likely that the mentally handicapped only are here meant: they did not constitute half the congregation. According to this passage, the "simple" are outside the Council of the Community, and according to the above the simple and other afflicted persons cannot govern or take part in the Meal ("come into the midst of the congregation", that is, the highest ranks). They are, however, in the membership: they may "say a word to the Holy Council" (through a representative, 1QSa 2:9-10). This means that they are allowed to the stage of

97

provisional membership, but not final initiation. It would follow that in 1QpHab 12:4 the name "the Simple" is used for the whole class of provisional members, who are not capable, for various reasons, of receiving full enlightenment into the higher doctrines of the sect, and so are like "beasts", less than "men" (=fully initiated, p.83). It may include others than the mentally and physically handicapped.

This observation illuminates CD 13:5-7:

> If a statute from the law of leprosy (Lev 13, 14) applies to a man (the context implies "member") the priest shall come and stand in the camp and the mĕbaqqer (who has close contact with the members of the camps, CD 13:7-22) shall instruct him in the interpretation of the Law (that is, the mĕbaqqer examines the man's body and reports to the priest if the symptoms of Lev 13, 14 appear). If the leper (not the priest, as most translators assume; this is shown by the repetition of hu') is a pĕtî (that is, a provisional member only, so forbidden all contact with the higher rank, the priests), the priest must still exclude him, for the law is for him to apply (the law of Moses concerning the priest's duty in cases of leprosy overrules the normal community practice of exclusion of provisional members from priests).

Thus there was a major class of members who were allowed to proceed only to the provisional stage, who could never have full membership, take part in the communal Meal and in government, and learn the higher secrets. It included all persons who were physically afflicted or of simple intellect.

The New Covenant: Admission of Proselytes

Both 1QS 6:13 and 1QSa 1:6 show that the man who begins the process leading to full initiation is "from Israel" and "born in Israel". This means that Jewish birth was not sufficient to entitle a man to membership of the community of the Future Time. Only initiation would give that privilege. As Jeremias, following H. W. Huppenbauer,[36] agrees, the Qumran sect discounted Jewish racial identity: "Die Zugehörigkeit zum Volk Israel an sich bietet keine Garantie mehr, denn der Schnitt geht nun durch Israel hindurch. Die Gleichung Gottesvolk = Israel ist aufgegeben".

Initiation into the community gave the "manhood" (pp.81-5) that was normally associated with circumcision. 1QS 5:5 shows that membership gave a spiritual circumcision: "to circumcise in the Community the foreskin of the inclination". As circumcision gave admission to the Jewish Covenant, so initiation made members of the Teacher's New Covenant (1QpHab 2:3). (Cf., possibly, Rev 3:9: "those . . . who say that they are Jews and are not" for a concept of bestowed Jewish identity.)

The symbol of "giving life" for initiation (1QS 3:7, cf. p.83) suggests that initiation was understood as a second birth into Judaism. The Teacher regularly uses the image of fatherhood in relation to the members, for example: "thou hast made me a father to the sons of grace" (1QH 7:20). Cf., in the same passage, his image as the Light (7:24-5) and "behold the Light of life", 1QS 3:7. In 1QH 8:16-27 he develops an image of spiritual fertility. The lifting or withdrawal of his hand gives spiritual fruitfulness or barrenness, and 8:16 plays on *yarâ* ("rain/teach") to show that his teaching gives spiritual life (accounting for his title, *môreh haṣṣedeq*, "teacher/ he who rains down righteousness"). He was the Anointed One who had made known the Spirit of holiness to the community (CD 2:12, see pp.65-71), and he himself possessed the Spirit. "Thou hast poured out thy Spirit of holiness upon me" (1QH 7:6-7). His own role as giver of fertility suggests that he was the means of transmission of the Spirit of holiness at initiation. As the Priest, he administered this form of final removal of sins, gave "life" to members, and made them Jews, in this being a second Abraham to them.

The consequence of the doctrine of the New Covenant was that *those who had not been born Jews could also be admitted,* as Jewish birth gave no privilege. CD 14: 4, 6,. lists proselytes *(ger)* as a fourth class in the community. 1QS 5:6 adds to the two Houses, of Aaron and Israel (forming a symbolic temple), another group, "those who joined" *(hannilêwîm),* playing on the word "levite", but not meaning levites as they are outside Aaron and Israel (cf. CD 3:21 - 4:3 for a parallel play). 4QpNah 2:9 speaks of the *ger nilweh* "proselytes who joined". Josephus confirms[37] that Greeks became members of the Essenes. "They irresistibly attract all who have once tasted of their philosophy." These would be required to be circumcised and to keep the Torah, in the communal interpretation.

There was reason also for Diaspora Jews to be admitted to the New Covenant, as a means of restoring Jewish identity in the face of the erosion caused by hellenization. They would form a bridge to the Gentile proselytes.

But 1QS 6:13-23, on the process of *full* initiation, concerns only Jews. There was an impediment to the full inclusion of Diaspora Jews and proselytes, under the Teacher's temple doctrine. In the Future Time, when the community priests again officiated in the temple in Jerusalem (p.70), it would be necessary for all members to attend the temple regularly. This was impossible for those who lived at too great a distance. 11QT 43:12-13 contains a law for those who lived more than three days' distance from the temple (they could bring money instead of offerings if the latter were too heavy to carry), showing special provision for them. This fact may be seen to account for the class of the "Simple of Judah who do the Law" in 1QpHab 12:4-5, who are distinguished from the Council of the Community (pp.97-8) and the "Simple of Ephraim" in 4QpNah 3:5. The class of the Simple are known to include the intellectually and physically handicapped who were given only provisional membership, baptized but not given the Spirit of holiness (p.98). In both the above contexts, the Simple are shown as subject to the persecution of rival teaching. It is unlikely that the class of the literally handicapped were so numerous or so significant that their subjection to false teaching was a major problem. The addition of "who do the Law" to "the Simple of Judah" suggests that the Simple include also proselytes and Diaspora Jews, who were not given full membership, only provisional membership, because of their distance from the temple. Only those "born in Israel" could proceed to full membership. In being denied full membership, the distant members were denied knowledge of the higher teachings of the community, being put in the class of the "Simple" and "beasts" who had not become "men" (initiated).

4QpNah 4:1 speaks of the "house of Peleg", who had gone over to the sect's enemies, and CD 20:22 of "the house of Peleg who went out of the Holy City and leaned on God" *(wayyissa'ēnû 'al 'el)*. The latter description is applicable to Diaspora Jews who have separated from Jerusalem and believe in a direct dependence on God rather than attendance at the temple.[38] The name "Peleg" is also suitable to one section of such a class. According to Gen 10:25-31, the earth was divided between two sons of Eber, a descendant of Shem. One was Peleg ("division"), the other was Joktan, who was the ancestor of all who lived in the territory "from Mesha in the direction of Sephar (Sippar) to the hill country of the east". 1QM 2:11, "Mesha beyond the Euphrates" uses the same division. All Semites were divided into these two groups (cf. 10:21: "Shem . . . the father of all the children of Eber"), west and east of the Euphrates. Peleg, the west, included Palestinian Jews, cf. 11:17-26, Peleg was an ancestor of Abraham. The divisions were also applicable to Diaspora Jews, throughout the "whole world". The House of Peleg was a suitable name for western Diaspora Jews and western Gentiles who had become Jews spiritually. CD 20:24-25 confirms that they were members of the community and that they had lapsed, like the House of Peleg in 4QpNah 4:1. They would be admitted back and judged in the "Holy Council". Cf. the Holy Council as the group to which the physically handicapped may send a representative in 1QSa 2:9.

It has sometimes been held that the Teacher's emphasis on separation meant that he led a small and isolated group who would have no interest in the inclusion of proselytes. The passages enjoining separation are, however, not as generalised as has been supposed. A study of the organisational terminology will show (p.149) that they refer to formal separation from the schismatics, former members of the community. For example, in 1QS 5:1-2 they are to separate from the "congregation *('edâ)* of the Men of Iniquity".

100

That these are the schismatics is shown by the law in the same passage, that the Men of Iniquity are not to "enter the waters to touch the Purity" (5:13), applicable only to lapsed members. The Teacher required separation from all impurity, including evil men, but gave to large numbers of people, through his doctrine of the New Covenant, the opportunity to form the membership of the pure community of the Future Time. As a *mebaśśer*, "preacher of good tidings" (pp.78-81), he proclaimed publicly the news of the coming catastrophe and of the appearance of the heavenly temple. His gift of oratory is noted in 4QpPsᵃ 4:27: " 'my tongue is the pen of a ready scribe' (Ps 45:1). Its interpretation] concerns the Teacher of [Righteousness . . .] God [. . .] him with an eloquent tongue [. . .]." As the coming of the Future Time was chronologically determined (p.68) and was expected in the lifetime of present members (p.70) the Teacher had every reason, and a suitable doctrinal basis, to admit as many members as possible into the community. They alone would survive the coming catastrophe and constitute a world-wide Kingdom of Jews.

NOTES

1. Some passages of the CD Laws contain legislation no different from that of the Teacher. See further below pp.191-5.

2. Milik, "Milki-sedeq . . .", 135. Milik states that it is in 4QDᵃ (formerly 4QDᵇ, see pp.45-6), the oldest copy of CD, and some missing words are completed by 4QDᵉ. He refutes Talmon (*RevQ* 1960 p.499, note 11), who challenges his view that the initiation ceremony was at Pentecost.

3. "Milki-sedeq . . .", 136.

4. See further Leaney, *The Rule of Qumran* . . ., 80-107.

5. *DJD* I, 152-5.

6. See further my forthcoming study "Qumran Initiation and N.T. Baptism".

7. Wernberg-Møller (*The Manual of Discipline* . . .' 107), following Kuhn, notes that *prostithēmi* is used in a similar way in Acts 5:14, 11:24.

8. Wernberg-Møller (*The Manual of Discipline* . . ., 107): "if he is amenable to ethics". "The intellectualistic ring of the phrase . . . should not be overlooked."

9. *yidrośuhu*. The whole community is referred to in the immediately preceding clauses. The plural is read by Lohse, Vermes, Leaney, Milik; the singular by Wernberg-Møller, J. van der Ploeg ("Quelques traductions du 'Manual de Discipline' des manuscrits de la Mer Morte", *BO* IX (1952), 127-133.

10. C. Rabin ("Private Property in the Qumran Community", in *Qumran Studies*, O.U.P., 1957) holds that *'arab* here means "to transact business with", as in 1QS 9:8-9 (in his interpretation). J. A. Fitzmyer (*Essays on the Semitic Background* . . ., p.286, footnote 25) finds Rabin's reasons "not very convincing"; *'arab* refers to the mingling of the individual's property

with that of the group, and corresponds to Josephus' expression *anamemigmenōn* (*J.W.* 2§122). See below p.175 on the meaning in 1QS 9:8-9: it also refers to mingling of property within the community.

11. *yiśśa'alu* "shall be asked about',' as also in 1QS 6:4. Wernberg-Møller (*The Manual of Discipline* ..., p. 102, n. 13): "one person puts the questions to the members, probably the president of the session."

12. The meaning of *sôd* will be discussed p.132.

13. 1QSa is on the rules for the Future Time, but as the present community would survive in material form (pp.62-4), the constitution is the same. As all the wicked would have been destroyed, there would be no more conversions. The various ranks are therefore related to age, as all members would proceed to initiation on maturity.

14. This passage of CD also contains legislation from the time of the Teacher (cf. note 1).

15. By Vermes (*DSSE*, 19), Wernberg-Møller (*The Manual of Discipline* ..., 107), E. Cothenet (*Textes de Qumrân* II, p. 201, n. 18), W. Brownlee, (*The Dead Sea Manual* ..., 25), M. Delcor ("Contribution à l'étude de la législation des sectaires de Damas et de Qumran", *RB* (1954, 533-53, p.541), H. H. Rowley (*The Zadokite Fragments and the Dead Sea Scrolls*, Oxford: Blackwell, 1956, p.37). Leaney (*The Rule of Qumran*, 196) thinks that the *paqîd* is the same as the *mĕbaqqer* of CD 13:7,11, 15:7-11, but not the same as the chief *mĕbaqqer* of CD 14:9. J. F. Priest ("*Mĕbaqqer*, *Paqîd* and the Messiah", *JBL* 81 (1962), 55-61, p.58) disagrees, holding that the *paqîd* is the head of the priests, on the basis of CD 14:6. But the noun is not used in CD 14:6, only the verb. P. Guilbert (*Textes de Qumrân*, I, on 1QS 6:12, n. 86, also distinguishes them.

16. *J.W.* 2§§137-9.

17. As Brownlee (The Dead Sea Manual ..., 49) and Rabin (Qumran Studies ..., 7) agree.

18. Wernberg-Møller, *The Manual of Discipline* ..., 96; S. Liebermann. "The Discipline in the so-called Dead Sea Manual of Discipline", *JBL* 71 (1952), 199-206, p.203.

19. Leaney, *The Rule of Qumrân* ..., 193-5.

20. Vermes, *DSSE*. Rabin ("The Novitiate", *Qumran Studies* ... 7-8) holds that the Purity is ritually pure food, but sees the emphasis on the purity of the food, not the privilege of communality expressed through the daily Meal.

21. Vermes, *DSSE*, 27.

22. Guilbert (*Textes de Qumrân*, I, p. 48, n. 98), following Milik, agrees that the Drink refers to the community meal of 1QS 6:5-6 and 1QSa 2:17-22. Leaney (*The Rule of Qumran* ..., 194-5) with Sutcliffe ("Sacred Meals at Qumran", *Heythrop Journal*, I (1960), 48ff.) takes the Drink to be different from the Purity, and sees its confinement to the highest rank as due to the fact that "liquids were the most powerful conveyors of uncleanness at a remove", so "the purity of the full members must be protected by prohibiting anyone other than a fellow full member to touch the drink which they shared".

23. Jeremias, *Der Lehrer* ..., 293-4. See further below p.169.

24. 1QS 7:18-25 shows that a fully initiated member of less than ten years' standing who becomes rebellious is given the chance to be reduced to

provisional membership and to go through the two years again. This would both give him an opportunity to repent and also be a device for returning his property to him if he chose to leave altogether. The member of more than ten years' standing who rebels is expelled. Others are not permitted to share the community property with him (25), i.e., his property is not returned.

25. B. Gärtner, *The Temple and the Community* . . ., 8.

26. *J.W.* 2§§143-4.

27. There is no information about the way the Spirit was given. It is to be noted, however, that D. Flusser ("Healing through the Laying-on of Hands in a Dead Sea Scroll", *IEJ* 7 (1957), 107-8) has pointed out that the only contemporary parallel to the NT practice of laying on of hands for healing of illness is found in the scrolls, in 1QarGen 20:21-22, where Abraham lays his hands on the head of Pharaoh and drives out the evil spirit which afflicted him. 1Q22 4:9 quotes Lev 16:21 on laying hands on the scapegoat; cf. also 11QT 15:18.

28. H. Braun, *Qumran und das Neue Testament* (Tübingen: Mohr, 1966), II, 6-7; M. Black, *The Gospel and the Scrolls* (Berlin, 1959), 565-579; O. Cullmann, "Secte de Qumrân, Hellénistes des Actes et Quatrième Evangile", in *Les Manuscrits de la Mer Morte* (Colloque de Strasbourg, Paris, 1957).

29. In M. Baillet *et al.*, "Le travail d'édition des fragments manuscrits de Qumrân", *RB* 63 (1956), 49-67, p.67.

30. *tabal = baptein* is not found in the scrolls. 1QS 3:4-5 implies total immersion.

31. Leaney (*The Rule of Qumran* . . ., 192-3), in his analysis of the passage, identifies step (a) with step (b), contrary to lls. 14-16, which show a separation in time for a period of instruction. He consequently identifies step (b) with step (c) and is left with only one more year before full admission, whereas Josephus gives two years.

32. Leaney, *The Rule of Qumran* . . ., 192.

33. Rabin, *Qumran Studies* . . ., 10.

34. Vermes, *DSSE, ad. loc.*

35. In 4QD^a, filling out the lacuna in the Cairo MS. See Milik, *Ten Years* . . ., 114.

36. Jeremias, *Der Lehrer* . . ., 331-2. H. W. Huppenbauer, "Der Mensch zwischen zwei Welten; der Dualismus der Texte von Qumran (Höhle 1) und der Damaskusfragmente. Ein Beitrag zur Vorgeschichte des Evangeliums", *ATANT* 34 (1959).

37. *J.W.* 2§158.

38. Cf. Klinzing, *Umdeutung* . . ., 11-20.

part three

The
Reconstruction

CHAPTER NINE

Starting-point and Methodology

We are now in a position to begin the work of detailed analysis of the writings in order to discover their relationship with one another, and the historical reason for the differences between them. This will be a very close study, but has the satisfactory result of yielding a solidly supported historical hypothesis. As explained in the Introduction, an assumption will be made that the use of terms is consistent, unless the opposite is proven. Specific meanings for apparently generalised terms will be looked for, as there is reason to suppose, from the usage of the *pesharim* in regard to scripture, that they frequently had such a sense.

Some further remarks must also be made concerning the starting-point and methodology.

The Starting-Point: 11QT and 1QM 2-9

We turn first to a major work which, while clearly a sectarian writing, shows no signs of the Teacher's doctrine or presence. The Temple Scroll (11QT)[1] sets out the plans for a temple, the organisation of its services, and the regulations for a new state. The question of its unity is still open, but for our purposes, it is unified by the fact that it contains no sign of the Teacher.

The temple of the scroll is physical, in its nature no different from those that had already been built on the sacred site in Jerusalem, except that this one was to be truly according to the divine plan, modifying or superseding the details of previous plans.[2] In its form, the work is a biblical book, using the language and long excerpts from the OT. The name Yahweh is used throughout, and Yahweh speaks directly as in OT books. The scribe took the text to be biblical, as he wrote the Tetragrammaton in the same script as the rest of the work. The intention is, as in the book of *Jubilees,* to revise the OT revelation in certain details, by offering a book claimed to be a biblical writing not previously known.

In 29:8-10 Yahweh is presented as saying: "I will sanctify with my glory my sanctuary, on which I shall cause my glory to dwell until the day of blessing *(yôm habbĕrakâ)* when I myself will create *('ebra' 'ănî)* my sanctuary to establish it for myself for ever, according to the covenant which I made with Jacob in Bethel". Yadin[3] suggests that it refers to two stages in the future. The temple of the scroll is to be built as that of the first part of the sentence, and in the eschatological period ("day of blessing") another sanctuary, corresponding to the temple of 4QFlor (4Q*174*), will be built. The material nature of the eschatological temple in Qumran thought (ch. VI) suggests, rather, that the temple of the scroll is that to be built *after* the "day of blessing". The one *before* the "day of blessing" is the present construction on the site, and all previous constructions. Yahweh, speaking in the time of Moses (cf. 44:5), anticipated the first and second temples as places where the Shekinah did dwell, but were not exactly according to his specifications. He promised that he would eventually build it as he had always intended. "I myself will create" shows that he will supervise it directly, as opposed to the imperfect builders of the first and second temples. This interpretation is supported by 4Q*174* 1:1-6, which contrasts the temple to be built by God himself with the temple destroyed in 587 BC.

11QT shows very close links with one section of 1QM. P.R. Davies,[4] following earlier observations of disunity in 1QM (notably by van der Ploeg)[5] has now given a convincing demonstration of the divisions and their order. In cols. 2-9 the warfare is nationalistic, the opponents are simply called "the enemy", and a single battle is envisaged. There is no developed dualism or any sign of a cosmic cataclysm. In 1 and 15-19 there is a greatly heightened dualism, the warfare is on a cosmic level, and the terms "sons of Light"[6] and "Kittim" are used. A seven-stage battle is described. Against Osten-Sacken,[7] he demonstrates that 2-9 must be earlier. It is inconceivable that a later section has simply ceased to use the terms and doctrines of 1, 15-19. "Would a second author, in attempting to expand an earlier work, simply allow obvious contradictions between his own work and the original to stand?"[8]

11QT supplies strong confirmation of the divisions in 1QM. In its organisational terms and structures, it has an extremely close relationship to 1QM 2-9, much less to the rest of 1QM. Terms in common are: the ḥigh/chief priest and his Second (M, 2:1, T 31:4;[9] twelve chief (head) priests, twelve chief (head) levites, twelve tribal heads (M 2:1-3, T 57:11-13); the three levitical families separate from the tribes (M 3:12 - 4:5, T 44:14ff); the use of the thousands, hundreds, fifties and tens in warfare (M 3:12 - 4:5, T 58:1-15); the office of *něśî'îm* (M 3:16, 4:1, T 21:5); the use of animal sacrifices (M 2:5,[10] T *passim*); restrictions on boys and women (M 7:3, T 39:7). 1QM 2-9 depends heavily on Num 1-10:10, as Davies shows.[11] 11QT 36-44 also draws on the organisation of tribes in the same section of Numbers.

The terms that are lacking in 1QM 2-9, but are found in the later stage of the work, are lacking in 11QT: "sons of Light", "Kittim", "Belial" (as a power of evil; in 55:3, quoting Deut 13:14, it is used of a "worthless person"). The doctrines that are absent from the first stage of 1QM are absent also from 11QT: dualism, cosmic warfare. There can be no doubt that 11QT and 1QM 2-9 have the closest connections. This fact makes untenable Davies' view[12] that the earliest stage of 1QM was not a sectarian document; a view in any case difficult to hold because of its close links with 1QSa. 11QT is clearly a sectarian document, emphasizing the liturgical calendar of the Qumran community (19:11 - 25: 10, 43).

11QT and 1QM 2-9 are, then, to be placed at an earlier stage than those writings which contain the dualistic terminology "sons of Light" and "Belial", eschatological doctrine (associated with dualism) or the idea of cosmic warfare, and the name "Kittim" for the enemy.

The eschatological writings (using the terms Future Time, Visitation, and expecting a cataclysmic event in the future), may all be seen to come from at or after the period of the Teacher of Righteousness (pp.70-1). CD refers back to him as a figure in the past, and the majority of the *pesharim* mention him. 1QH was partly written by him, and the other hymns show dependency on his hymns. 1QS has close links with both 1QH and CD, and 1QSa is dependent on 1QS.[13] *It may therefore be taken as a starting-point for the analysis that 11QT and 1QM 2-9 precede the period of the Teacher of Righteousness.*

The Methodology

A satisfactory reconstruction of Qumran history must depend on a very close analysis of the text. The primary data are the words of the writings themselves, and all plausible conjectures must be controlled by them. The aim of the researcher should also be to construct a single hypothesis, bringing in all the evidence, without resort to additional hypotheses at isolated points. One unified hypothesis, supposing a history whose different phases flow directly from one another, will, by its economy, carry more conviction than one requiring numerous additional supports.

The methodological procedure used by P. R. Davies, and endorsed also by J. Murphy-O'Connor and J. Pouilly,[14] is to study the meaning and distribution of organisational terms, and to observe the differences of the various rules from one another. The conflicting rules concerning the control of property in 1QS 5:2-3 (where both priests and laymen control it) and 1QS 9:7 (where priests only control it) are a firm indication that there are different levels, and that they may be discovered by the method of comparison. The writings may be grouped together in terms of their differences, and a history of the different stages read from them. With the knowledge that 11QT and 1QM 2-9 are earlier than the stage of the Teacher, a valuable starting-point has been obtained.

A preliminary observation of the distribution of nine organisational terms and one topic, through a number of the sectarian writings, may here be made, in order to illustrate the usefulness of the procedure. It may be set out in tabular form, showing by + the presence of the term in the writing or section of a writing.

DISTRIBUTION OF SOME COMMUNITY TERMS

Key. — 1. *Yaḥad* as a name for the community. 2. *'edâ, qahal* as names for the community. 3. *edâ, qahal* as names for the the schismatics. 4. "The Poor" *('ebyônîm)* as a name for members. 5. "Sons of Light" as a name for members. 6. "Volunteers" *(niddabîm)* as a name for members. 7. Sons of Zadok. 8. Presence of priests. 9. First Ones. 10. Presence of schismatics.

	1	2	3	4	5	6	7	8	9	10
11QT		+						+		
1QM 2-9		+						+		
1QS 3:13-4:14					+					
1QS 1:1-3:12	+				+	+		+		
1QS 5:20b-7:25	+	+				+		+		
1QSa	+	+					+	+		
1QSb	+	+					+	+		
1QM 10:8b-13:16		+		+	+			+		
1QS 5:1-20	+		+			+	+	+		+ª
Hymns of Teacher[b]		+	+							+
Rest of 1QH	+	+								+
4QpPs[a]	+	+		+				+		+
1QpHab		+	+					+		+
1QS 8:1-15	+							+		+[c]
1QS 9:12-26	+						d			+[e]
1QS 8:16b-9:11	+							+		+[f]
1QM 1, 15-19			+		+			+		+
4Q174-77	+				+		+	+		+
CD 7:10-21a		+								+
CD 2:14-7:10			+				g	h	+	+
CD 7:21b-8:21			+						+	+
CD 20:1-13a		+							+	+
CD 20:17b-27a										+[i]
CD 10:10b-12:22a										+
4QpNah			+					+		+
CD 1:1-2:13			+						+	+
CD 19:7b-15a			+					+		+
CD 19:32b-20:1	j							+		+
CD 20:13b-17a	j							+		+
CD 20:27b-34	j									+
CD 15:1-15								+		
CD 16:1-18								+		
CD 9:1-10:10		+						+		
CD 12:22b-14:22		+						+		
4Q266[k]								+		

109

a See p.149.
b See p.71 footnote 4.
c See p.166.
d See p.168.
e See p.169.
f See p.175.
g See p.183 (Symbolic only).
h See p.183 (Symbolic only).
i See p.157.
j See pp.195-6.
k See p.180.

The table contains some valuable indications for further investigation. *Yahad* as a name is found in the writings reflecting the eschatological doctrine of the Teacher of Righteousness (1QS, 1QSa, 1QSb), but not in 11QT and 1QM 2-9, before his time, or in CD, after his time. This means that it reflects his organisation, and other works using it are to be grouped with works from his time. *'Edâ* and *qahal,* however, are not exclusively his terms. They are used, not only for the community, but in a negative sense, for the schismatics. This fact, and the fact that they were used before his time, may tell us something about the nature of the schism: was it a return to a previous form of organisation?

The name "the Poor" *('ebyônîm)* is found in three out of four cases in documents directly connected with the Teacher. This may bring 1QM 10:8b-13:16, in which it is a prominent expression, into close connection with him. 4Q*174-7,* already linked with the Teacher through *yahad,* is further linked through "sons of Light". This, then, strengthens the links between 1QM 10:8b-13:16 and the Teacher, as it also contains "sons of Light". "Volunteers" is exclusive to the Teacher: it may be connected with *yahad.* The "sons of Zadok" further link 4Q*174-7* with the Teacher, and are exclusive to him.

The priests appear almost continuously, as is to be expected, but there is a surprising absence of literal priests from a large section of CD: cols. 1-8 and some sections of the Laws. But in these same sections, the First Ones appear. Are they a substitute for priests?

The schismatics do not appear in many parts of 1QS, nor in 1QSa and 1QSb. But their presence is continuous in the historical part of CD, after the Teacher's death. They appeared, therefore, after the beginning of his career. Those writings reflecting the Teacher's doctrine but not mentioning the schismatics are to be placed early in his history.

We proceed, now, to follow up these and very many other organisational terms, beginning with 11QT and 1QM 2-9 as containing a form of organisation preceding the Teacher of Righteousness. A large number of pieces of data will be studied and traced through all the sectarian works, in order to group the various writings and sections of writings, put them in the order indicated by signs of development, and read a history from them. The test of the procedure will be in its ability to produce a single hypothesis whose component parts are integrally related to one another.

NOTES

1. Edito princeps: Y. Yadin, *Mĕgillat-hammiqdaš* (Jerusalem: Israel Exploration Society, 1977).
2. Eg. in the allocation of the twelve gates to the different tribes (see p.120).
3. Yadin, *Mĕgillat-hammiqdaš*, vol. 1, 140-144.
4. P. R. Davies, *1QM. The War Scroll* . . .; "Dualism and Eschatology . . ."
5. J. van der Ploeg, *Le Rouleau de la Guerre* (Leiden: Brill, 1959).
6. "Sons of darkness" appear in 3:6,9 as a designation of the wicked, but not "sons of Light".
7. P. von der Osten-Sacken, *Gott und Belial*.
8. Davies, *1QM, The War Scroll* . . ., 14.
9. See Yadin, *Mĕgillat-hammiqdaš*, vol. II, p.95.
10. Cf. Klinzig, *Umdeutung*, p.84, n.31.
11. Davies, *1QM, The War Scroll* . . ., 28.
12. Davies, *1QM. The War Scroll* . . ., 58-65.
13. Osten-Sacken, *Gott und Belial*, 234-238.
14. J. Pouilly, *La Règle de la Communauté de Qumrân: Son Evolution Littéraire* (Cahiers de la Revue Biblique, Paris: Gabalda, 1976); "L'évolution de la législation pénale dans la Communauté de Qumran", *RB* 82 (1975), 522-551.
    Pouilly follows up the analysis of 1QS made by J. Murphy-O'Connor, in "La Genèse Littéraire de la Règle de la Communauté", *RB* 76 (1969), 528-549. The main criterion is the observation of the differences in the rules. There can be no doubt that this is the correct method. It may be remarked, however, that they have not always used the method of close analysis of the text. E.g., they hold that 1QS 8:1-15a is the earliest level, following the suggestion of E. F. Sutcliffe (*The Monks of Qumran*, London: Burns and Oates, 1960) that the twelve men and three priests of 8:1 were the small group of original followers of the Teacher who made the original move to Qumran. This hypothesis encounters a difficulty in 10b-12a

of this passage: "When these are established in the *yĕsod* of the Community for two years in perfection of way, they shall be separated as holy in the midst of the men of the Community . . .". This rule supposes a larger group holding the same discipline from which these men are to be separated after two years. J. Pouilly treats the passage as an interpolation (p.18), attaching it to 8:16b-19 as an introduction. Its removal is supported by pointing out that without it there is a harmonious literary structure. But this argument is only valid if such harmonious structures are regularly observable in 1QS, which is not the case. Pouilly's rearrangement also makes the new section, 8:10b-12a with 16b-19, begin "when these are established . . ." without a referent for the pronoun. In its present position it offers no grammatical difficulty.

Murphy-O'Connor has made a series of analyses of parts of CD (I, "An Essene Missionary Document? CD II, 14-VI, 1", *RB* 77 (1970), 201-229; II, "A Literary Analysis of Damascus Document VI, 2-VIII, 3", *RB* 78 (1971), 210-232; III, "The Critique of the Princes of Judah", *RB* 79 (1972), 200-216; IV, "A Literary Analysis of Damascus Document XIX, 33-XX,34", *RB* 79 (1972), 544-64). The results of his analysis of CD and 1QS are brought together into a historical hypothesis, in "The Essenes and their History", *RB* 81 (1974), 215-244. The outlines of his reconstruction are: the Essene movement was founded in Babylon following the Exile. In the Maccabean period a group of the members moved back to Palestine, where they began the period of bewilderment ("blindness") of CD 1:9. The Teacher of Righteousness, the expelled Zadokite high priest, then joined them, and provoked a split in the movement, with the result that he led a small group of his followers to Qumran, where the numbers later increased. The other party of Essenes remained outside Qumran, and were attacked as being associated with the group of dissidents led by the "Man of a Lie".

The analyses of CD frequently suppose interpolations, i.e. new hypotheses are introduced. Examples are in 4:19-20 and 8:12-13. In both places there is a reference to those who followed the Man of a Lie, making the passages 4:12b-5:19 and 8:3-18, in their present form, refer to the schismatics. Murphy-O'Connor holds, however, that both refer to Jews generally, and come from the time when the returning Essenes tried to convert their fellow-Jews. In the second of these, a close analysis of the text (made also by G. Jeremias, *Der Lehrer* . . ., 111) shows that the conduct of the subjects, the "princes *(śarim)* of Judah" is being compared, point by point, with the precepts for community members, set out in CD 6:11 - 7:6. This, with the fact that both "*śarim*" and "*Judah*" are community terms (Murphy-O'Connor bases his argument for 4:11 on "House of Judah" being a name for the community) means that the "*śarim* of Judah" are apostate members of the community, and the sentence on the Man of a Lie confirms this. The following table shows the details of the comparison:

6:11 - 7:6	8:5-8
7:1 to separate from sexual impurity *(zonot)*.	8:5 they wallowed in the ways of sexual impurity *(zonot)*.
6:15 to separate from wicked wealth *(hôn hariš'â.*	5 and wicked wealth *(hôn riš'â)*.
6:21 - 7:2 each to seek the peace of his brother . . . and not bear a grudge.	5-6 they bear a grudge, each against his brother.
6:20 each to love his brother.	6 each hates his brother.
7:1 not to sin against his near kin.	6 each sins against his near kin.
6:16 not to rob the poor of his people.	7 acted high-handedly for riches and gain.
6:14-15 to withdraw from the sons of the Pit.	8 they have not separated from the people.

With Jeremias, the two passages 4:12b - 5:19 and 8:3 - 13 are to be treated as sources for the schismatics.

CHAPTER TEN

$\mathcal{T}he\ \mathcal{R}econstruction$

A list of contents of this lengthy chapter may be useful. Attention is directed to the sections marked * , drawing together the findings of preceding sections.

THE ESSENES: 11QT 116
        Table 1: Organisation of 11QT 122
THE CONGREGATION: 1QM 2-9 122

THE COMMUNITY (YAḤAD) 125

Stage I: THE TEACHER OF RIGHTEOUSNESS 125

A. Before the Schism 125
    The sources 125
    The leadership structure 126
    The high priest 127
    The new roles of the laity 128
      (a) Symbolic priests and levites 128
      (b) Symbolic warriors 130
    Lay ranks 131

        Table 2: Lay Ranks in the Community 133
    Priests and levites 133
    The Messiah of Israel 135
    The third leader 137
    The *mĕbaqqĕrîm* 137
    The *yaḥad* 139
        Table 3: Ministry of the Community, Stage 1A 141
    Comparison with 11QT and 1QM 2-9 142
    The Teacher's View of Warfare 142
    * *Synthesis: The historical hypothesis* 145

B. After the Schism 148
    The sources 148
    Nature and reasons for the schism 150
    Further evidences 153
    The hellenizing policy of the rival party 156
    Results of the schism 160
    * *Synthesis* 165

Stage II: THE LAW-INTERPRETER 166
Stage III: THE LAW-INTERPRETER, THE CHIEF PRIEST, AND
    THE WARRIOR 171
    * *Synthesis* 178

        Table 4: Stages of the Schism 179

THE NEW COVENANT IN THE LAND OF DAMASCUS 180

The Sources 180
Phase I. The Law-Interpreter and the Warrior, and
Phase II. The Law-Interpreter 180
  * *Synthesis* 191
Phase III. The Messiah of Aaron and Israel 191
  * *Synthesis* 196

SUBSEQUENT HISTORY 196

THE ESSENES: 11QT

The close links between 11QT and 1QM 2-9, and their differences from the other sectarian writings, have been set out above (pp.105-7), together with the reasons for placing them before the eschatological writings and the Teacher of Righteousness.

There is also a major difference between these two documents: 11QT plans for a new state in peaceful conditions, in which there would only be defensive warfare (cols. 57-58), while 1QM 2-9 plans for an offensive war, resulting in world conquest (2: 6-14). With the plan for holy war are found organisational terms not in 11QT: "saints" *(qĕdôsîm,* "holy ones", 3:5, 6:6), "camps" (of the saints, of God, 3:5, 4:9), "named men" *('anšê haššem,* 3:4). It is unlikely that the plan for war would have been formed then abandoned, with its organisational terms. 1QM 2-9 is readily understood as the result of the addition of a plan for war and its organisation to the structures of 11QT.

The plans for the new state of 11QT are worked out on a biblical basis, using biblical terminology, but sometimes showing distinctions that are not apparent in the OT. There are also alterations in detail, e.g., the different order of tribes on the four sides of the central temple (39:12, 40-41), when compared with Num 2:3-2 and Ezek 48:32. The leadership practice of the post-exilic period has been drawn upon to support the constitution of a religious state under the supreme authority of the high priest, *hakkôhen haggadôl* (15:15 *et passim).*

A division into priests, levites and laity is fully illustrated. For example, at the feast of New Oil the leaders of each of the three classes, priests, levites and tribes, are to be given the same portion (one ram, one sheep) to eat (22:11-13); the king's council is to consist of twelve priests, twelve levites, twelve chiefs of the laity (57:11-13). In 61:8, the scroll adds "levites" to the "priests and judges" of Deut 19:17.[1]

The three courts, each a perfect square, into which the temple area is divided,[2] correspond, as is to be expected, to grades of holiness. The inner court surrounds the temple itself. Into the middle court, "no woman or boy will enter" (39:7, cf. 1QM 7:3). In the outer court, however, women and proselytes are admitted (40:6). It is on the wall of the outer court that booths are to be built for the tribal leaders at the Feast of Tabernacles (42:7-17); they represent the laity.

In the outer wall of the middle court there are twelve gates, corresponding to the twelve tribes, as there are also in the outer wall of the outer court. In the inner wall of the middle court there are four gates only, leading into the inner court around the temple.

The plan is certainly related to that of Ezekiel (45:1-5; 48:8-20), who set apart within the land a holy territory, a square, divided into three adjacent rectangles, for the priests, levites and people, respectively. The middle court of the temple area in the scroll corresponds to the levites in the community structure.

In Ezekiel's plan, the temple is placed in the priestly rectangle, so that the rectangle of the levites acts as a barrier between the temple and the laity. 11QT shows an important difference: the temple is placed at the centre of three concentric squares, showing that holiness lies at the heart of the whole community. The series of gates from outer wall to inner court give access to it. The access is through the court of the levites, which on one side is tribal (twelve gates) and on the other is not tribal (four gates), and leads into the temple court. The tribe of Levi, in the OT sources, was both tribal and priestly. It was the only group capable of being placed between the priesthood and the laity, if such a group were required. The plan of the middle court shows that the levitical class is understood as an intermediate group in the community, as in Ezekiel, but, unlike Ezekiel, it is also understood as a bridging group. The two sets of gates allow access from the outer to the temple court while preserving the difference between tribes and temple. The transition from the lay to the priestly order takes place within the levitical class.

Col. 44 contains a description of the chambers on the outer wall of the outer court, occupying the sixteen spaces from corners to gates and between gate and gate. Eleven of these are for the "sons of" the lay tribes after whom the gates are named. The two spaces to the right and left of the central gate on the east, the gate of Levi, are to be for the priests. One of each of the spaces on the south, west and northern walls are to be for the three groups of levitical families, the sons of Kohath, Gershom and Merari, following the directions of Num 3:21-27. Cf. the addition of the three levitical families to the twelve tribes in 1QM 3:13 - 4:5.

In 44:14 the scribe originally wrote, after "sons of Kohath", *mibbĕnê hallĕwîyîm,* "from the sons of the levites".[3] Two letters of the first word *(b,y)* have subsequently been erased, giving *min hallĕwîyîm,* "from the levites". The correction shows that "sons of levites" were not quite the same as levites. Yet in 1 Chr 15:15 "sons of levites" is used for the three levitical divisions.

22:4 reads "the sons of Levi *(bĕnê lewî)* will slaughter *(šaḥaṭ)* . . .". In the following line the sons of Aaron are differentiated from them as the ones who will sprinkle the blood. The reference is to Ezek 44:10-11, where Ezekiel's second ministerial class, the levites who went astray, are appointed to slaughter *(šaḥat)* the sacrifice. But where MT reads *hallĕwîyîm,* "levites", in Ezek 44:10, 11QT has "sons of Levi". In view of the regular use of *lĕwîyîm* for the second class throughout 11QT, the difference is striking. That Ezekiel means levitical priests is shown by the parallel between 44:10 and 40:45.

63:3, in reproducing the law of Deut 21:1-9 (a rule concerning the cities of Israel), uses the phrase of Deut. 21:5, "the priests the sons of Levi" *(hakkôhănîm bĕnê lewî).* In three instances before this, the scroll shows independence in the matter of terminology for the levites: it departs from the biblical text in the Ezek 44:10 quotation (above); it adds "levites" to the text of Deut 19:17, giving "priests, levites and judges" in 61:8; and it alters the apparently appropriate "sons of the levites" to "the levites" in 44:14 (above). The term "the priests the sons of Levi" must, then, be taken as fully intentional here, not simply an imitation of the biblical term. In a work regularly including levites, who were not priests in the second temple, the term is significant.

The organisation of the chambers on the outer wall (col. 44) shows a distinction between sons of Aaron and remaining members of the tribe of Levi. The sixteen spaces are to be occupied by (a) sons of Aaron, in the two spaces on either side of the gate of Levi, in the centre of the eastern wall ("All the right of the gate of Levi and all the left, for the sons of Aaron" (5) stresses that sons of Aaron are on both sides, and there are no other sons of Levi, although the gate is of Levi); (b) sons of Kohath, Gershom and Merari, one in each of the southern, western and northern walls (44:14, 45:01-04); (c) eleven tribal leaders, counting Ephraim and Manasseh as one, beside the gate of Joseph (44:13).

These facts put together may be taken as meaning that in 11QT there are two priestly classes, primary and secondary. The sons of Aaron are the primary class, and are separated from the tribes, the laity; they correspond to the inner court of the temple. But the levitical class, the middle court, are also priests, of a secondary order. They are grouped with the tribes, taking part in the affairs of the ordinary laity, the inhabitants of the cities of Israel (63:3). Corresponding to the fact that the levitical court is tribal on one side and non-tribal on the other, the sons of Levi, secondary priests, form a bridging class, linking the laity with the priests and the priests with the laity.

The alteration of the original version of 44:14, and of the MT in Ezek 44:10, shows that a distinction was also made between sons of Levi/sons of the levites and levites. 15:17-18, naming both "priests" and "elders of the priests" shows a distinction between priests on the ground of age (cf. 2 Kgs 19:2). In 1 Chr 23, levites, who are there distinguished from priests, are divided into two classes:

(a) those over twenty years of age, who (i) work in the temple, and (ii) act as singers (27-32).

(b) those over thirty, who add to these two duties those of (iii) judges and *šôṭerîm,* and (iv) gatekeepers. The four kinds of work are listed in 23:3-5.

The senior levites here add duties requiring contact with the laity, while the juniors remain in the temple. The names and functions in 11QT are consistent with this distinction. "The priests the sons of Levi", involved in lay rule (63:3), correspond to the senior levites. The "sons of Levi" assist in the temple (22:4) as do senior levites, and do the work of Ezekiel's levitical priests. As "sons of the levites" in 44:14 would exclude the juniors of Kohath, it is altered to "levites", which is used, here and in 21:4, 24:11, 61:8 and 57:12, to cover all members of the class, according to the usage set out pp.93-4: in a pair belonging to a class, the lower rank term embraces . both lower and higher ranks, while the higher rank is distinguished by its specialist term. In 60:12-15 the law of Deut 18:6-8 is reproduced, concerning a levite *(hallewî)* who comes from one of the towns to the temple, where he may minister "like all his brothers the levites". The form of words is not inconsistent with his being a junior who ministers with other junior levites in the temple, "levites" here being used in its lower rank sense.

Deuteronomy, Ezekiel and Chronicles offer varying testimony on the subject of priests and levites. In Deuteronomy, there are levitical priests: "the priests the levites, all the tribe of Levi" (18:1). In the light of a later distinction between priests and levites, some passages may be seen as referring to a lower order, levites who were not priests, e.g. in 16:14, 18:6, 12:12, 19, levites are ranged with the slave, the widow and the orphan. R. Abba[4] has recently argued that there was a secondary class of levites in the first temple. In Ezekiel, the levitical priests are secondary to the sons of Zadok: the latter only are allowed at the altar, the innermost place 40:46, 44:15), while the former are allowed in the temple but not at the altar (40:45). In 1 Chr 23 the levites (called both "sons of Levi" and "levites") are no longer priests, but remain secondary (to the sons of Aaron) and continue to do the work of the temple, while the seniors add lay duties.

The definitions of 11QT may be understood as a combination of all three, following from the Essene view of the unity of scriptural testimony. Following Ezekiel, who uses "levites" and "levitical priests" interchangeably (40:45, 44:10), the priesthood of levites is retained. Following Chronicles and Ezekiel, the secondary status of levites is held; as priestly, they are in the temple, but excluded from the highest place. In accordance with Chronicles on senior levites and Deuteronomy on levitical priests, they are tribal priests: they are first among the laity but second in the temple. The difference between levitical priests and levites, evident from a comparison of Ezekiel and Chronicles, is maintained by a distinction between "sons of Levi the priests" and "levites" in terms of duties, reflecting seniority. "Levites" means both "junior levites" and "sons of Levi plus junior levites," in accordance with normal Qumran usage, and most scriptural uses of "levites" are covered by either meaning.

The organisation of the laity is likewise based on the OT. Ranked below priests and levites, laymen are in twelve tribes, grouped in threes called "divisions" *(dĕgalîm)* (21:5), around the four walls of the temple area (E. Simeon, Levi, Judah; S: Reuben, Joseph, Benjamin; W: Issachar, Zebulun, Gad; N: Dan, Naphtali, Asher (39:12, 40-41). Judah is ranked immediately below the levites as the first tribe, cf. 24:10-11: "the sons of Judah after the levites", and 23:10.

The leader of the laity is to be the king *(melek,* 56:13). He is clearly subordinated to the high priest; the final decision whether to go out to war is made by the high priest, consulting the Urim and Thummin (58:16-20). Nor is the king a ruler of the laity in his own right; he reflects a democratic structure of lay government, ruling under the advice of a council of thirty-six, who arė in "session" *(yôšebîm)* with him, "together" *(yaḥad,* adverb only). He "shall not lift up his heart from them, and he shall not do anything, on any matter of council, without them" (57:14-15). He is simply their executive officer and chairman.

Beneath him as leaders of the laity are twelve *nĕśî'îm* (57:11), part of his council of thirty-six. They are divided into groups of three, corresponding to the tribes, cf. *"nĕśî'îm* of the divisions" (21:5). Their title, "lifted up (from the people)" *(nasa'* "to lift up") shows that they also are only first among equals. 42:13-15 supplies two further titles for them: "heads of fathers' houses for the sons of Israel" and "elders of the congregation".

There would sometimes be need for an army, when the state was attacked by Gentiles (57: 7, 11). From the laity are to be selected twelve thousand especially worthy, "men of truth who fear God" (57:8), and purified as "men of war" *('anšê milḥamâ,* 57:6), "mighty men of the army for war" *(gibbôrê ḥayil lĕmilḥamâ,* 58:16). When not needed in the field they will be the king's bodyguard, "with him always, day and night" (57:9-10). For purposes of war the twelve thousand are to be subdivided into thousands, hundreds, fifties, tens, the numbers being used in proportion to the size of the attacking army (58:1-15). Their leaders are called *śarîm* ("chiefs, princes"), of thousands, hundreds, etc. (57:4-5); there were therefore twelve leading *śarîm,* 120 below them, etc. 42:15 shows that the *śarîm* are to be ranked after the *nĕśî'îm,* the tribal heads. The latter are for permanent government, the former for war only, a secondary role in the peaceful state planned in this document.

The king's advisory council consists of the twelve lay *nĕśî'îm,* also "from the priests, twelve, and from the levites, twelve" (57:11-13). Each of the two priestly classes is to be drawn upon for twelve leaders. The intermediate position of the levites, both tribal leaders and secondary priests, maintains a balance between lay and priestly interests.

In 1QDM (1Q22, a piece with similar characterists to 11QT)[5] the phrase "head fathers for the levites" *(ra'šê 'ăbôt lallĕwîyîm)* is found (1:3), and 1QM 4:1 names the *naśî'* of Merari. The twelve lay *nĕśî'îm* are called "heads of fathers' houses" in 11QT 42:13-15. The titles reflect the tribal leadership of the levites, balancing their priestly titles with those of the lay leaders. They are intended as the class in which both sides of the community meet; cf. the plan of the levitical court.

At the top of the leadership structure is the high priest, and in 31:4 "the Second Priest" is named. The title suggests that he is in a levitical relationship to the high priest. Cf. also 2Q24 ar fr.4:16: "[the high] pr[iest] with him, and let the other (loaf of bread) be given to his Second who stands apart."

The whole membership are called the *qahal* ("assembly", NT *ekklēsia,* 16: 15, 16, 18; 26:9) or "people of the *qahal*" (26:7-9), the name used for gatherings of Israel for worship (2 Chr 20:5) or self-government (1 Kgs 12:3). "Congregation" *('edâ)* is sometimes used (42:14, 22:02, 39:6).

TABLE 1

Organisation of 11QT

LAITY		PRIESTS
		High priest
King		Second Priest
		12 sons of Aaron
12 tribal heads (also called "něśî'îm", "head fathers")	12 sons of Levi (secondary priests, also called "head fathers for the levites", "něśî'îm for the levites")	
12 śarim of thousands		
120 śarim of hundreds, etc.		

THE CONGREGATION: 1QM 2-9

The plan for offensive war in 1QM 2-9 is in marked contrast with the expectation of a normally peaceful state in 11QT. But the ministry, described in 1QM 2:1-6 as that to be set up in the seventh year of the war,[6] is able to be related at every point to that of 11QT, with one significant difference.

1QM 2:1-6 continues the missing part of the previous column:

[. . .] (1) fathers of the congregation, fifty-two. They shall rank the head priests after the Chief Priest (*kôhen haro'š*) and his Second, twelve heads, to be ministers (*měśarětîm*) (2) in perpetuity (*bětamîd*) before God. The heads of the *mišměrôt* (priestly divisions), twenty-six, shall minister (*śaret*) in their *mišměrôt*. After them the head levites are to minister perpetually (*tamîd*), twelve, one for each (3) tribe. The heads of the *mišměrôt* shall minister, each man in his office (*ma'ămad*). The heads of the tribes and the fathers of the congregation after them are to stand (*hityasseb*) perpetually in the gates of the temple. (4) The heads of the *mišměrôt* with their attendants (*pěqûdîm*) are to stand, for feasts, new moons, sabbaths, and every day of the year, aged fifty and upwards. (5) These shall stand at burnt-offerings and sacrifices ,to prepare incense-offerings as a sweet-smelling gift to God, to atone for all his congregation and to participate before him perpetually (6) in the table of glory.

The Chief Priest and his Second correspond to the high priest and the Second Priest (see further below). After them come the twelve head priests, corresponding to those of 11QT, together with lower Aaronites, the twenty-six heads of *mišměrôt*.[7]

122

The twelve levites follow them, their number linked with the tribes, in accordance with the role of the sons of Levi as tribal priests (pp.117-20); "levites" is used for them as representatives of the whole class, and to distinguish them from the superior priests. The twelve heads of tribes (3b) complete the thirty-six heads of priests, levites and laity.

Šaret, "minister" is used only for the high priest and his Second, the twelve priests, the twenty-six heads of mišmĕrôt[8] and the twelve levites, totalling fifty-two, the number of weeks in the year (exactly) according to the solar calendar of 364 days. The number fifty-two is found at the beginning of the column, preceded by "[. . .] fathers of the congregation", that is, the fathers are included in the total. The fathers of the congregation appear with the tribal heads in the next section (3b) as "standing" *(hityasseb)* in the gates of the temple, that is, not in the temple itself. In 11QT and 1QDM, both the levitical heads and the tribal heads are called "fathers" pp.120-1). If the fathers are the twelve levites here, then their inclusion in the total of fifty-two, and their difference from the tribal heads are accounted for. They have the same dual role as in 11QT, included with the priests in temple service, and with the lay leaders in tribal rule.

They are, however, placed *after* the tribal heads: "the heads of tribes and the fathers of the congregation after them" (3b), whereas the superiority of priests in 11QT implies that the levitical priests are second in the temple but first in the tribes. If the tribal leaders are also "fathers" in this ministry, the usage of pp.93-4 confirms that the levites are subordinate to them: both groups are fathers, but only the lower rank are called by this name. This is consistent with the differences in titles of the supreme leaders, priestly and lay. The supreme priest is now called the Chief Priest *(kôhen haro'š),* and the king is called Naśî' of all the Congregation (5:1). Both have been reduced in status, so that neither is superior according to title. But the lay leader now has an overall rule which is not given to the Chief Priest. He is still "lifted up" from the laity, but is over "all". There is an equality of status, with much greater power given to the lay ruler. The superiority of the twelve tribal leaders to the levitical leaders outside the temple reflects this arrangement. It is a consequence of the plan for holy war, which requires holiness and power from the laity also.

The following passage, 2:6-7, reads: "In the remaining thirty-three years of the war, the *'anšê haššem* (lit., "the named men") called to the *mô'ed* ("meeting for worship, feast", cf. the concept of holy war), and all the head fathers of the congregation, shall choose for themselves men of war for all the lands of Gentiles". Cf. also 3:3-4: "the named men (and)[9] the head fathers of the congregation, called to the house of *mô'ed"*. On their trumpets will be written "testimonies of God for the Holy Council *('āṣat qôdeš)"*.

"All" does not appear with the levitical fathers in 1QM 2:3, and is not known to appear before the same group in 2:1. This expression may be taken as confirming that the twelve tribal heads are also "fathers". "All the head fathers" are the twenty-four of 2:3, the twelve tribal heads and the twelve levites (levitical priests). As lay leaders, they meet with the named men in a lay council for the purpose of planning war, choosing the "men of war", as in 11QT 57:6-8.

The "named men" are those whose names are listed in the *serek* ("register of ranks"): cf. 4:6, "the *serek* of the list of their names". They are the men capable of warfare. This reflects the selection of a special, numbered group of men for warfare in 11QT (pp.120-1). They now have a more prominent role, meeting with the twenty-four fathers in a lay structure called the Holy Council.

Their leaders are still the *śarîm* of thousands, hundreds, etc., who now appear more frequently, as their central occupation is warfare. The *neśî'îm,* the tribal leaders who are superior to them in 11QT (p.120) are found as leaders of ten thousands in 3:16. All male members of the tribes are now engaged in aggressive warfare, not merely the selected group of twelve thousand in 11QT.

The holiness necessary for religious warfare is required of the laity. The members are called "saints" (3:5, 6:6). The rule of 11QT 39:7 concerning the exclusion of boys and women from the holier areas of the temple is applied to the battlefield (7:3). The new term "camps" is applied to the sub-groupings of thousands, hundreds, fifties, tens (3:5), and the tribes are again in groups of three (3:14). The three levitical families are additional to the tribes (3:14-4:5).

The name the Congregation *('edâ)* is now regularly used for the whole community (2:5, 2:9, 3:2). "All the congregation together *(yaḥad,* adverb)" appears in 2:9. *Qahal,* more appropriate to the worshipping community, is found only once (4:10).

In 2:1-6 *tamîd,* "perpetually" is used for the service of both priestly-levitical and lay members of the thirty-six, but not for the twenty-six lower Aaronites. Service at the different times of the calendar is described only for them (lls. 4-6). They are the ordinary cultic ministers, officiating at the different occasions of worship, while the ministry of the thirty-six is perpetual, that is, it means constant dedication.

The two essential differences between 11QT and 1QM 2-9 are, then, aggressive warfare and greater lay authority, with a reduction of priestly supremacy. They are related to one another as required by holy war. They have been added to the plans of 11QT, resulting in the synthesis of 1QM 2-9. There must be a historical reason for the combination, yet radical change. Further, there must be a reason why these two writings are so different from the eschatological group, which expect a much more fundamental change in human conditions. This difference may also point to an event in the history. The next step is, therefore, to analyse the organisational terminology of the group of writings connected with the Teacher of Righteousness, in order to be in a position to bring all three groups together for the formation of a historical hypothesis.

THE COMMUNITY (YAHAD)
STAGE I: The Teacher of Righteousness

A. Before the Schism

The Sources

1QS, 1QSa and 1QSb are closely linked in organisational terminology, and were part of the same scroll. 1QSa concerns the community of the Future Time (1:1), but as the life of the members would be the same then as now, in a world cleansed of all evil, its description of the future community is a source for the present organisation.

The eschatology of 1QSa and of parts of 1QS (3:13 - 4:14, 4:15-26) links them with the Teacher of Righteousness. The three documents all use the name *yaḥad*, the Community (lit. "togetherness', NT *koinōnia)*, not used as a name in 11QT and 1QM 2-9. It may be seen as entering with the Teacher (p.110).

The continuity between this group and the previous two stages is apparent in the terms "congregation" (1QS 5:20, 1QSa 1:1 *et passim)*, "Holy Council" (1QSa 2:9), *qahal* (1QSa 2:4), "named men" (1QSa 2:11), "camps" (1QSa 2:15), "head fathers" (1QSa 2:25), *śarîm* of thousands, etc. (1QSa 1:29-2:1).

1QSa and b, and some of the documents assembled in 1QS, contain no hint of the schism in the community that figures in other writings of the Teacher's time, and those after his death. They are a source for the early part of his career.

1QS 5:1-20a, 8:1-15a with 9:12-26, and 8:16b - 9:11 (the latter not in 4QSᵉ) describe an organisation different from that of the Teacher; they will be studied separately. The sources describing the early organisation of the Teacher are:

    1QS 3:13 - 4:14
         4:15-26
         1:1 - 3:12
         5:20b - 7:25
    1QSa
    1QSb
    4QpIsaᵈ
    4QPB

The leadership structure

According to 1QSa 1:24, the congregation is "under the authority of the sons of Zadok the priests and [all the h]ead fathers of the congregation". Cf. also 1:2: "under the judgement of the sons of Zadok the priests and the men of their covenant". In 4QpIsaᵈ 4, twelve priestly persons (the word after "twelve" is missing) are interpreted as the suns/pinnacles *(šimšôt)* of the temple, "giving light in judgement by the Urim and Thummim". 11QT 58:18-19 shows that it is the duty of the high priest to give guidance by the Urim and Thummim, and 4QTestim 14 also gives this task to the priestly leader. The twelve in 4QpIsaᵈ are like "agate", and 1QSb 3:25 describes the sons of Zadok as a "brilliant jewel". There appear to be twelve sons of Zadok, the superior priests in the community, in the rank below the high priest, corresponding to the twelve priests of 11QT and 1QM 2-9.

1QSa 1:22-25 reads: (22) "The sons of Levi shall stand, each in his office *(ma'ămad)* (23) under the authority of the sons of Aaron, to cause the whole congregation to come in and go out, each in his rank, under the hand of the head (24) fathers of the congregation, as *śarîm*, judges, *šôtěrîm*, according to the number of all their hosts, under the authority of the sons of Zadok the priests (25) and all the head fathers of the congregation".

The "head fathers" of lls. 23-24 cannot be the same as "all the head fathers" of 25. In 1QM 2-9 a similar distinction has been found: the "fathers" of 2: 1- 3 are the twelve levites, while "all the head fathers" of 2:7 are the twenty-four leaders of the laity, the twelve levites and twelve tribal heads. All twenty-four are "fathers". The usage here is consistent with this. The fathers of 23-24 are the twelve lay leaders, who rule the congregation beside the sons of Levi of 1.22. "All the head fathers" of 1.25, who rule with the sons of Zadok, are the whole twenty-four, making with the sons of Zadok a supreme council of thirty-six.

The same meaning may be seen in the order of ranking of the meetings of the Many, 1QS 6:8: the priests first, the elders second, and then "all the rest of the laity". The elders or fathers include the twelve levites, so levites are not named, and they include also twelve lay leaders, accounting for the phrase "all the rest of the laity".

Lay leaders include heads of tribes (1QSa 1:29),[10] and *śarîm* of thousands, hundreds, fifties, tens (1QSa 1:29 - 2:1, 1:14-15, 1:24. These also are as in 11QT and 1QM 2-9.

Sons of Levi rule the laity, but themselves are under the authority of the sons of Aaron (1:22-23); both the name and rank are the same as the sons of Levi in 11QT (pp.117-20). They are secondary priests who are first over the laity, and rule in conjunction with the twelve tribal leaders as a structure of twenty-four elders (the name in 1QS 6:8).

But whereas in 1QM 2:3 the levites are given the lower rank title of "father" (p.123), it is the lay leaders who are called "fathers" in 1QSa 1:23-24, while the sons of Levi are called by their specialist term. The relative ranking of priesthood and laity is here the same as in 11QT and different from 1QM 2-9: levites are above all laymen.

The wider body of superior priests are sons of Aaron (1QS 5:21, 1QSa 2:13). The two opposite sectors in the community are priests and laity: sons of Aaron and the multitude of Israel (1QS 5:21-22), sons of Zadok and the heads of tribes (4QpIsa[d]).

It may be concluded that the Teacher's leadership structure corresponds to that of 11QT and 1QM 2-9, and shows the priestly supremacy of 11QT.

The high priest

In the important passage 1QSa 2:11-22, two figures are named: the Priest, and the Messiah of Israel. The first is clearly the superior: "For he (the Priest) blesses the firstfruits of (both) the bread and the new wine. He stretches out his hand over the bread first. After this, the Messiah of Israel stretches out his hand over the bread" (19-21). As K. G. Kuhn[11] remarks: "in such a context the reference to 'the priest' takes on significance". It means the high priest, and priestly Messiah. Kuhn points to Lev 4 as the source of the simple title "the Priest"; in this chapter, the high priest is first introduced as the Anointed Priest *(hakkôhen hammaśiah),* and referred to in subsequent verses (6, 7, 10) simply as "the priest". The Teacher is called the Priest in 4QpPs^a 2:17, 3:14, and it has been shown (ch. VII) that as high priest he expected to become priestly Messiah in the restored temple. 1QSa illustrates, then, his present position within the community, and future position as head of the surviving community of the Future Time.

Unlike the Chief Priest of 1QM 2:1, he has clear supremacy over the whole community. He takes precedence over the Messiah of Israel, the leader of the laity, at the Meal. In 1QM 5:1 the lay leader was called "the *Naśî'* of *all* the Congregation", but in 1QSa 2:12 the high priest is "the Priest, the head of *all* the congregation of Israel". 1QSb 4:23-24 confirms that he has taken the place of the *Naśî'* as supreme ruler of the laity also: "to lift thee up (root *naśa')* at the head of the saints and thy people . . . under thy hand are the men of the Council of God (lay structure, below pp.131-2, and not under the hand of a *śar* (lay leader, p.127).[12]

The high priest is now, again, at the supreme head of the community, as in 11QT. But the statements that he is to be head over the laity imply a new closeness to them. Yet the separateness of priests, still maintained (1QS 7:2-3), would make such contact difficult. A change in the status of laity is implied; it will be examined below.

The high priest is a "light *(ma'ôr)* for the world" (1QSb 4:27, and the Teacher says of himself "I have shone forth in sevenfold light" (1QH 7:24-25). He is likened to the Menorah, the seven-branched candlestick in the temple. The consequences of this image, in relation to the "sons of Light", will also be considered below.

The new roles of the laity

(a) Symbolic priests and levites

One of the duties of the sons of Aaron in 1QM 2:4-6 was to atone for the people by the performance of sacrifices; another was to officiate at all the appointed times of the calendar (pp.124-5). Symbolic versions of both these tasks are now given to the *laity.*

1QS 3:6-8 shows that righteousness atones: "in a spirit of true counsel concerning the ways of a man they shall atone (root *kipper)* for all their iniquities . . . in a spirit of uprightness and humility his sin will be atoned for". The whole community, represented by both kinds of leaders, are now to atone for the land by their righteousness in keeping the Covenant. "The men of his Council who keep his Covenant in the midst of wickedness to atone on behalf of the land" (1QSa 1:3). Similarly 1QS 5:3-6, 8:6-7, 8:2-4 (all later sources).

On entering the Covenant, initiates vow "not to transgress one word of God's commands concerning the periods of time, and shall not advance their times and not be behind for any of their feasts" (1QS 1:13-15). They are to be as conscious of the calendar as the priests, although in 1QM 2:1-6 only the priests served at the appointed times.

The ages at which, in the Future Time, they will receive initiation and entry into the ranks of government, twenty and thirty respectively (1QSa 1: 8, 13) are the same as distinguish the two kinds of levites in 1 Chr 23; these distinctions have been suggested to have been used in 11QT (p.119). At thirty, they act as judges and *sôterîm* (1QSa 1: 15, 29), the work of senior levites in 1 Chr 23:4.

At initiation and the receipt of the Spirit of holiness, the righteousness of God is given to members, who have prepared for it by their repentance. "With God is my justification, and in his hand is the perfection of my way . . . he will remove my sin through his righteousnesses, for he has opened up my light from the source of his knowledge" (1QS 11:2-3). They are *given* righteousness. At the same time, they are given "light". They "behold the light of life" (1QS 3:7). This gift is a consequence of the fact that the high priest is the Light. 1QSb 4:27: the high priest is "a light *(ma'ôr)* . . . for the world". The Teacher says of himself: "I have shone forth in sevenfold light, with [the light which thou hast est]ablished for thy glory". His light was derived from God: "for thou art an everlasting light to me" (1QH 7:24-25). In giving them life, a second birth as Jews (pp.98-9) he gives them light (1QS 3:7). Light stands for priesthood, as the priests know the secrets of the heavenly bodies and the calendar; the twelve priests in 4QpIsa[d] "give light by the Urim and Thummin" (lights and perfections). In receiving light at initiation, members receive from the high priest a symbolic priesthood. This makes them "sons of Light", the name emphasised in the initiation document, 1QS 1:1 - 3:12. By the righteousness which they also receive at initiation, they are able to perform the priestly task of a symbolic atonement. Levitical gradings and roles are also appropriate to them.

This doctrine is an extension of that which gives all members a bond with the heavenly temple (pp. 60-5). All the members of heaven perform

129

the priestly service of continually worshipping God; the sons of Light, having a bestowed "priesthood" are able to be members of their company with their brethren, the literal priests and levites. It also enables the high priest and superior priests to enter into a form of contact with them. The obligation of practising righteousness in order to atone for others gives laymen a new responsibility for leading a virtuous life.

Literal priests are also initiated and must practise righteousness: 1QS 2:19-20 shows that they are included in the *serek,* the register of the names of the initiated.

(b) Symbolic warriors

A number of expressions and practices normally having a military association are found in the context of initiation. Those who come for initiation are "volunteers" *(niddabîm,* 1QS 1: 7, 11; 5:21, 22; 6:13) and members are "elect ones" *(běhîrîm)* (1QH 2:13, 1QM 12:1). The initiated are called "named men" (1QSa 2:11) and their names, at initiation, are written in a *serek* (1QS 6:22). Men who go through the grades of initiation are members of the "hosts" *(ṣeba'ôt).* These expressions reflect both the "named men" and the *serek* of army members of 1QM 2-9 (p.124) and the selection of a special group fit for war, of 11QT.

1QM 12:1-5, containing the Teacher's doctrine of membership of heaven (p.62) shows that the angels also have a military definition. In heaven, there is a multitude of saints *(qědôšîm),* the hosts *(ṣeba'ôt)* of angels, whose service is through praising God's name. The book of the names of "the elect ones of the holy people", the earthly members, is kept in heaven. To the list of their thousands and ten thousands (military formations in 11QT) are added together *(yaḥad)* the names of the angels, who are "the elect ones of heaven" (5). With the fact that the terms are used in the context of initiation by the Teacher, this means that the "army" of members is a spiritual one only. They become soldiers for righteousness at initiation.

Symbolic priesthood gives to the laity a role to which they were not born; but membership of a spiritual army takes from them the literal role of warriors. The first is a significant difference from 11QT, the second from 1QM 2-9.

Members are "sons of truth" (1QS 4: 5, 6), "volunteers for truth" (1QS 1:11), belong to a "Community of truth" (1QS 2:24), walk in the ways of truth" (1QS 4:17). These expressions may be seen, in the light of the above, as reflections of the "men of truth" of 11QT 57:8, the specially selected men for war.

The list of exclusions is appropriate to both the priesthood and the army. Women and children are members of the *qahal,* the name used in 11QT for the whole worshipping community, but are not initiated into the "hosts" (1QSa 1:4-6). They are permitted to hear the reading of the laws in order that they may not err in their conduct (1QSa 1:4). 1QSa 1:11 may mean that married women (cf. *teqabbel,* fem. prefix) have a lay ministry (cf. *hityasseb* with 1QM 2:3) of testifying *(ha'îd,* reciting?) to their husbands the laws of the Torah, of a particular group *(mišpetôt* for *mišpetîm).* Unclean persons are outside the *qahal* altogether (2:3-4).

Physically handicapped men may be baptized, but are not allowed into the Holy Council (1QSa 2:9), that is, to be fully initiated (p.100). They may not receive the Spirit of holiness, or take part in the Meal (p.97). This is because their presence would break the laws of priestly purity now applicable to all members (Lev 21:16-24). The Meal was called the Purity, and both elements were taken only by those who had received a final purification at full initiation (pp.92-4). If the handicapped wish, as baptized members, to participate in the affairs of government, they may send an oral communication (1QSa 2:4-11).

The intellectually handicapped, the Simple, are also not capable of full membership (p.97). According to 1QSa 1:21 they are given *mas,* ("task-work"); it is not clear what this means.

Lay ranks

Appropriately to their membership of a spiritual army, men are promoted through a series of grades from the time of first entry, the promotions being rewards for righteousness. The grades of initiation have been set out pp.91-6. The process covers three years: a year outside the community, with contact only with a *paqîd,* leading up to baptism on the Day of Pentecost completing that year. The baptism gives "fleshly" membership only: two further years are required before full initiation. Partial privileges (participation in the bread of the Meal, and placing one's property in reserve) are given at the end of the second year, and at the end of the third year the Spirit of holiness for full initiation is given, property is fully surrendered, and both elements of the Meal taken.

The most frequently occurring organisational term is "Council of the Community" *('ăṣat hayyaḥad).* Its uses are consistent with the meaning: "all baptized members who have begun to progress through the stages of promotion". The members of the Council of the Community of 1QSa 1:27 - 2:3 are to be aged from twenty years (1:27), the age of baptism in the Future Time (1:6-9), but are all leaders. In 1QpHab 12:4, the Council of the Community excludes the group who are initiated but incapable of further promotion, the "Simple" (pp.97-8). The Council of the Community is the ladder of promotion; baptism is the first rung. Those for whom there are impediments to promotion do not begin to climb it.

1QS 1:1 - 3:12, the initiation document,[13] uses "Holy Council" and "Council of God" as the structure into which members come at full initiation. At the final initiation, members give their counsel *('eṣâ)* as one of their gifts to the community (1QS 6:22-23). The Holy Council or Council of God is the higher rank within the Council of the Community. In 1QM 3:4 the Holy Council is for planning war.

Sôd, "company" is also used for the ranks of fully initiated members, as opposed to baptized members (1QS 6:18-19, 2:25). The term is frequently found in the Teacher's writings: it plays on "foundation" (1QH 6:26, 7:9) and "secret" (1QH 4:28).[14] In 1QH 14: 18, 21 and 1QS 11:8 it is a name for the members; in the latter text, in their relationship with the members of heaven. For the Teacher, to have become a member of the *sôd* at full initiation has considerable significance: it is to be "set upon a rock" (1QH 6:36, 7:9), that is, to have received certain salvation. Members are therefore "strengthened" or "confirmed *(haḥāzîq)* at this stage (1QSa 2:5). Higher secrets of the doctrine are also given at this stage, as shown by the meaning "secret".

Five years after baptism (in the Future Time, 1QSa), men enter the *(yesôdôt,* the ranks of government, reaching the top five years later (1QSa 1:12-15). The *yesôd* is the governing structure, above the *sôd.* At the top rank, they become tribal heads and *śarîm* of thousands, hundreds, fifties, tens (1QSa 1: 14-15, 24), "in their camps and marches" (2:15). Both *śarîm* and "camps" no longer have a military significance, but are the groupings of lay members under lay leaders. They also become judges and *šôterîm* (1: 14-15, 24).

TABLE 2

Lay Ranks in the Community (yaḥad)

All higher ranks incorporate the lower ranks

Year of Initiation		Structure
10	Twelve heads of tribes (head fathers, elders). Sarîm of thousands, hundreds, fifties, tens.	Yĕsôd
5		Yĕsôdôt
3	Full initiation (Spirit of holiness, wine at Meal, surrender of property).	{ Holy Council
2	Preliminary full initiation (bread at Meal, property reserved).	} Sôd
	Physically and mentally handicapped persons, and proselytes and Diaspora Jews proceed no further.	
1	Baptism.	Council of Community
	Women and children.	Qahal
	Unclean persons.	

Priests and levites

Although the laity are now symbolic priests, the literal sons of Aaron are kept apart in a separate priestly sector. Priests and laity each have their own *yaḥad:* " . . . under the authority of the sons of Aaron, who volunteer in a *yaḥad* to restore his Covenant . . . and under the authority of the multitude of Israel, who volunteer to return in a *yaḥad* to his Covenant" (1QS 5:21-22).

Sons of Aaron are superior to both sons of Levi and the tribal leaders (1QSa 1:15-16 with 1:22). Their work is that of inspection, "visitation": "to inspect (root *paqad*) all his decrees, which he commanded to do" (1QS 5:22). Coming from above, as God would do on the Day of Visitation *(pĕquddâ),* they ensure that the commandments are kept. Each year they record in the *serek,* the register of members' names, their assessment of their spiritual state, and members are promoted accordingly (1QS 5:23-24, cf. also CD 14:6-7).

1QSa 1:15-16 and 22-24 show that the members of the ruling ranks of the laity, the *yĕsôdôt,* are under the immediate authority of the sons of Aaron, while the ordinary members of the laity are under the sons of Levi. The *sôd,* the body of fully initiated members only, is "under the authority of the priests and the multitude of the men of their covenant" (that is, the twenty-four elders, cf. 1QSa 1:2). It is only at full initiation and receipt of the Spirit of holiness that members may have contact with priests, who are holy; prior to this they meet only levites (below p.134).

The new closeness of priests to lay members, expressed through the Teacher's rule of the whole congregation (above p.128) and the symbolic priesthood of the laity, is given its main expression through the meetings of the Many *(harabbîm)* and the associated Meal. During the present time, while the priests of the Community are debarred from officiating at the Jerusalem temple, they meet daily with the members in a ceremony celebrating their unity with heaven. "In Community *(yaḥad)* they shall eat, in Community they shall bless (pray), in Community they shall take council" (1QS 6:2-3). The meetings are held in each local group, wherever there are at least ten men (1QS 6:3, 1QS 2:22), and are called a Session *(môsab)* of the Many (1QS 6:8, 1QSa 2:11). They extend from six p.m. to ten p.m. every evening ("a third of every night of the year" (1QS 6:7). If 1QS 6:2-3 gives the order of events, the Meal was held first, followed by prayers, then debates on government, the conduct of which is described in 6:8b-13a.

The Meal is used as a means of discipline; breaches of the rules are punished by exclusion from it (e.g. 7:18-20). It is, therefore, the main sign of membership, showing also membership in heaven. Priests take a leading role in it as the representatives of the standards of heaven. It has no sacrificial aspect: the law of Deut 12:15-25 against the drinking of blood is repeated in 11QT 53:1-7.

A priest must always be present: "in every place where there are ten men from the Council of the Community there shall not be absent from them a priest. And they shall sit before him, each according to his rank" (1QS 6:3-4). He blesses first the bread and the new wine (1QS 6:5-6).

A formula parallel to that used for the priest introduces another leader at the Meal: "there shall not be absent from the place where there are ten men a man interpreting the Law *('îš dôreš battôrâ)* day and night" (6:6). The parallel with the priest suggests that he is a levite. This is supported by Neh 8:7-8: "The levites helped the people to understand the Law, while the people remained in their places. And they read from the book, from the Law of God, clearly, and they gave the sense, so that the people understood the reading". The Teacher has retained the sons of Levi as secondary priests (above pp.126-7). They are therefore able to be involved in the Meal, in a secondary role. Appropriately to their position as a bridging class, and as levites, they bring the heavenly Law to the people by its reading and interpretation.

Those who wish to become members are prepared for baptism by the *paqîd* at the head of the Many (1QS 6:14). Cf. also 1QSa 1:8-9: the novice of the Future Time, at the age of twenty, comes to the *pĕqûdîm*. *Pĕqûdîm* are assistants to the Aaronite heads of the *mišmĕrôt* in 1QM 2:4; they are levites, who here perform the levitical work of instructing the novice in the rudiments of the Law and of washing his flesh in baptism. The levite in each community is "at the head of the Many" because all levites are superior to all laymen. The sons of Levi rule the ordinary laity (1QSa 1:22).

The Messiah of Israel

1QSa 2:11-22 describes an occasion in the Future Time when the Priest (the priestly Messiah) and the Messiah of Israel are present. It is called a Session *(môšab)* of the "named men", that is, the initiates (p.130), a *mô'ed* of the Council of the Community (12), that is, it is a copy of the evening meetings of the Many, at which all baptized members are present, and the initiated take part in the full Meal. The final sentence (2:22) repeats the rule about the minimum of ten men, applicable to the local meetings. In the Future Time, the close links between priests and laity, now expressed in the evening meetings, will be retained; priests will not return to an entirely separate life in the temple. The two Messiahs will also be closely involved with the initiated laity.

The rite of blessing the two elements in the Meal is carefully described: "No man shall stretch out his hand over the firstfruits of the bread and the new wine before the Priest, for he blesses the firstfruits of (both) the bread and the new wine. He stretches out his hand over the bread first. After this, the Messiah of Israel stretches out his hand over the bread". Both the titles of the two Messiahs, and the elements in the Meal, are understood according to the pyramidal hierarchical structure, whereby each higher rank incorporates the lower ranks, but has a special function which the lower rank does not have. Both leaders are Messiahs (cf. 1QS 9:11), but the superior one has, in addition, the high priesthood, and is called by his specialist title, the Priest. He blesses both the bread, the subordinate element (p.93), and the new wine, the higher element, which is reserved for his blessing alone. It is emphasised that he blesses both, and that he proceeds upwards from the bread ("he stretches out his hand over the bread first"): he is not separated from the lower rank. The Messiah of Israel, however, stays at the subordinate level, blessing only the bread, the subordinate element.

The action of the Priest is exactly parallel to that of the priest in the local meetings: "the priest shall stretch out his hand first to bless the first-fruits of the bread and the new wine" (1QS 6:5-6). The assistant of the local priest is the law-interpreter, and there is good reason to believe that he is a levitical priest (above pp.134-5). The fragment 2Q24 ar fr. 4:16, in a broken context, reads: "[the high] pr[iest] with him, and let the other (loaf of bread) be given to his Second who stands apart". In 11QT and 1QM 2-9 the high or chief priest has a Second Priest, in a levitical relationship to him (pp.121-2). The parallel between the action of the Messiah of Israel, who blesses the bread in a subordinate position to the Priest, and the position of the law-interpreter at the local Meals, suggests that the Messiah of Israel is a levitical priest, the levite to the high priest.

He is also a layman. 1QSb 5:20-29 develops his warrior role as Sceptre (šebeṭ). "May he make your horns of iron and your hooves of bronze . . . as a sceptre" (26). He is here called Nāsî' of the Congregation, with the "all" removed (cf. 1QM 5:1) because the high priest is now leader of all the congregation (p.128). He has a covenant of kingship (1QSb 5:21), as does the king in 11QT 59:13-21. 4QPB describes his davidic kingship. He has the sceptre (šebeṭ, also meaning "tribe") of Judah, the first of the tribes, and the ruler's staff, mĕḥôqeq, symbolizing kingship (2, 4). He will be the Messiah of Righteousness, the shoot of David (3-4).

Priesthood and membership of the different tribes depended on physical descent; members were initiated into the class or tribe in which they were born. It would not be impossible, although rare, for a man to have both davidic and levitical ancestry, cf. Luke 3:23-31 and 1: 5, 36. The requirement that the Messiah of Israel should have both may be suggested to account for the much-disputed expression in the description of the messianic Meal: 'im yô[lî]d ['el] 'e[t] hammašîaḥ 'ittam (1QSa 2:11-12).[15] It means "when God causes the Messiah to be born with them", that is, when God brings to the community a man with the correct genealogy.

The requirement that the Messiah of Israel should be both priestly and davidic would also account for the importance given to the Star and Sceptre prophecy of Num 24:17-19: "a Star shall come out of Jacob, and a Sceptre shall rise out of Israel". In 4QTestim 12-13 and 1QM 11:6-7 it refers to the davidic Messiah only (not in CD 7:18-21), see below p. 182). To be a Star was to have the priestly quality of Light. The verse, in these places, was used as a prediction of the special character of the Messiah of Israel.

The development is consistent with the Teacher's giving a symbolic priesthood to the laity, and with his retention of the levitical class in a bridging role. The second leader of the Community, formerly the Second Priest, is now a combination of the Second Priest and the King, expressing the new unity of priesthood and laity. As a levitical priest, he cannot take the place of the high priest, as he has not the correct ancestry (Zadokite-Aaronite). But he brings the laity into contact with the high priest, and the high priesthood into contact with the laity, in a way that does not defile the purity of the traditional priesthood, in this fulfilling the role of the levitical class found also in 11QT.

As Messiah of Righteousness (4QPB) he bestows the righteousness at initiation, while the high priest gives the Light; both qualities needed for the "priestly" duty of atoning by righteousness (pp.128-9).

A new organisational term, *kĕneset* ("gathering") is found in connection with him in 4QPB 6: " . . . the Law with the men of the Community, for [. . .] it is the *kĕneset* of the men of [. . .]."

The third leader

Both 11QT and 1QM 2-9 plan for three supreme leaders: two priests and a king. There is one piece of evidence that the Teacher retained the number, although with different definitions. In 1QH 3:9, in a passage dealing with the messianic doctrine (below, pp.155-6), a third male figure, the *zakar* ("male") is mentioned beside the *geber,* the priestly Messiah (4QpPsᵃ (3:14, above p.85) and the *gibbôr,* the Warrior, the davidic Messiah (Wondrous Counsellor, 10, cf. 1QM 12:9). No separate third leader is named at the messianic Meal, however. But at this occasion, "all the head fathers", the twenty-four elders, are ranked after the Messiah of Israel (1QSa 2:15-16). The head of these was the first of the sons of Levi, the head of the tribe of Levi, superior to the twelve tribal heads (who presumably counted Ephraim and Manasseh as two for this purpose). He would be an appropriate third leader, representing the intermediate levitical class only, while the Messiah of Israel also represented the laity. Cf., possibly, 5Q*13* fr.2:7: "Thou hast [sanctified] Levi and given him (the power) to bind and to loose".

The mĕbaqqerîm

The *mĕbaqqer* ("overseer", NT *episkopos*) is found in 1QS 6: 12, 20, and in passages of CD (15:7-15, 9:16b-23, 12:22 - 14:22) which contain the same definitions of priests and levites as in the Teacher's organisation (see further below pp.191-5).

In CD 15:7-15 and 13:11-12a the *mĕbaqqer* over the Many (cf. 15:8) is given the same duty as the *paqîd* over the Many of 1QS 6:14 performs: receiving novices, instructing them, and bringing them to the first stage of initiation, including baptism. It has been shown p.135 that the *paqîd* is a levite, performing the fleshly washing appropriate to levites. In CD 13:1-7 there are two parallel laws; in the first, the priest who must be present with a local community of ten (cf. 1QS 6:3-4) may not be experienced in the knowledge required to rule the laity, and in this case a "man from the levites" *('îs mehallĕwîyîm,* 3) may instruct him and rule the congregation, performing the work of the levitical law-interpreter. In the second, a priest comes to a "camp" (local community) and examines a leper, but does not touch him himself; in his place the *mĕbaqqer* examines him and reports if the symptoms of Lev 13-14 are present.[16] The relationship of the *mĕbaqqer* to the priest is a levitical one; he is the same as the "man from the levites" (the term reflecting the distinction between sons of Levi and levites, cf. Jer 33:18). In 4Q275, fr.3:3[17] *mĕbaqqer* is used interchangeably with "levite" (as he utters the curses of the covenant on sinners, the work of the levite in 1QS 2:4-10). The minimum age of the chief *mĕbaqqer* is to be thirty (CD 14:9, the age of the senior levites in 1 Chr 23:3). The *mĕbaqqer* is a son of Levi.

This accounts for his role of intermediary between the ruling authorities and the laity. CD 14:11-12: "if any man has any matter to speak to the *mĕbaqqer* concerning dispute or judgement, let him say it". In 9:16-23 he is the one to whom a community member goes when he has a complaint of sin against another member that is not yet proven by the evidence of other witnesses. The *mĕbaqqer* cannot yet act, but records the grievance, and if further evidence, supported by witnesses, is produced, will present the case as complete. In a related law, witnesses of an offence are to inform the *mĕbaqqer* as soon as the offence is committed (9:22). He acts as a representative of authority immediately accessible to individuals, as an outer gate of a court of justice.

The special skills of the superior *mĕbaqqer* are to enable him to be in communication with all members. He is to be "master of all the secrets of men and of all the languages of the clans".

The title *mĕbaqqer* is drawn from Ezek 34:12: "As a shepherd seeks out (root *baqar*) his flock when some of his sheep have been scattered abroad, so will I seek out my sheep". The image of "care" in both "father" and "shepherd" is appropriate to the work of levites, who had the care of the temple property (1 Chr 23:28).

All of the twenty-four leaders, twelve levitical and twelve tribal heads, are called "fathers" and "elders" (p.127). In 1QS 6:8 the list of members of the Many is: priests first, elders second, all the rest of the people third. In 1QS 2:19-21 the list present at the initiation is: priests first, levites second, all the people third; cf. also CD 14: 4, 5, for all Sessions of "camps". "Elders" includes levites, but the interchangeability of the lists suggests that the twelve tribal heads, members of the twenty-four elders, are also levites. If this were the case, then the omission of the levites from 4QpIsa^d is accounted for. As Baumgarten has noted, there is no room for them between the "pinnacles", the twelve priests, and the "gates" (cf. Isa 54:12), who are the twelve tribal heads.[18] If they are levites, their interpretation as "gates" is understandable: levites are gatekeepers in 1 Chr 23:5.

There appears to be reason for supposing that the Teacher has required that both the Messiah of Israel and the twelve heads of tribes should have levitical as well as the appropriate lay ancestry. What is required of the Messiah of Israel should be required of at least the supreme lay leaders. "Fatherhood", originally a lay, tribal image, like "elder", has taken on priestly associations through its use by the sons of Levi as tribal leaders. They are also levitical priests, caring for the laity. The next step has been taken by the Teacher, in bringing priesthood and laity closer together: the lay fathers are to be levitical fathers. The new term *mĕbaqqer* is found for them, meaning neither levite nor layman, but one who is both, and in close contact with the "sheep", living among the laity.

The yaḥad

The name *yaḥad* enters the literature with the Teacher of Righteousness. It is a reflection of his eschatological doctrine of the heavenly temple. "God . . . has caused them to inherit the lot of the holy ones, and with the sons of heaven he has joined their *sôd* to be a Council of the Community *(yaḥad)*" (1QS 11:8). The *sôd* (of initiated members (above, p.132)) is part of the Council of the Community, the whole structure of promotion (pp.131-2). The Council of the Community includes also the members of heaven; it is a ladder going from earth to heaven. To be a member of the *yaḥad* is to have commonality with the heavenly priests.

139

1QS 5:21-22 shows that there is a *yaḥad* of priests and a *yaḥad* of laity: they are parallel but separate (p.133). The *yaḥad,* therefore, is triangular. At its apex are the heavenly priests, of one class only. At its base are the two present classes, the priests and the laity. The laity are able to be members of it because they are symbolic priests, but must still keep apart from the literal priests.

The Council of the Community, as listed in 1QSa 1:27 - 2:3, contains no priests, only lay leaders and levites. It is "under the authority of the sons of Zadok the priests" (2:3). This suggests that the Council of the Community is the lay-levitical *yaḥad,* while the superior priests, in their own *yaḥad,* have a different structure of promotion.

4QpIsa[d] 2 has sometimes been thought to read: "the Council of the Community, the priests and the pe[ople . . .]".[19] Strugnell and Yadin,[20] however, read: "(they have founded) the Council of the Community [on] *(bě)* the priests". There is room for a word of two letters between *yaḥad* and *kôhănîm.* With the following *w-h-'* [. . . . . .] *'ădat běḥîrô,* the reading may have been: "they have founded the Council of the Community with *('im)* the priests, and the Council *(w-h-'[-ṣ-t])* of the Community . . . is the Congregation of his Elect One", that is, the high priest. The two structures, priests and Council of the Community, are separate, although both form the foundation.

The rules concerning property also show that the two structures are kept separate. *Yaḥad* means "commonality", and all gifts brought to it by members are owned by the whole community, no longer retained as private property. "All who volunteer for his truth shall bring all their knowledge, their strength, and their property *(hôn)* into the *yaḥad* of God" (1QS 1:11-12) (Cf. 1QS 6:22-23). This text also shows that the three gifts are treated differently. Knowledge is purified in the truth of God's decrees, strength is made stronger by perfection of way, and property is brought into the Council *('eṣâ)* of Righteousness. "Council" is used for lay structures only, and the davidic Messiah, the lay-levitical leader, is distinguished from the priestly Messiah as the Messiah of Righteousness (p.137). Financial matters are "fleshly" concerns. The Teacher's doctrine of spirit and flesh, underlying all his organisation, would require that the priests, the most spiritual of members, should not have contact with the fleshly work of dealing with money.

The *měbaqqěrîm* are responsible for the handling of money. A year after baptism, and a year before full initiation, the member hands over his property to the *mèbaqqer* over the income of the Many (1QS 6:20). In CD 14:12-15 the *mèbaqqer,* with the judges, is to receive from members the earnings of two days a month, which he will distribute to the poor and needy. He is to be informed by members of any commercial arrangements they have made (CD 12:15-16). The significance of the fact that all *mèbaqqèrîm* are sons of Levi is now apparent. They are members of the levitical-lay Council of the Community (cf. "[heads of tr]ibes" and "levites" in the list of 1QSa 1:29 - 2:1). As secondary priests, they are able to represent priestly interests in the Council, leaving the sons of Aaron free from contact with fleshly concerns. The property still remains that of both priests and laity, while the superior priests are kept apart.

The Council of the Community is the lay structure, yet its leaders, the twenty-four elders, are all levitical priests (p.139). The temple, the central image of the Teacher's organisation, has two rooms, the Holy of Holies and the Holy House, the latter the less holy place (1 Kgs 6:16-17). The only reference to this image in the sources for the early organisation of the Teacher is in 1QSb 4:28: the high priest is the "crown of the Holy of Holies", and in the parallel between the whole temple area and the community in 4QpIsa[d]. The image is found in three other writings, however (1QS 5:6, 1QS 8:5-6, 1QS 9:6). It would follow from the levitical priesthood of the twenty-four elders that they formed the "Holy House", while the superior priests, sons of Zadok and sons of Aaron, formed the "Holy of Holies", of the "temple" consisting in the members. In Ezek 40:45-46 the levitical priests are permitted into the temple, but only the sons of Zadok are permitted at the altar, the innermost place.

The term "last priests", found in 1QpHab 9:4, is an appropriate one for the levitical priests, the leaders of the laity and the members of the Holy House, and the "Last Priest" of 4QpHos[b] fr.2:3, is an appropriate one for the Messiah of Israel. Cf. 11QT 21:4: "[the priests shall minister there] as the first ones *(ri'sônîm),* and the levites [. . .]".

TABLE 3
Ministry of the Community, Stage 1A

The high priest, son of Zadok
The Messiah of Israel, son of David, son of Levi
Holy of Holies: 12 sons of Zadok
                    Sons of Aaron
Holy House: 24 elders, *mèbaqqĕrîm,* fathers, comprising:
                    12 sons of Levi
                    12 heads of tribes, sons of Levi
12 *śarîm* of thousands
120 *śarîm* of hundreds, etc.

141

Comparison with 11QT and 1QM 2-9

The characteristics of the Teacher's organisation, as assembled in the foregoing, enable a comparison to be made with those of 11QT and 1QM 2-9. His central image is that of the temple. In heaven, the angelic priests are continually engaged in worship of God, and the members of the community are brought in to a *yaḥad* with them, so that they are themselves members of the heavenly temple. They are in two sectors: literal priests and symbolic priests (laity). Binding together the two sectors is the intermediate Holy House of levitical priests, part of the temple but not its most holy part. The linking of priesthood and laity occurs within the Holy House, through the combination of lay and levitical descent in the twelve tribal leaders. The Messiah of Israel combines both kinds in himself, making an indissoluble bond between priesthood and laity.

The function of the levitical class as a bridge has been developed even further than in 11QT, by the introduction into it of the lay leaders. The effect is to disseminate priestliness or holiness right through the community, in the persons of the members themselves, not simply by means of the plan of the temple courts, as in 11QT.

Yet the separateness and superiority of literal priests is still retained. With the dominance of priestliness as an image, priestly superiority is reinforced. The high priest exercises authority over all the congregation because of the priestliness of all, and the davidic king has been brought into even greater subordination to the high priest through being made his levite, by scriptural definition his inferior.

The separate authority of the laity of 1QM 2-9 is no longer held, and they are symbolic warriors only.

The Teacher's view of warfare

In 1QH 6:24-35 the Teacher relates his eschatology to two kinds of warfare. The community is described with the imagery of Isa 28:14-22: "I was like one who comes to a fortified city . . . thou wilt set its foundation on a rock, a basis by the measuring-cord of justice, and by the plumb-line of truth thou wilt lay the tried stones . . . ". The present community is a guarantee of the certainty of the New Jerusalem to come, as its members are bonded to the heavenly temple (ch. VI). The Isaiah passage contrasts trust in political alliances with trust in the temple, and the Teacher makes a similar contrast: outside the walls are the "troops with their weapons of war", but the "swords of the wars of wickedness" will be destroyed (28-29).

In the Period of Judgement the sword of God will be unsheathed. Then all the sons of his truth (the sectarians) will awaken to destroy wickedness. With them will appear the Warrior *(gibbôr)*, who will bend the bow, and weapons of war will be drawn. The warriors of wickedness will be destroyed (29-33). Those who fight on the side of right are "those who lie in the dust" *(šôkebê 'apar)*. The Teacher holds that warfare in the present is conducted only by evil men; the members of the community remain safe inside their "walls". But at the Judgement there will be a great battle, conducted by the divinely sent Warrior, with the aid of the sectarians, an entirely supernatural battle which will result in the destruction of all wicked men. Supernatural warfare is opposed to natural warfare, and the former is a part of his eschatological expectation.

With this passage is to be linked 1QM 10:8b - 13:16,[21] not in the Teacher's style and vocabulary,[22] but containing a development of the same doctrine. It does not describe a physical battle. Those on the side of right are "those bent to the dust" (11:13) and the Poor *('ebyônîm)* (11: 9, 13; 13:14), a term found elsewhere as a name for the community only in 1QpHab, 4QpPs[a], 1QH 3:25, all associated with the Teacher, and in the Teacher's hymns (1QH 5: 16, 18, 22). These columns of 1QM show that battle is in the hands of God alone, and that victory will be achieved by his davidic Messiah alone, not by human warfare. "For indeed, the battle is thine . . . Thou didst deliver Goliath of Gath, a mighty warrior, into the hand of David thy servant, because he trusted in thy great name and not in the sword, nor the spear, for thine is the battle" (11:1-2). Those who overcome evil will be "the Poor, whom thou hast redeemed", likened to the Israelites before Pharaoh (9-10), that is, they have no military strength and trust only in God. 12:1-5 sets out the doctrine of the union with heaven, the basis of the Teacher's eschatology. 12:6-18 describes the Royal Warrior (King of Glory (8), Mighty Warrior (9)) who is with them: it is he who will overcome the enemy, and cause Jerusalem to open its gates to the conquered kings of the nations, that is, lead Israel to victory over the world. The times of the wars have been predicted by the prophets: they are chronologically determined (11:7-8).

4QpIsa[a] frs.8-10 contains a parallel doctrine of the davidic Messiah. It also draws upon the first Isaiah (10:24 - 11:10) to show that the davidic Messiah, the "axe" (6-8) will be God's instrument, bringing down the great political power. He will come in the *'aḥarît hayyamîm,* the Future Time (17), an expression from the Teacher's eschatology. It is further linked with 1QM 10:8b - 13:16 by the use of Magog as a name for the enemy (20, cf. 1QM 11:16, Gog).

143

It is clear that the Teacher repudiates warfare for the present time, and holds that membership of the community is a sufficient means of security. All that is necessary is to wait for the appointed time, and the davidic Messiah would be used by God in a supernatural battle to destroy all wicked men. In this the second leader would exercise his role of the Sceptre, and God's Anointed, the instrument of divine rather than human action.

As has been shown p.99, there is direct evidence in 1QS 5:6, 4QpNah and CD of the presence of a class of proselytes in the community; admission of proselytes is consistent with the Teacher's doctrine of the New Covenant. These are not sources for the Teacher's early organisation, but there is indirect evidence that he did include them from the beginning. According to 1QpHab 11:16 - 12:5, the "Simple of Judah who keep the Law" were, with the Council of the Community, the subjects of attack by the leader of the schismatic party (the Wicked Priest, see ch. II). Reasons have been given why the "Simple who keep the Law" are Diaspora Jews and proselytes (pp.99-100). As the schism occurred in the lifetime of the Teacher (p.111), this special class of members had already been added in his time.

It would be consistent with the Teacher's giving symbolic warriorhood and priesthood to the laity, and with the requirement of levitical priesthood for the lay leaders, if he held that *proselytisation was a substitute for literal warfare.* Priests took part in battle, but only performed ritual duties (1QM 7:9 - 9:9); direct contact with the slain was forbidden them (1QM 9:7-9). To "conquer" proselytes by conversion would be an exercise of symbolic warriorhood and priesthood. If the davidic Messiah and tribal leaders were levitical priests, they would be able to baptize them. By a campaign of proselytisation of Gentiles, the Teacher could hope to subdue them in a different way than by destruction. Cf. 1QM 12:14-15, Gentile kings will bow down before Jerusalem, 1QpPs frs. 9 - 10:1-3, the kings of the Kittim will bring presents to the temple in Jerusalem. At the appointed time in the future, those who had not "succumbed" and remained in their wickedness would be destroyed by the davidic Messiah, now in his role of Sceptre.

If this were the case, then there would be further signs that warfare was understood symbolically. The use of the word "violence" is such a sign: it regularly means "false teaching". The main complaint against the leader of the schismatics, the Man of a Lie, was that he had led the sectarians into apostasy. In 4QpPs[a] 4:13-14, the "wicked violent person" *(raśaʿ ʿarîs)* of Ps 37:35 is interpreted of him, and in 2:12-14 the members of the "house of Judah" (part of the community, below pp.175-6) who had become apostate are called "the violent ones of the Covenant" *('arîṣê habbĕrît);* cf. also 4:1-2. 1QpHab 2:6 also uses "the violent men of the Covenant" for the same group; 8:11 speaks of "men of violence who rebelled against God" *('anšê ḥamas 'ăšer marĕdû bĕ'el).* The Teacher calls those who mock him "violent men" *('arîṣîm,* 1QH 2:11) and the schismatic party[23] "the congregation of vanity and the assembly of violence" *('ădat [šaw'] ûmissôd ḥamas),* 1QH 6:4-5). To "shed blood" is also a metaphor in 1QpHab 10:6-13. Hab 2:12, "Woe to him who builds a city with blood" is interpreted of the building of the rival "city", the alternate congregation of schismatics.[24]

The use of physical violence is not precluded by the term, cf. 1QH 2:21: "violent men *('arîṣîm)* seek my life", and 4QpPs[a] 2:17-18, 4:8. But the regular use of the term in a symbolic sense reveals an assumption that "warfare" is normally conducted through words and teaching. "Violence" is false teaching, taking away the "life" of members, who have been given "life" at initiation into the community. Those who give false teaching are engaged in "violence"; those who "conquer" others through true teaching are, presumably, engaged in "holy war".[25]

*Synthesis: The historical hypothesis
We are now in a position to consider the implications of the three successive kinds of organisation that have been studied. 11QT, 1QM 2-9, and the early organisation of the Teacher are clearly continuous. But each has been shown to have a different character and emphasis. Their essential points may be summarised:

(a) 11QT plans for a rebuilt temple in Jerusalem, and a religious state under high priestly supremacy. It is simply expected in the future, on the Day of Blessing (29:9). It will be a society in which present conditions continue: there is no sign of a catastrophe and a radical change. Defensive warfare, such as is necessary in any state, is the only kind envisaged.

(b) 1QM 2-9 plans for a forty years' war against all nations of the world. In the seventh year, the temple ministry will be established (2:6 cf.8), that is, the temple will have been gained at the end of the first seven year period of the war. There is a balance of priestly and lay leadership, and the lay leader is over all the congregation.

(c) The Teacher plans for the destruction of all wickedness at a chronologically determined time, in a supernatural battle in which the davidic Messiah will be God's instrument. In the meantime, spiritual warfare is con-

145

ducted in the form of a campaign against unrighteousness, including proselytisation of Gentiles. The "temple" is present now in the community, as all initiates have been made members of the heavenly temple. In the Future Time, the heavenly temple will come to earth, and the community priests will officiate in it under their supreme leader, the high priest/priestly Messiah.

Two separate kinds of change are illustrated in the three successive organisations:

(i) In each phase, there is a different view of offensive warfare (no war; literal war; symbolic war).

(ii) In the first and third phases, priestly superiority is planned; in the second, there is a reduction in priestly power and an independent lay authority.

Literal warfare goes with priestly-lay equality, but priestly supremacy is associated only with spiritual warfare or no offensive war at all.

What is the reason for this series of dramatic changes in policy in a movement which still shows continuity between the successive phases?

The Essene movement was undoubtedly founded at the time of the illegal adoption of the high priesthood by the Hasmonean house, and opposed their action on the grounds of biblical law. The significance that was attached in the Teacher's time to Zadokite descent is shown in the importance of the sons of Zadok in 1QS and 1QSa. The Teacher's doctrine implied an expectation that the Zadokite high priesthood would be restored to power in the Jerusalem temple (ch. VI).

A further relevant fact is that the Teacher appeared twenty years after the foundation of the Plant-root, and that for these twenty years the members were "like blind men, groping for the way" (CD 1:8-10). Murphy-O'Connor[26] interprets this as a time of bewilderment, when they were unable to impose their ideas on other Jews; he is thus selecting the latter part of the image. But "blindness" has a specific meaning in the Qumran symbolism. "Light" is a symbol of truth. As sons of Light, the community members possessed knowledge of the heavenly secrets. If they were "blind", they were in doctrinal error. The twenty years was a time when, from a later point of view, the members were sincerely seeking the truth (cf. "sought him wholeheartedly", CD 1:10), but had still not reached the full truth that was made available to them later. There was, in other words, a radical revision of the doctrine under the Teacher of Righteousness.

In the light of this fact and the central concern with the restoration of the Zadokite high priesthood, a hypothesis may be put forward accounting for both the series of changes and the continuity. The first phase (a), that of 11QT, comes from a time when there was no strong feeling of danger to the country, and when something occurred to raise the hopes of the Essenes that the Zadokite high priesthood, and their control over the religious life of the country, would be restored. They believed that there was reason for planning the rebuilding of the temple, and they put forward their plans in the form of a lost biblical book. The new state would be under high priestly supremacy, in accordance with their priestly outlook.

There followed, in phase (b), the intrusion of a major threat to the country from a great foreign power. It was so serious that the Essenes turned to a plan for war, necessary to drive off the enemy and fulfil their intention of regaining control of the state. There was no possibility of their fighting alone; they were forced into a coalition with a group of others, who did not share their views on priestly supremacy. In exchange for their support, the Essenes accepted a greater equality of priests and laymen, and lay independence. The combination of Essenes and the lay group, a new formation from the Essene movement, was called "the Plant-root".

Twenty years later, it was apparent that there was no possibility of defeating the foreign power: it was too strong. The Teacher, a member of the Essene wing of the Plant-root, and a Zadokite, appeared as leader and raised the disappointed hopes of the new community by promising that the longed-for victory and recovery of the temple would be achieved by eschatological means, through a divine intervention at a chronologically determined time. He was also able to restore priestly supremacy, as the lay wing had not fulfilled the promise of military victory. Both the military method and the lay-dominated organisation of the Plant-root had been, from the Essene point of view, erroneous, although their intention of recovering the temple was sound. The Teacher, with his eschatological and priestly doctrine, corrected their "blindness".

On pp.50-7 some evidence has been brought forward for the conclusion that the Teacher lived in the Roman period, some time after 63 B.C. and before 68 A.D. It was also suggested that if he led a related but different movement from the Essenes in that time, it would account for his absence from the contemporary histories. The present hypothesis may be brought together with those findings. The major world power which has been conjectured to account for the series of dramatic changes would readily correspond to the Romans. Their presence from the beginning of their era meant a loss of Jewish independence, unlike the danger presented by the Seleucids. 4QpNah 1:3 has been seen to reflect this fact (p.26). Stages (b) and (c), the Plant-root and the Teacher, would fit an experience of such intrusion on the part of Rome that war against them was planned, followed by twenty years' further experience with them, in which their real strength became known, and the early hope of a victorious war against them in all their dominions was replaced by the hope of the intervention of the only power that could save, that of God himself.

Our proposal is, then, that the changing phases in the community from the time of 11QT were brought about in reaction to the presence of the Romans. At the appearance of a major threat from them, the peaceful, this-worldly project of 11QT was set aside, and a new community formed from a coalition of Essenes and lay militarists. The date of its formation was taken to be a significant one historically, the beginning of the Period of Wrath, that is, Roman oppression. The Teacher led this new group, appearing twenty years later.

The question of the precise point in the Roman era when the threat was identified will, at this stage in the reconstruction, be left open. It may be noted that from 63 B.C. Roman control was exercised with different degrees of directness: (1) rule through the high priests, 63-37 B.C.; (2) representation by Herod the Great, giving relative independence, 37 BC - 4 B.C., and his sons, 4 B.C. - 6 A.D.; (3) the imposition of direct rule by the procurators, 6-69 A.D., except for the reign of Herod Agrippa I, 41-44 A.D. The intrusion in question would fit either their first appearance under Pompey, who entered the Holy of Holies of the temple, or the third stage. But the hypothesis has yet to be tested against the remainder of the Qumran material. If it is capable of accounting for the remaining data, it may be claimed to have some strength. It is possible that the further study may also supply more precise indications of the date.

Through all the remaining writings runs the thread of the great schism in the community that occurred in the lifetime of the Teacher. As it had such a lasting impact, it was of considerable magnitude. It could not have been unrelated to the history that has been supposed. Is there any evidence linking it with that history?

B. After the Schism

The Sources

From a study of 1QpHab, CD, 4QpPs[a], 4QpIsa[b] and 1QpMic, G. Jeremias[27] has established that during the lifetime of the Teacher of

Righteousness, a large number of his followers split off from his community under the leadership of the man variously known as the Man of a Lie *('îš hakkazab)*, He who Drips Lies *(mattîp hakkazab)*, Ṣaw and the Man of Scoffing *('îš hallaṣôn)*. Names for the schismatics, his followers, include: the Traitors *(bôgĕdîm)*, the Wall-builders *(bônê haḥayiṣ)*, the Men of Scoffing *('anšê hallaṣôn)*, the Removers of the Bound *(massîgê haggĕbûl)*.[28] The rival leader established his own "city", that is, he founded a "New Jerusalem" like that of the Teacher, a religious community with similar ideals.

With the conclusion of ch. II above, that the Wicked Priest of 1QpHab and 4QpPs[a] was the same person as the Man of a Lie, new data is added for the study of the schism.

The analysis of the organisational terms also adds new sources. "Men of Iniquity" *('anšê ha'awel)*, an apparently general term for all evil-doers, is found only in sections where it is also used with the community organisational terms, *'edâ*, "congregation", and *môšab*, "Session". These are in 1QS 5:2, "separate from the congregation of the Men of Iniquity", and cf. "Men of Iniquity" in the same section, 5:10; 1QS 8:13, "separate from the midst of the Session of the Men of Iniquity"; and 9:17 (in 9:12-26, linked with 8:1-15a, see pp.167-8 below): "to hide the counsel of the Law from the midst of the Men of Iniquity". In 1QS 5:11-14, the "congregation of Men of Iniquity" (5:10 with 5:1-2) are forbidden to "enter the waters to touch the Purity", that is, take part in the Meal, "until they have repented of their wickedness". This prohibition is only appropriate to former community members, as is seen by those[29] who exclude 13b-14 as an interpolation on the grounds that "men of iniquity" is a general term. The use of *'edâ* to refer to the schismatics is recognized in 1QH 6:5, 7:34, where the Teacher calls them a "congregation of vanity".

Cols. 2-4 of 4QpNah were not available to Jeremias.[30] Reasons have been given in ch. III why the Young Lion of Wrath in its col. 1 is not Alexander Jannaeus. Cols. 2-4 attack enemies called "Ephraim" (2:2) and "Manasseh" (3:9). Ephraim is a name for the schismatic party in CD 7:10-14, and the wicked men of Ephraim and Manasseh of 4QpPs[a] have also been shown to be the apostate members (p.14). The enemies in 4QpNah 2-4 have a *qahal* (3:5), another community organisational term (p.131), also an *'edâ* (2:5). The House of Peleg, a name for a part of the community in CD 20:22, is said in 4:1 to have joined "Manasseh". 4QpNah is also, therefore, a source for the schism.

1QM 15:9 refers to a "congregation *('edâ)* of wickedness" who have a *qahal*. *4Q180-181* - 11QMelch[31] refers to a *yaḥad* of wickedness (4Q*181*

149

fr. 1:2). 4QTestim attacks "one of Belial" *('ahad běliya'al)* after a series of messianic proof-texts. He "builds a city" and "commits a horrible thing in Ephraim" (21-30); as shown pp.9-10, this is also a source for the Wicked Priest, the rival leader. 4QpHos[b] mentions the Young Lion of Wrath of 4QpNah, and "the Last Priest, who puts forth his hand to smite Ephraim" (fr.2:2-3). These writings are also part of the data.

The additional material opens up the possibility of adding to the conclusions of Jeremias further observations on the identity and history of the schismatic group.

Nature and reasons for the schism

The rival party are formed into an *'edâ,* a *môšab,* a *yahad* and a *qahal* (above). All of these are organisational terms in the Teacher's community. All refer to the whole community together, not priests alone. The *qahal* is the entire community, including women and children (p.131). The schismatic party were, then, not the priestly sector, nor were they the initiates alone.

There are a number of accusations that they had taken the property of the community, of the schismatics themselves, and of others. 1QpHab 12:9-10: "the cities of Judah where he (the Wicked Priest) robbed the Poor of their possessions"; 8:11-12: "he amassed the riches of the men of violence who rebelled against God" (that is, of the false teachers, his own followers: see pp.144-5). He also "took the wealth of the peoples", in the same text. The "last priests of Jerusalem", his successors, "amassed property and wealth by plundering the peoples" (9:5). Cf. also 4QpNah 1:11-12: "the wealth which the [prie]sts of Jerusalem am as[sed] which they will give [. . .] Ephraim".

There are reasons for supposing, as shown pp.139-41, that the property of the community was controlled by the Council of the Community, the levitical-lay sector, whose leaders formed the Holy House. The priests, as the more spiritual sector, did not deal with the fleshly concerns of money, but their interests were represented by the fact that the members of the Holy House were secondary priests. The two sectors, levitical-lay and priestly, were kept apart, each in its own *yahad.* If the schism were of the lay-levitical sector, separating from the priestly sector, the accusations concerning property would be a consequence of the fact that the seceding sector held two out of the three classes in the community (levites and laity) and could therefore claim to be the true community, the legal owners of the property. If they continued to initiate (cf. their *yaḥad*, 4Q*181* fr.1:2) they would continue to receive property from new members according to the rules of the community.

The successors of the leader, those who "amassed wealth", are called the "last priests" (1QpHab 9:5). It has been suggested p.141 that "last priests" would fit the levitical priests, the Holy House; there is some evidence that the sons of Aaron were "first ones".

These indications give reason for supposing that the schism in the community was of the levitical-lay sector, breaking away from the priestly sector.

This would be consistent with the hypothesis set out above, that the Teacher had taken a community that had been formed out of Essenes and laymen in an emergency situation, and had re-imposed priestly authority. The priestly Essene wing, the upholders of the Zadokite high priesthood, would accept his change of policy, while the laity, with their levitical leaders (pp.137-9), who had accepted the coalition on the terms of lay independence, did not accept it.

The name "Wall-builders" for the rivals (CD 4:19, 8:12)[32] reflects the role of Nehemiah in relation to Ezra, and accords with a lay rather than priestly emphasis. In 4QpIsa[d] the lay leaders are the "gates" of the temple, and its stones are "all Israel", the laity (l.1); this may mean that the "wall" of the Isa 54:12 lemma were proselytes, the next rank below "Israel" (CD 14: 4, 5). To "build a wall" would be to gain proselytes. Cf. the "city" of the rival party, 1QpHab 10:10. Laity (rather than priests) were permitted contact with Gentiles.

The schismatic group are most frequently called "Ephraim", some-times "Ephraim and Manasseh" (CD 7:10-14, 4QpPs[a] 2:17-19, 4QpNah 2:2). They had "led Ephraim astray" (4QpNah 2:8), and the Last Priest of 4QpHos[b] 3 will "put out his hand to smite Ephraim", that is, Ephraim was a former section of the community, which had been attacked with false doctrine. Cf. CD 7:10-14, likening the community to Israel in OT times, when there had been a split between southern Judah and northern Ephraim. One of the names for the leader, *Ṣaw,* is taken from Hos 5:11, "Ephraim was determined to follow after *Ṣaw"*.

Ephraim was the biblical name of the whole of the north of the country, or, with Manasseh, was a tribal name for a large part of the north, from just above Jericho to the Plain of Esdraelon, and also the Transjordan, from shortly below Pella to below Damascus. Opposition to priestly supremacy from members living in the northern part of the country followed from the position of Jerusalem and the temple in the south, and from the tradi-tional north-south tension. A southern and priestly bias for the Essene party is related to the position of Qumran.

There is no difficulty in supposing a national scope for the movement; both Josephus and Philo give the number of Essenes as four thousand.[33] The identification of the schismatics with Ephraim gives a new fact: that *the party of lay militarists with whom the Essenes had joined were from the northern part of the country.*

The identity of the leader of the seceding group, the man called by various epithets, including the "Wicked Priest" and the "Man of a Lie", is the next aspect to be considered. Intense hostility is shown to him as an individual, not just to his cause.

The clues are: the terms "Last Priest" of 4QpHos[b] 3 and *kĕneset* of 4QpNah 3:7; the original position of the twenty-four elders (the "last priests" or levitical priests who had seceded (above)); and the context in 4QTestim of the passage on the "one of Belial" (21-30), who, as argued pp.9-10, is the same as the Wicked Priest.

The Last Priest "will put out his hand to smite Ephraim", that is, to lead Ephraim astray into doctrinal error (above, p.151); he is the rival leader. The name is related to his title "the Wicked Priest". The Wicked Priest is linked with the schismatic "last priests" in 1QpHab 9:5. The name "last priest" is appropriate to levitical priests, and the charge of taking the property of the community, held by the levitical priests, is also appropriate to this status (p.151). Now, the Messiah of Israel, the second-in-command described in 1QSa 2:11-22, is defined as a levitical priest (pp.135-7). The twenty-four elders, the secondary priesthood, are in the same passage placed after the Messiah of Israel as his subordinates; he is their leader (1QSa 2:14-17 and p.137). It is to be expected that their secession would be under his authority. Confirmation is given by the placing of the passage on the "one of Belial" after three messianic proof-texts in 4QTestim. This implies that he was, according to the writer, an anti-Messiah, the counter to the three messianic figures whom scripture predicts. The charge is appropriate if he were originally a Messiah in the community. Final proof is given by the organisational term *kĕneset*, used for his followers in 4QpNah 3:7. This term is found with the description of the davidic Messiah in 4QPB 6.

Once the organisational terminology is understood, there is good evidence that the Teacher had actually appointed a second-in-command, to be the future Messiah of Israel, the leader of the levitical-lay sector. He had both davidic and levitical ancestry; God had "caused him to be born" (p.136) with the correct qualifications to unite the laity with the priesthood, and to be king over the future world community, under the headship of the priestly Messiah.

The historical hypothesis gives a coherent explanation of his conflict with the Teacher. As the lay leader, he represented the northern sector, with its traditional lay emphasis. He was the natural focus of dissidence, once the Teacher restored priestly supremacy. The two parties that had originally formed the Plant-root could no longer be held together once the priestly-lay balance was disturbed, and the inevitable split occurred. The second leader separated, holding two out of the three classes in the community, the levitical priests and laymen. This meant that he held a majority. The property, already owned by the levitical priests, was legally under his control. The priestly class, although the superiors, were left as an isolated minority group. Moreover, the Teacher's hopes of restoring the Zadokite priesthood at the head of a new religious state were destroyed by the schism. It was a devastating blow, bringing to an end the project of recovering the temple, and uniting the country, that had been under way for more than twenty years. Its significance fully accounts for the intense hostility shown to the rival leader and his party.

Further evidences

Two further passages, 1QS 5:1-20a and 1QH 3:7-18, are able to be fully accounted for in the present context.

1QS 5:1-20a shows an organisation with two significant differences from the previous ones, and also contains rules concerning the schismatics. The list of injunctions to members includes that of separating "from the congregation *('edâ)* of the Men of Iniquity (1-2). In 11-16, they are to "separate from all the Men of Iniquity walking in the way of wickedness. For they are not reckoned in the Covenant . . . they have treated the revealed things high-handedly . . . He shall not enter into the waters to touch the Purity of the holy men, for they have not been purified — unless they repent from their wickedness. For everyone who transgresses this word is unclean. No one shall be joined *(yiwwaḥed)* with him in service or in property, lest he assume their guilt . . . none of the men of the Community shall accept their authority on any matter of law or judgement".

As shown above (p.149), this is an edict of discipline for the schismatics. They use the community organisational term *'edâ,* and exclusion from the Meal is only applicable to initiated members. They are not, however, excommunicated finally: cf. "unless they repent from their wickedness".

There are two differences in the constitution: (a) property is now under the direction of the sons of Zadok in conjunction with the laity. They are "a Community in Law and in property . . . under the authority of the sons of Zadok the priests . . . and the multitude of the men of the Community" (2). "Under their authority (that of the priests and the leading laity) shall be issued every statement concerning Law, property and judgement" (3). The property of the schismatics is unclean (20). This fully supports the indications (above) that the schismatics were the levitical-lay sector, holding the property of the community, and retaining it at the schism. Some laymen loyal to the Essene wing have remained. Under the title of "the multitude of the men of the Community" (not "all the head fathers") they now form a leadership body with the sons of Zadok, and the property is controlled by both sectors. The lessons of the schism have been learned, with further serious consequences to the Teacher's doctrine of the separation of the fleshly from the spiritual, as the superior priests now handle money.

The second difference (b) is in the definition of the two Houses of the community "temple". Previously, the Holy of Holies had consisted of the priests, the sons of Zadok and (presumably) the sons of Aaron. The Holy House, the less holy part, had consisted of the levitical priests, both pure sons of Levi and levitical-laymen (p.141). Now, it consists of "all who volunteer for holiness in Aaron, and a House of Truth for Israel" (6). The first is called neither a Holy of Holies nor a Holy House, but simply (the place of) holiness, and the second House is not holy at all. Holiness, for the Teacher, is synonymous with literal priesthood, at least in a temple image. With the loss of the levitical Holy House, the two Houses having holiness are combined into one, "for Aaron". There is only one class of priests, and there can no longer be a distinction between the Holy of Holies and the Holy House. The lay leaders, as levitical priests, had previously formed part of the second House. The new lay leaders, who were not levitical priests, could still form a second House, but it must have a new name. "House of Truth" reflects the laity, as the name "men of truth", previously used for the selected men for the army, had been re-applied by the Teacher to the initiates. The former military associations of the term suggest the identity of the new lay leaders. In view of the hierarchical structure, they could not be immediately raised from the ranks, but must have already held leadership. The second rank of lay leaders were the twelve *śarîm* (p.141), whose title also had a former military association; they were the leaders of the "men of truth" in 11QT (pp.120-1). If it is the case that they had not seceded, the schism is to be seen as a re-arrangement of the issues that had been held together in the coalition. These were (a) priestly supremacy, (b) priestly-lay equality, (c) militarism. The presence of the *śarîm* would mean that (a) and (c) had combined, and that the schism was entirely on the question of priestly supremacy, the levitical-lay Holy House having accepted the Teacher's doctrine of spiritual warfare. See further below p.159, p.163.

The placing of purely lay leaders in a second House, even if it is not a Holy House, is a step towards the development of a lay ministry, an extension of the Teacher's doctrine of symbolic priesthood.

1QH 3:7-18, one of the most baffling passages in the Teacher's hymns, is able to be placed in the context of the schism and the reduction in the supreme leadership.

7-12 may be translated:

(7) I was in distress, like a woman bearing her first-born child;
For her pains have come, (8) and violent pangs upon her birth-passage/waves,
To bring anguish upon the first-born// in the womb/furnace of the pregnant one.
For sons have come to the birth-passage/waves of death,

(9) And she that is pregnant with a Man *(geber)* is distressed in her pains.
For from the birth-passage/in the waves of death she causes to escape a Male *(zakar)*,
And in the throes of hell there shall spring (10) from the womb/furnace of the pregnant one a Marvellous Counsellor with his strength,
And a Man *(geber)* escapes from the birth-passage/waves.

At his conception (11) all wombs/waves shall stir,
And at their birth there shall be violent pains,
And she who bears them/teaches shall be in terror.
And at his birth, all pangs will come (12) upon the womb/furnace of the pregnant one.

The Teacher likens an experience of anguish to the labour-pains of a pregnant woman. The passage is characterised by double meanings, a mark of the Teacher's style.[34] He, as the "woman giving birth", is bringing forth the first-born *(bĕkôr)*/in the furnace/womb *(bĕkûr)* of the pregnant one (8). He is pregnant with a *geber (hărayat geber*, 9), a name for the priestly

155

Messiah (4QpPs^a 3:14). Although he is pregnant with a singular "first-born", "sons" (plu.) have come (perfect tense) to the birth-passage/ waves *(miśbarîm)* of death (8), and from the birth-passage/waves of death is born (a) a male (sing., *zakar)* (9); (b) a Marvellous Counsellor with his strength *(pele' yô'eṣ 'im gĕbûratô)* (10), a name for the davidic Messiah (Isa 9:5, changed from *'el gibbôr,* "mighty God", as the second Messiah was a subordinate leader); (c) a *geber* (10). L.11 speaks of the pains of "their (plu.) birth, and the terror of teaching them/being pregnant with them (play on *yarâ,* "teach" and *harâ,* "be pregnant". In the next phrase is "his (sing.) birth". The constant fluctuation between singular and plural may be understood as meaning that the Teacher, who had expected to "give birth" to the priestly Messiah only (that is, the priestly Messiah within him would be revealed at the Future Time), must now "give birth" to all three leaders, a priestly and davidic Messiah, and a *zakar* (third leader, possibly the head of Levi, see p.137). He would have to adopt all three roles himself. As priestly, he must rule, and conduct the full initiation ceremony; as levitical, he must baptize. The play on birth passage/waters of death may refer to the imagery of initiation as a "second birth" (pp.98-9).

The second section of the passage, on the *hărayat 'ep'eh,* "the one pregnant with vanity" would then refer to the seceding Messiah. The foundations of his city (his rival New Jerusalem (cf. 1QpHab 10:10) are as insecure as a ship in a storm (12-13). His lay followers, "those who dwell in the dust" (cf. 1QM 11:13 for this as a name for the Teacher's followers) and his "wise men" (lay leaders, cf. 1QSa 2:16) will be like sailors in a shipwreck (13-14). They will be finally swept on their waves (baptism) into the gates of Hell (17-18).

There is, then, further evidence in favour of the historical hypothesis set out pp.145-8. The nature of the schism supports the view that an Essene-lay coalition had been formed later in the history of the Essene movement. While priestly and lay leadership were held in equal balance, the coalition stayed together. But with a restoration of priestly supremacy under the Teacher, the lay wing seceded, in the form of the twenty-four elders, the secondary priests who also included the twelve tribal leaders, together with the Messiah of Israel, the lay-levitical leader.

The hellenizing policy of the rival party

There is further information on the reason for the schism in some of the writings from after the Teacher's death. These show that they had the adherence of a large sector of the proselytes. As argued pp.99-100, the name "the Simple" was used for a class who were excluded from full membership, Diaspora Jews and proselytes, who would not be able to attend the temple in the Future Time. They themselves had little loyalty to the temple (cf. the house of Peleg who "went out of the holy city and leaned on God", CD 20:22-23), but joined the movement in order to re-establish or gain Jewish identity. According to 4QpNah 2:9, 4:1, proselytes and Peleg had joined the rival party, and in 3:5, the Simple of Ephraim had done so. The reason for their attraction may be seen, not only in their lack of sympathy with the temple and priestly rule, but in a further aspect of the rival party's policy, as shown in CD 4:12 - 5:19.

This passage, on the three nets of Belial, is tightly structured, and is able to be separated from the context as an independent piece. Its structure is:

12b-19a: The basis of the argument: Isaiah (24: 17-18) spoke of three *paḥ*-(snares). Some escape from *paḥad* (terror) and fall into a *paḥat* (pit), then escape that to fall finally into a *paḥ (snare)*. These are the three nets which, according to Levi,[35] Belial sets up to catch Israel. Israel is caught because they appear to be three kinds of righteousness *(ṣedeq)*. The three nets are (i) sexual immorality, (ii) wealth, (iii) defilement of the sanctuary, temple *(miqdaš)*.

19b-20. The Wall-builders, who have followed *Ṣaw* (the rival leader), are caught in two of them, (i) and (iii).

20-5:6. On (i). They commit polygamy.[36] There are three (indirect) arguments from the Torah against it: (a) Gen 1:27, (b) Gen 7:15-16, (c) Deut 17:17. David, who practised it, did not have access to the Torah.

5:6-14. On (iii). They commit three kinds of defilement:

(a) intercourse during menstruation

(b) niece-marriage. The law against aunt-marriage applies

(c) defilement of their holy spirit *(rûaḥ qodšehem)* by saying that the Law is not established *(lô' nakônû,* 12).

5:14-19. Warning to have nothing to do with those who practise these sins, supported by OT precedents: (a) punishment of a rebellious people; (b) punishment of two brothers, rebellious leaders.

The second "net", greed for wealth, is omitted.[37] But in 8: 5, 7 the *śarîm* of Judah, who are also Wall-builders, that is, schismatics, are accused of it. The Wall-builders in the present passage are the ordinary members, while the *śarîm* are leaders, who were responsible for the decisions regarding property and the "theft" ((according to the remaining party's viewpoint) of the community funds.

Although the "sins" described were common in the Judaism of the hellenistic period,[38] the fact that they were set up as three kinds of righteousness *(sedeq)* shows that they were claimed to rest upon the community teachings, as the community alone had *sedeq,* given at initiation (pp.128-9). Cf. "sons of righteousness" (1QS 3:20, 22, 9:14), "the ways of righteousness" (1QS 4:2), the "chosen ones of righteousness" (1QH 2:13). To "defile the sanctuary", one of the three "nets", is apostasy from the community in CD 20:23. Cf. also 1QpHab 12:8-9, the rival leader "defiled the sanctuary". They had broken the laws regarding holiness, thus defiling the community "temple". But they held that this was "righteousness"; it was in conformity with the community teachings. This could be claimed by taking to an extreme the teaching that ritual washing was secondary only to the cleansing of the soul (pp.65-6). Ritual matters, from being secondary, were disregarded altogether.

There may be a further reference to this attitude in CD 3:6. Israel in the wilderness "ate blood", not a significant feature in the OT history, and possibly referring to the schismatics typologically (cf. also 3:8, "they did not listen . . . to the commands of their Teacher"). Acts 15:20 shows that it means eating meat not prepared in accordance with ritual law, and was a temptation of hellenizing Jews.

The fact that they broke the laws of sexual uncleanness,[39] and that they committed polygamy, together with their use of the organisational term *qahal* (4QpNah 3: 5, 7), may mean that their anti-ritual attitude was extended to anti-asceticism, and included a rejection of the exclusion of women, who in the original community were not admitted to initiation and formed only the *qahal* (p.131). Celibacy was an aspect of the Essene practice, although there is no direct evidence for it in the scrolls.[40] The rival leader is accused of drunkenness (1QpHab 11:8-14), possibly connected with anti-asceticism (cf. Matt 11:18-19).

A disregard of ritual requirements would be a further attraction to many Diaspora Jews, who, with other hellenizers, made a distinction between moral and ritual law (1 Macc 1:11-15). It would also attract some proselytes, who had joined because of their respect for the ethical values rather than the ritual requirements of Judaism. The third kind of defilement of the sanctuary, defilement of their holy spirit by saying that the Law is not established (5:12), may refer to allegorical interpretation of the Torah, also reflecting the interests of hellenizing Jews. The charge is paralleled in 1QH 4:15-18, where the Teacher complains of "prophets of lies" who say of the "vision of knowledge, *lô' nakôn*, "it is not established". Cf. also CD 1:16, 5:20, the rivals "removed the bound" of the Law. The Teacher had shown that the scriptures were a source of mysteries (1QpHab 7:4-5), and the *pesher* method encouraged the seeing of hidden meanings in the words of the prophets, a step towards the allegorical method practised by hellenizing Jews. Philo[41] finds in Num 21:17 an allegory of knowledge as the Well, cf. CD 6:3-4, where the same allegory is found for the Law, and he attributes to the Essenes the allegorizing method he used himself.[42] This method, in some hands, could have been used to deny the literal meaning, the "establishment", or solidity, of the ritual laws, while holding them as transparent of allegorical truth. The charge that they "watched for breaks" (in the wall, Isa 30:13) (CD 1:18-19) would be appropriate to such a procedure.

The second "net", also represented as righteousness, was greed for wealth, committed by the leaders (above). This is consistent with the hypothesis: the schismatic party held the legal ownership of the property.

A hellenizing policy on the part of the rival party would account for the name "seekers-after-smooth-things" *(dôrešê hahălaqôt)* used in 4QpNah both for their group (2:2, "the city of Ephraim, the seekers-after-smooth-things") and for the party of the hellenizing Alcimus, who had allied himself with Demetrius I (see p.25). All Jews who "sought smooth things", that is, only the easier aspects of the Law, were given this title by the rigorists.

The support of the rival party by proselytes strengthens the suggestion made pp.154-5 that they had retained the Teacher's view of spiritual warfare, leaving the militarists in the coalition to ally themselves with the priestly party. A military policy would not attract those living under the rule of Rome.

The Teacher's party, however, retained some proselytes and Diaspora members. 1QS 5:6 names them after the two Houses, and in 1QpHab 12:4 the Simple of Judah "who keep the Law" are, with the Council of the Community, oppressed by the rival leader. Cf. these with the Simple of

159

Ephraim who followed him in 4QpNah 3:5. The two sectors in the community would attract two different kinds of proselytes: those who wished to keep the ritual law and those who did not. The suggestion made p.100 that proselytes were divided into Peleg, the west, and Joktan, the east, would account for proselytes from the east staying with the Teacher's party, despite its militarist faction, while Peleg joined the other party. Easterners had less reason for loyalty to Rome and greater hope of Semitic domination.

Results of the schism

The Teacher complains in 1QH 4:6-9 that the schism has caused him to go into exile. "Teachers of lies . . . have led them astray; I am despised by them and they have no esteem for me . . . they have banished me from my land like a bird from its nest; all my friends and brethren are driven far from me and hold me for a broken vessel". Cf. also 1QpHab 11:6, the Teacher in his "House of Exile". A loss of the north, "Ephraim", would allow him to retain the southern sector. Qumran had been a place of retreat or exile for the Essenes since their separation from the Hasmoneans. While the Zadokite heirs, in Essene ranks, worked to displace the Jerusalem high priesthood, they would be obliged to retain it as their headquarters. As it was close to the border of Transjordan and Nabatea, allowing rapid escape if necessary, it was a suitable House of Exile. While the united community existed, Judea was not the Teacher's "land"; rather, the whole country, although he may well have made Qumran his centre. The schism, however, would have driven him from his "land" and confined him to the south.

In several sources, the rival party are shown to have established themselves in Jerusalem. In 4QpNah 2:2, they have made Jerusalem (=the biblical Nineveh) the "city of Ephraim"; 2:4, they "rule" in Jerusalem; 1QpHab 9:4, "the last priests of Jerusalem" 4QpNah 1:11, "the [pri]ests of Jerusalem [. . .]Ephraim"; 4QpIsa^b 2:6-7, "the Men of Scoffing who are in Jerusalem"; 4QpIsa^c 2:10-11, "the seekers-after-smooth-things who are in Jerusalem". That the rival leader himself was in Jerusalem is shown by 1QpHab 12:7-9: "Jerusalem, where the Wicked Priest committed abominable deeds and defiled the sanctuary of God". But in 1QpMic frs. 8-10: 5-6 the Teacher of Righteousness is associated with the high places of Judah and Jerusalem, while the rival leader is associated with Samaria.

1QpHab finds two significant events of the schism in the prophecy of Habakkuk. In 5:9-12, the House of Absalom, who are the "traitors" of Hab 1:13, had been silent[43] when the Teacher of Righteousness had been chastised (bĕtôkaḥat môreh haṣṣedeq) "and did not help him against the Man of a Lie, when he flouted the Law in the midst of their whole congregation". In 11:4-8, the Wicked Priest had "pursued after the Teacher of Righteousness, to swallow him up in his venomous wrath, to his House of Exile. Then, at the Period of the Feast of Rest, the Day of Atonement, he manifested himself *(hôpîaʻ)* to them to swallow them up and to cause them to stumble on the day of fasting, their Sabbath of Rest". The sentence structure of 11:4-8 shows that it refers to two parallel events rather than a single event. As argued p.19, the verb means that the rival leader offered himself as high priest in the absence of the Teacher on the Day of Atonement, when the Law required that a high priest should be present.

A split between the north and south defeated the purposes of the coalition, which had aimed to gain control of the temple and state from the hands of the present establishment. If the Teacher became high priest, he would reign only over the southern portion of the country, with no hope of going on to gain the world for Judaism. The northern party, although it had the majority of numbers and the western Diaspora members, did not have Jerusalem and Judea. They could gain part of the world, but not for Judaism, which was capable of uniting east and west. Only Jerusalem could be the capital of world Judaism.

The rival leader's occupation of Jerusalem is able to be accounted for as a means of reuniting the separated northern and southern sectors of the community, and pursuing the original purposes of the Teacher. He had not accepted the necessity of the schism, and came south, regaining much of the southern party with the exception of a small group of loyalists to the Teacher. He had thus taken the place of the Teacher as head of almost the whole community. The frequent references to his occupation of Jerusalem are support for this interpretation. By this action, he had become supreme leader and brought about a fundamental revision of the doctrine, while still preserving the aim of establishing a world-wide Jewish spiritual kingdom. In thus deposing the Teacher and confining him to a small group of followers, he had "pursued after the Teacher . . . to swallow him up in his furious anger, to his House of Exile" (1QpHab 11:5-6).

The original aims, however, had included leadership by a high priest, appropriate to a religious kingdom. The Teacher was identified with Jerusalem in 1QpMic because he was to reign there as high priest. The northern party had retained priesthood, although in the form of the lowly levitical priests; the function was retained in a lowered status. It was also necessary to have the high priesthood in order to continue to initiate, as the Spirit of holiness was given through him (p.99). Priestly leadership was necessary, even when less significance was given to the temple. But the rival leader was not a Zadokite. He was a levitical priest only, and a son of David. If he reigned as king, it would be more difficult to achieve the Teacher's aim of a spiritual kingdom. It was necessary that his status should be that of a high priest.

The Day of Atonement after the schism had occurred gave him h's opportunity. It was absolutely necessary, according to the Law, that the high priest should be present on this day. With the Teacher separated from them in his "House of Exile", the levitical subordinate of the Teacher "manifested himself" to his followers, claiming the glory of the high priest. H's claim succeeded, and he was accepted as the supreme priestly ruler of the new Israel (p.18). Those who accepted him were "caused to stumble" because of the illegality of his action.

Further evidence that he adopted the high priesthood is in 1QpHab 11:12: "his (the Wicked Priest's) shame was greater than his glory *(kabôd)"*. The high priest, as the Light (p.128) had glory. CD 19:25 says that he "walks in wind" *(hôlek rûaḥ)* possibly a play on his claim to give the Spirit of holiness as high priest. The pseudonym *haṣṣaw (Ṣaw,* CD 4:19b), as well as being drawn from Hos 5:11, may also have been understood as the first letter of *haṣṣedeq (ṣade* with *waw,* cf. *taw* with *yod* and *waw* as a name for the letter in CD 19:12), the Righteous One, a name for the Teacher (4QpPs^a 4:8).

The basis on which the claim was made, and accepted, is apparent from the analysis of the Teacher's organisation. The Messiah of Israel was also a levitical priest. The Teacher required literal priests to be initiated (p.130), and initiation bestowed Jewish identity. It was only a step from this to the *bestowal* of priesthood, although the Teacher had not taken it. His giving of a symbolic priesthood to the laity at initiation also supported the development, as did his doctrine of the indwelling heavenly high priest. As in the case of the attitude to the ritual law and the interpretation of scripture, the rival's action simply carried the Teacher's doctrine to its logical conclusion.

In 1QpHab 5:9-12 the House of Absalom failed to speak out against the action of the rival leader when he "flouted the Law in the midst of the'r whole congregation". The levitical priests, the twenty-four elders, had two loyalties, to the priests and to the laity. As they were two-thirds priestly (twelve pure sons of Levi, twelve who were both sons of Levi and tribal leaders), they should have supported the priestly party in the case of a flagrant breach of the law of Zadokite descent. But by establishing a levitical high priesthood, the rival leader was able to gain their sympathies as levitical priests. They would be the superior rank in a community which preferred a lowered status for priests. As their vote was the crucial one, their action deposed the Teacher; they thus became the "House of Absalom", fulfilling the type of the treacherous heir who attempted to establish a northern kingship (1 Sam 15:10).

Both leaders of the community were opponents of the established government, as they aimed at replacing it and taking control of Jerusalem/the temple and the state. But that government itself was divided, as, following the arrival of Pompey, the territory of the Hasmoneans was reduced to Judea, and scattered communities of Jews in Samaria, Galilee and Transjordan lacked real cohesion.[44] This was true, in different degrees, in both the earlier and later periods of Roman intrusion (p.148). If the military faction had stayed in the Teacher's party, as suggested pp.154-5, the Teacher was an enemy of the southern government on the grounds of militarism and an attempt on the temple, and of the northern governments on the grounds of militarism. The rival leader, who did not retain the military faction, was an enemy of the southern government only, on the grounds of an attempt on Jerusalem. While his aims were centred on Jerusalem, he would be able to make use of the traditional north-south tension to gain a measure of support with the northern governments. This may be the reason for the situation of 4QpPs[a]. The Teacher and the men of his Council are about to be judged (4:7-9, 2:18). "Council" is a lay structure (pp.131-2), and the Teacher's surviving laymen may have been the *sarîm*, with a traditional military association. An arrest of the Teacher on the grounds of militarism could have been made by either north or south. The *pesharist* suspects that "Ephraim and Manasseh", the northern party, "will seek to put forth a hand against the Priest and the men of his Council in the time of trial that is coming on them" (2:17-18) and that the Wicked Priest is plotting to slay him. They would have some opportunity to do so if a northern government had arrested him.

The rival leader was in danger from the southern government. Although he was not a Zadokite, he had the majority of the Teacher's community, including the laity, who gave popular support to his claim to the high priesthood. The Hasmonean house had gained the high priesthood, although they were not Zadokites, through their popularity as liberators of the people. In actually establishing himself in Jerusalem, the rival would inevitably come into conflict with the Jerusalem high priesthood. In 4QpPs[a] the writer expects that both the Wicked Priest and the men of Ephraim and Manasseh will be punished by the terrible Gentiles (2:17-19, 4:8-9). The established government had no alternative but to support Rome, and would be able to call on their help against enemies of the state.

1QpHab 8:13 - 9:12 reveals that the rival leader had in fact met his death at the hands of the Gentiles. Those who put him to death are the "oppressors" of Hab 2:7-8a, parallel to "all the remnant of the peoples" in the same lemma; the latter are the Kittim. The manner of his death is referred to in 9:1-2. After the quotation of the Habakkuk verse on the punishment by the oppressors, and a lacuna of about a line, the sentence continues: "[. . . . .] his chastisement *(negô'ô)*, by judgements of wickedness. They inflicted on him horrors of evil sicknesses *(mahălîm,* root *halâ,* possibly a play on *halal,* "defile"), and vengeance on his body of flesh". Cf. also the following section: the Wicked Priest was "delivered into the hands of his enemies, in order to humble him by a destructive scourge *(nega' lĕkalâ),* in bitterness of soul" (10-11). His death was accompanied by severe physical suffering.

In 4QpNah, whose cols. 2-4 deal at length with the schismatics, using for them the name "seekers-after-smooth-things" in 2:2, the death by crucifixion of some "seekers-after-smooth-things" is referred to in 1:6-7. The Young Lion of Wrath, a Roman ruler of Jerusalem (pp.27-30) had "brought vengeance on them" by this means. Their connection with the schismatics is further shown by 1:11-12: the "prey" of the Nah 2:14 lemma, applied to those put to death, is "the wealth which the [prie]sts of Jerusalem amass[ed] which they will give [. . .]Ephraim".

1:8-9, after the statement that "seekers-after-smooth-things" (plu.) had been crucified, continues: "for of the man hanged alive *(talûy)* upon a tree it reads ([*yiqq*]*are'*): 'Behold, I am against [thee]' ",[46] followed by the rest of Nah 2:14. *Talûy* is the passive participle, meaning "the man hanged", not "the act of hanging". The victims of the Young Lion, the schismatics, are now narrowed down to one, who is proven in this way to be the object of God's special wrath. Deut 21:23, "a hanged man is accursed by God", is in the background, as is recognized. The single victim referred to is surely the leader of the schismatics. The passage is to be brought together with 1QpHab 8:13-9:12, on the painful death of the rival leader at the hands of Gentiles, as evidence that *he was crucified by a Roman ruler of Jerusalem.*

As suggested pp.28-9, the law of 11QT 64:6-13, recommending crucifixion for a man with Gentile, hellenizing sympathies, may have been in the mind of the pesharist. If so, the writer of 1QpHab disagrees with him:

he considers it to have been "judgements of wickedness" (9:1), an illegal punishment.

Although the death of the rival leader is described as having already occurred in 1QpHab 9:10 *(nětanô,* perfect tense), 12:5 speaks of his destruction as a future event: "God will condemn him to destruction *(yeśôpětennû 'el lěkala').* It has been argued pp.51-2 that the writer took the repetition of the biblical verse "because of the blood of men . . . " as support for a prediction of a second death for the rival leader. His influence was still sufficiently strong at the time of writing of 1QpHab to lead to the hope that he would again be destroyed at the Day of Judgement.

* Synthesis

There has now been brought to light, from an analysis of the organisational terms and doctrines, a coherent history. At a certain point after the expulsion of the Zadokite dynasty, the Essenes formed the hope of its restoration in a rebuilt temple. The subsequent appearance of a grave threat to the state from the Roman power led them to form a coalition with a party of northern laymen for military purposes. The plan for war was frustrated because of the greater power of the Romans, and twenty years later the Teacher put the hope of recovery of the temple on an eschatological plane. The military plans were transformed into a campaign of proselytisation, to prepare a world-wide community for the coming Future Time. The Teacher's restoration of priestly supremacy then led to the secession of the northern party from the coalition. The schismatics had also introduced a hellenizing approach to the Law, giving them the support of Diaspora and proselyte members. There are some signs that they retained the Teacher's doctrine of spiritual warfare, leaving those with military sympathies in the Teacher's party after the separation. The Teacher's arrest may have been due to this fact. The leader of the seceding party was the Messiah of Israel, who had been the second leader. In order to retain the southern sector and fulfil the Teacher's purpose of winning the world for Judaism, he established himself in Jerusalem as the sectarian high priest. Although he was not a Zadokite, he was able to support his claim by an extension of the Teacher's doctrine of second birth, being accepted by the levitical priests, the twenty-four elders. His claim to leadership of the state led to conflict with the Jerusalem authorities, and he was crucified by a Roman ruler of Jerusalem.

165

It is necessary to complete the analysis of the texts before turning to a consideration of whether this history can be matched with the events of the Roman occupation of Palestine. There still remain parts of 1QS, the whole of CD, and further pieces. Only if. the subsequent stages are consistent with this history can it be said that the hypothesis gives a unified account of all the data.

THE COMMUNITY (YAḤAD)

STAGE II. The Law-Interpreter

The manuscript of 1QSa[47] contains a series of marginal marks. The simpler kind, a horizontal stroke with an angled projection downwards, are found frequently and appear to mark divisions in the subject-matter, not sources. There are two very elaborate marks, several parallel lines with further embellishments, at 7:25 and 9:2. In both cases, there follows a passage on the community "temple", 8:1-16, and 9:3-11. There is none beside another passage on this subject, 5:1-20.

8:16b - 9:11, including one of the marked "temple" passages, is missing from 4QSᵉ,[48] which Milik considers to be the oldest MS of 1QS. It continues directly from 8:15a to 9:12. 1:1 - 7:25 form a complete corpus of documents reflecting the Teacher's organisation, and 5:1-20, referring to the schism, is to be placed near its beginning, as the rebels are considered to be still under the discipline of the community (pp.153-4). These facts support the division of 1QS into three distinct stages, each with a different "temple" structure, that is, a different definition of leadership and policy. They are:

Stage I. 1:1 - 7:25. The Teacher of Righteousness.

Stage II. 8:1-15a with 9:12-26. The Law-Interpreter.

Stage III. 8:16b-9:11 (not in 4QSᵉ), added in 1QS. The Law-Interpreter, the Chief Priest, and the Warrior.

In 8:13, the members are enjoined to "separate from the Session (môšab) of the Men of Iniquity". The Session is the local meeting for the Meal and government (p.134), including laity, and the Men of Iniquity are the schismatics in 5:1-20. This passage follows the schism.

8:1 reads: "In the Council of the Community there are to be twelve men (ʾîš) and three priests, perfect in all that is revealed from all the Law, to do truth, righteousness, justice . . . ". In 4-5: "When these are in Israel,

the Council of the Community is established in truth, as an eternal Plantation *(matta'at)*, a Holy House for Israel, and a *sôd* of the Holy of Holies
for Aaron, witnesses of truth for justice, and Elect Ones of his will, to
atone . . . ".

There is a striking change from the definitions of 1QS 5:1-20, which
are understood (pp.153-5) as an adaptation of the Teacher's ministry
following the loss of the levitical Holy House. At that point, consistently
with the Teacher's separation of literal and symbolic priests, there had been
only one "holy" structure, containing the superior priests only, and laymen
had been formed into a House of Truth.

There are now, once more, two holy Houses, a Holy of Holies and a
Holy House. The three priests of 8:1 form the Holy of Holies, for Aaron,
as in the Teacher's original system. The Holy House is "for Israel": this
name was possible while it contained the levitical priests, of whom twelve
were also the tribal leaders. But it now contains twelve "men" (8:1). The
word means laymen only. 8:10-11 sets out a new rule for them, confirming
that they are a newly created rank. "When these are established in the
yèsôd of the Community for two years in perfection of way, they will be
separated as holy in the midst of the Council of the men of the Community".
After reaching the top of the *yèsôd,* the lay governing ranks (p.132), they
are to be trained two further years. The requirement of perfection is found
in a further name for their House, "the House of Perfection and Truth"
(8:9). To "separate as holy" is to give them a form of priestliness. Twelve
laymen have now been promoted to a newly created rank and have been
made lay ministers. Laymen have, for the first time, been permitted into
the "temple" itself; the Teacher's division of literal from symbolic priests
has been abandoned.

There is still a difference between the priests and the lay ministers:
the former are a *sôd* of the Holy of Holies (8:5). The *sôd* is the Company
of members who have received the Spirit of holiness, and so can make
contact with priests for the first time (pp.133-4). The priests still form the
superior rank, containing the Spirit of holiness. This implies that the twelve
laymen perform the work of levites, including baptism of members two
years before full initiation.

1QS 9:12-26 is linked with 8:1-15a by several almost identical phrases:
the command to go into the wilderness (8:13-16, 9:19-20); the ideal of
9:17-20: "walking perfectly, each man with his neighbour, in all that is
revealed to them", cf. 8:1-2; the use of "Elect Ones" for the ministers (8:6,

9: 14, 17-18). It refers to those whom the *maśkîl* separates and weighs as *běnê haṣṣadôq* (9:14). The reading in 4QS^e is *běnê haṣṣedeq*. There is a play on "sons of Zadok": the fifteen ministers are now symbolic "sons of Zadok/righteousness". This means that the three priests are not literal sons of Zadok, only sons of Aaron. The presence of sons of Zadok would be inconsistent with a lay ministry, lowering the status of priests.

The alternative title for the House of Israel, "House of Perfection and Truth" (8:9) suggests a link with the House of Truth of 1QS 5:1-20. "Truth" appears frequently in the description of the fifteen: to "do the truth" is the first duty required of them in 8:2; the Council of the Community is "established in truth" in 8:5, cf. also "witnesses of truth", 8:6. The 4QS^e reading of 8:13 is "to prepare in the wilderness the Way of Truth".

The fifteen are also called "the Elect Ones" (8:6, "the Elect of his will"). In 9:14 they are "the Elect Ones of the time (calendar, see below on the preoccupation of the leader with the calendar), and 9:17-18, in 4QS^d, calls them "the Elect Ones of the Way". As shown pp.130-1, the Teacher had used military terms, "elect", "truth", "volunteers", *śarîm*, in a spiritual sense, in accordance with his doctrine of spiritual warfare. The use of "House of Truth" and the leadership of *śarîm* in the Teacher's organisation following the schism (1QS 5:1-20a, pp.154-5) was suggested to mean that the military faction had remained in the Teacher's party, and this was supported by the details of the Teacher's arrest (p.163). The new lay ministers, the Elect Ones, and the House of . . . Truth, use the old military terms. They are also called "the Plantation" (8:5), possibly reviving the old military name "Plant-root". The fact noted p.110 may also be brought in here: the name "volunteers" is only found in the writings describing the Teacher's organisation. It ceases altogether in this and subsequent documents. These are indications of the policy of the new stage of the community. The military faction is in control. "Volunteers" has come to be so associated with the proselytising organisation that it ceases to be used. But the old military terms, "elect ones" and "men of truth", given a literal sense with the rise to power of the *śarîm*, have become titles. The new lay ministry are part of an organisation dedicated to holy war,, on a physical level.

The difference between Stage II of the Community and the rival party whom they condemn in 8:13, is then accounted for. Both represent the northern, lay emphasis; both are opposed to priestly supremacy. But the hellenizing outlook of the rival party would not be compatible with a plan for war against Gentiles. The northern warriors are now in the remnants of the Teacher's party, leaving the schismatic followers of the Wicked Priest to continue the Teacher's programme of proselytisation.

The members, under the fifteen Elect Ones, are therefore commanded to "separate from the Session of the Men of Iniquity, to go into the wilderness to prepare there the Way" (8:13); and cf. also 9:19-20: "this is the time for the preparation of the Way to the wilderness". The Community, Stage II, is sharply in disagreement with the schismatics on the question of asceticism, necessary for physical war; an outlook not encouraged by a hellenizing approach to the Law. The name "the Way" is now developed and used absolutely (9:18, 21) to express the lay ascetic ideal. Although already resident in the wilderness (Qumran) the members are more conscious than ever that they have retained the wilderness ideal, as against their rivals in Jerusalem (p.160), and are ready at any time for holy war.

This interpretation of the terms will be supported by further indications of a military policy (below, p.172).

Both the priests and the laymen are to form the Council of the Community (8:1; 8:5: "when these are in Israel, the Council of the Community is established in truth"). This emphasizes the change that had occurred in 1QS 5:1-20, when the property was brought under the control of both the priests and the laity, no longer separated into a levitical-lay Council of the Community. There are no longer two separate sectors; the Community is all one. This makes it possible for it to be led by a single leader, as also in 1QS 5:1-20, when the Teacher was forced to adopt all three leadership roles.

8:11-12 introduces "the man, the Interpreter" *('îš haddôreš)* as the one who gives the secrets to the new ministers, and his duties are set out, under the title of the *maśkîl*, in 9:12-26. The purpose of the community is now to "interpret the Law". This is given as the meaning of the Way: "prepare the Way . . . this is the interpreting of the Law *(midraš hattôrâ)"* (8:14-15). The verb *haśkîl* and its derivatives are regularly associated with the levites, and *maśkîl* occurs in the titles of the Psalms, a further link with the levites, who looked after the music in the temple.[49] The law-interpreter, in the local meetings, is the levitical priest who assists the Aaronite priest in the duties of the Meal (pp.134-5). Law-interpreting is in accord with a lay-levitical, rather than priestly emphasis.

The special knowledge of the *maśkîl* concerns the calendar. The word *'et,* "time", now appears frequently. In 9:12, he is to "walk . . . according to the regulations of the different times" *(tikkûn 'et wa'et),* that is, the

169

calendar. The rules of the Way include "doing all that is revealed of the different times" (8:15). The determination of the calendar is a priestly duty, connected with their image of "light". Both priests and levites are "lights"; the former are the superior luminaries, twelve in number (4QpIsa^d)[50], while the latter are "stars", cf. the Star and Sceptre prophecy for the levitical-davidic Messiah.

The fifteen ministers, including the twelve laymen, are the Elect Ones of the Time (calendar) (9:14). The Interpreter is to reveal to them what is hidden from (the rest of) Israel, and not conceal it from them "out of fear of a spirit of apostasy" (8:11-12). The knowledge of the calendar is revealed from the Law (9:13). He is to share the priestly secrets of the calendar with laymen, as they are now "temple" ministers and take part in the services at the appointed times. This confirms that he is a levitical priest, standing between the superior priesthood and the laity. He is now the sole leader of a community in which priests and laymen have been joined, and there is a new lay ministry. The Teacher is no longer in power, and as, at the time of writing 4QpPs^a, a fear was expressed that he would be put to death following his trial, it may be presumed that he is now dead. The requirement that the twelve men are to undergo two further years' instruction implies that the new ministry was set up at least two years after his death.

The identity of the Law-Interpreter will be discussed below p.176.

His commitment to a war policy is confirmed in 9:23: the *maśkîl* is "a man zealous *(mĕqanne')* for the decree, and his Time *('et)* is for the Day of Vengeance". The Day of Vengeance was the term used in 1QM 2-9 (7:5) for the day of victory as the result of physical warfare. It is never found in the Teacher's writings: he speaks of a Visitation (1QS 4:18-19), as the defeat of wickedness was to be brought about by a divine intervention, not through human warfare. The Teacher's eschatological expectation has now been abandoned, leading to a return to militarism.

The reasons for the change of policy may be found in 1QpHab, written after the death of the Wicked Priest (9:10) and probably of the Teacher. The Teacher's eschatological terms are frequently used: "Future Time" (2:5, 9:6), "Last Period" (7:7, 12). His authority concerning the times predicted by the prophets is affirmed in 7:1-2: he knew the *gĕmar haqqes,* "the end of the Period", unknown to Habakkuk. There has, however, been a delay in the fulfilment of his expectations. The Last Period has been pro-longed (7:7). A prediction of this is found in Hab 2:3: "the vision still exists *('ôd ḥazôn)* for the Season: it puffs *(yapîaḥ)* to its end and does not lie". This is seen to mean that the prediction still stands, but it is bigger than expected: "it exceeds *(wèyeter)* everything that the prophets have said" (7:5-8). A greater fulfilment will require a greater time. As the *pesher* is being written, the Romans are marching across the land. "From afar they come, from the islands of the sea, to devour all the peoples" (3:10-11). "They shall march across the plain, smiting and plundering the cities of the earth" (3:1). This conjunction of events: the disappointment of the Teacher's chronological scheme, and a renewed threat from Rome, would be a reason for the rise to power of the lay-military faction in the Teacher's party. 1QpHab is written by a priestly supporter of the Teacher, but his arguments were not strong enough to prevent a return of the military policy.

THE COMMUNITY (YAHAD)

STAGE III. The Law-Interpreter, the Chief Priest, and the Warrior

1QS 8:16b-9:11, not found in 4QSᵉ, contains at least three new elements:

(a) "They shall be judged by the first laws *(mišpaṭîm harišônîm)* by which the men of the Community began to be disciplined" (9:10). This clearly refers back to the original stage of the Community, under the Teacher. It claims continuity with his constitution, although allowing for some development, cf. "began".

(b) There are rules for both "holy men" *('anšê haqqôdeš)* (8:16b-19) and "perfectly holy men" *('anšê tèmîm haqqôdeš)* (8:20-9:2): for the latter, there is a much stricter discipline. The "Purity of the holy men" of 8:17 is found also in 5:13, where it replaces the "Purity of the Many" of the phase before the schism (1QS 6:16, 25, 7:3, 16, 19). But no distinction between two grades of holiness was found in the Teacher's stage.

(c) "Only the sons of Aaron are to rule in judgement and in property" (9:7).

In 9:11, there are to be three messianic figures. There is no d'fference in the time of their coming; all are grouped together. They are: the Prophet *(nabî),* the Messiah of Aaron, and the Messiah of Israel. The messianic doctrine (ch. VII) implies that statements concerning the future Messiahs refer also to the present leaders, who will become Messiahs in the Future Time.

4QTestim is copied by a scribe who is either the same, or has closely similar characteristics, to the scribe of 1QS. It sets out texts predicting the

171

same three messianic figures: a Prophet like Moses (Deut 18:18-19); a davidic Messiah who is the Star and Sceptre of Num 24:15-17, (cf. the definition of the Messiah of Israel (p.136); and a Levi who holds the Urim and Thummim, that is, has the high priestly power (Deut 33:8-11).

It has been established that 1QM 1 with 15-19 contains the final stage of 1QM.[51] It sets out a plan for physical warfare against the Romans. The ritual duties are given to a Chief Priest *(kôhen haro'š,* 15:4, 16:13, 18:5), the name for the leading priest used in the first stage of 1QM (p.123). It implies a leadership with priestly-lay equality. This is supported by 15:6: the priest is "appointed for the Season of Vengeance under the authority of all his brothers". He is *primus inter pares* with his fellow-priests, reflecting the lay doctrine of leadership. There is also a davidic leader, shown to have exactly the same definition as the Messiah of Israel of the Teacher, as the hymn concerning him from the Teacher's stage of 1QM (10:7-18) is reproduced in 19:1-8. Levites are included (15:4).

The war plan of 1QM 1, 15-19 is compatible with that of Stage II of the Community (pp.168-9) and its leadership is compatible with that of Stage III and 4QTestim. If the ministry of Stage III is compatible with that of Stage II, then it may be held that the Prophet of Stage III is the Law-Interpreter of Stage II (cf. the theme of Moses in both names), who has now allied himself with two new leaders, a Chief Priest who will become Mess'ah of Aaron, and a Warrior *(gibbôr* (davidic leader, 1QM 19:2)) who will become Messiah of Israel. They plan to carry out the intention of regaining political power by means of war, and to use the name "Messiah", although without an eschatological association.

The "perfectly holy men" of 8:20-9:2 are evidence of continuity between Stages II and III. The twelve men of Stage II are a House of Perfection and Truth (8:9). Perfection of way is frequently required of them (8:1, 10, 9:19). In 8:10, their perfection is tested by their two extra years' training. They are now incorporated into the new structure. There is good reason to believe that the Law-Interpreter is the same as the Prophet.

9:3, "when these are in Israel", is linked syntactically with the rules for the perfectly holy men. It calls them a *"yĕsôd* of the Spirit of holiness for eternal truth". They are to atone for sin, a duty performed also by laymen (pp.128-9). It is to be done by prayer, as a substitute for sacrifices: "without the flesh of burnt-offerings and the fat of sacrifice, for the offering of the lips according to the law is an acceptable fragrance of righteousness" (4-5). Their righteousness also atones (5). The duty of prayer for the lay "priests" is set out in 1QS 1:14-15, and is developed here for the lay ministers. There is a further significant development. The *yĕsôd* of lay ministers (governing ranks, in which they are two years above other leading laymen) is "of the Spirit of holiness". In Stage II, the priests as the *sôd* were distinguished from the twelve men. The former gave the Spirit of holiness at initiation, the latter the levitical washing. The twelve lay ministers have now been enabled to give the Spirit of holiness, as it is possessed by all who are fully initiated. This means that there is no distinction between the fleshly and spiritual initiation, in terms of the ministers or priests involved. The breaking down of the difference is consistent with both 1QS 5:1-20 and the rule in 9:7: the priests are given the fleshly duty of control of money.

The development of the lay ministry may be summarised as follows:

(a) In 1QS 5:1-20, following the schism, but still in the time of the Teacher, the twelve *śarîm* were promoted to be the leading laymen to take the place of their immediate superiors, the twelve tribal heads, who had gone over with the twenty-four elders. The twelve tribal heads had been levitical ministers. The twelve *śarîm* were now made a House of Truth, that is, given some ministerial functions, but could not enter the "temple", even the Holy House (pp.154-5). Their ministerial functions made them "holy men", having some qualities of literal priests. The name Purity of the Holy Men now replaced Purity of the Rabbim (5:13).

(b) In 8:1-15a the "holy men" became "perfectly holy men", by the addition of two further years.

(c) In 8:16b - 9:11 the ministerial function of the perfectly holy men is developed, so that they give the Spirit of holiness. This gives a new significance to other laymen, all of whom possess the Spirit of holiness if initiated. They now become the "holy men", and the name Purity of the Holy Men is retained for them (8:7). There is still a distinction between them and the perfectly holy men, as the latter are of a higher rank. Rules for the two grades are set out in 8:16b - 9:2.

This interpretation is supported by the insertion of 8:16b - 9:11 between 8:15a and 9:12 in the manuscript of 1QS. This is the appropriate point at which to insert the rules on the perfectly holy men, the twelve men of 8:1.

The "temple" structure of 9:5-11 is different from both the previous ones, for it contains three Houses. "At that time the men of the Community shall separate a Holy House for Aaron, to be united *(lĕhiwwaḥed)* to a Holy

173

of Holies, and a House of Community *(yaḥad)* for Israel, those walking in perfection." There is a considerable difference from Stage II, in which the three priests were a Holy of Holies for Aaron, and the twelve laymen a Holy House for Israel (p.167). Aaron, the priests, are now a Holy House: they have gone down in status. The new third House consists of those walking in perfection, that is, the twelve lay ministers. They have also gone down in status, as formerly they were the Holy House. The reason is the appearance of a new Holy of Holies, to be connected with the appearance of the Chief Priest (9:11 with 1QM 15:4, p.172). A superior grade of priests has now joined the community, with their leader, the Chief Priest, who has the role if not the title of high priest (handling the Urim and the Thummim, 4QTestim 14). The sons of Zadok, not present in Stage II, and presumably forming a third party, holding the Teacher's viewpoint, have now come back. But the lay ministry is established, and is incorporated in Stage III. There are therefore two kinds of ministry, side by side. The priests, only, form the Holy of Holies and the Holy House, as in the days of the Teacher. For this reason, continuity with the Teacher's constitution, the "first laws", can be claimed in 9:10. But the difference between them is only that between two ranks of superior priests, not superior priests and levitical priests. The Holy House of Aaronites is "united" to the Holy of Holies of Zadokites. Beside them, there is a House of the *yaḥad,* representing the ideals of the *yaḥad,* the laity here finding their place as symbolic priests. For the other members of the House of the Community, see below p.175.

The sons of Zadok were present in 1QS 5:1-20, but not in Stage II (p.168). Their appearance in Stage III may be connected with the inclusion of sons of Levi in the list of protagonists in the war (1QM 1:2 "sons of Levi, sons of Judah, and sons of Benjamin" form the complete list). The sons of Levi, as the bridging class, exercise the casting vote, as they represent both priestly and lay interests. At the time of the schism, the decision of the "House of Absalom" had given the twenty-four elders to the rival leader (pp.162-3). If some of the sons of Levi now decided to return from the rival party, in response to the new pressures to military activity, they would bring with them some of the priestly class. It contained two points of view, as shown by the different attitudes of the writer of 1QpHab, still upholding the Teacher's eschatology, and the three sons of Aaron who joined the Law-Interpreter in Stage II, accepting his plan for war. The priestly third party has now been divided by the decision of the sons of Levi, and some of its members have come back to join the sons of Aaron in a plan for war. They have accepted a lowered priestly status, shown in the title Chief Priest for their leader.

As they are capable of changing sides, the sons of Levi are not placed in the Holy House. Their instability accounts for the rule of 1QS 9:7: "only the sons of Aaron shall rule in judgement and in property". It is intended to exclude the sons of Levi from control of the finances, to prevent a repetition of the financial losses of the schism. The money still belongs to both laity and priests, making them a *yaḥad*: it is "the property of the holy men walking in perfection" (8). But the sons of Aaron alone have the power to determine its use. The name "House of the *yaḥad*" for the third House suggests that it is here that the sons of Levi have been placed, forming a community with laymen. They are grouped with the lay ministers, as before, but now represent the priesthood in the separate lay ministry, making it a *yaḥad*, a commonality of two kinds. This is supported by the law of 9:8-9: "the property (of the holy men walking in perfection) shall not be mingled with the property of the Men of Deception who have not cleansed their way to be separated from iniquity, to walk in perfection of way". If some of the sons of Levi had come back, they would have brought with them some of the property that they had taken over to the rival party (p.150). It was necessary to make a formal division in the funds that had once formed a single resource. This law makes the division. The two sums cannot be mixed, because that held by the rival party is unclean (p.154). The law indicates that there is still not a final separation between the two parties.

In 1QM 1:2 the list of protagonists in the war is given: "the sons of Levi, Judah and Benjamin": three tribes only, connected by no special pattern except that they are southern tribes. P. R. Davies remarks:[52] "the mention of three tribes here is most curious", and supposes a theory of the return of the lost tribes, understood as the return of further members of the sect from Babylon.

The inclusion of Levi in the list has been suggested above to mean that some of the levitical priests had returned from the rival party at the threat of war. The tribal heads, members of the Holy House of twenty-four elders, had also gone over to the rival party (p.151). There are signs, however, that there had been a division within the tribe of Judah: some had gone over, and some had remained. This is shown by 4QpPs^a 2:13-14: "the violent ones (false teachers, pp.144-5) of the Covenant in the House of Judah who will plot to destroy those who do the Law *('ôśê hattôrâ)* in the Council of the Community", and 1QpHab 7:17 - 8:3; "(the righteous who live by their fidelity to the Teacher of Righteousness) are those who do the Law *('ôśê hattôrâ)* in the House of Judah". Cf. also 1QpHab 12:4, the proselytes of Judah are still in the Teacher's party. The tribe of Judah is almost synonymous with the south, the House of Judah, according to the ancient tribal boundaries. Part of it, with its tribal head, had gone over and become

175

"the violent ones of the Covenant in the House of Judah"; part of it remained to be "those who do the Law in the House of Judah". Those members of it who remained are the "Judah" of 1QM 1:2.

There is no evidence, however, that any of the sons of Benjamin had remained, only that they had all gone over with the twenty-four elders who included their tribal leader. The inclusion of Benjamin in 1QM 1:2 would mean, then, that Benjamin and their leader had returned, with some of the sons of Levi. This supplies a satisfactory explanation of the expression "Returnees" (šabîm).[53] Šûb, "return" is used for going over to the rival party in CD 20:14; it means "change one's allegiance", in either direction. The šabê yisra'el, "Returnees of Israel" of CD 4:2, 6:5, 8:16, are, then, the lay members of Benjamin, who had come back from the rival party. The Returnees of the Wilderness of 4QpPs^a 3:1 are the same group, returning to the ascetic discipline of what is now the military party. This passage shows that they had returned during the Teacher's life-time, when 4QpPs^a was written.

The identity of the Law-Interpreter is suggested by this conclusion. As a law-interpreter, he was a levitical priest (pp.134-5). But he was not a leader of the returning sons of Levi, who were not with him in Stage II, as they are not named with the three priests (Aaron) and the twelve men. If he were a leader, as suggested by the fact that he was accepted as supreme leader in Stage II, he must have been one of the twenty-four elders who were tribal heads and levitical priests. Was he the head of Benjamin, who had originally gone over to the seceding party because of their militaristic background, but who, when they persisted in the Teacher's policy of spiritual warfare, and added anti-asceticism, decided to return, after a very short time? His introduction of a lay ministry may well have been borrowed from their extension of the concept of a bestowed priesthood, the basis of their non-Zadokite high priesthood.

The title of Prophet was possibly given by the Teacher to the third, non-messianic leader (p.137). The original Prophet, the zakar, appears, from 1QH 3:7-18, to have gone over in the schism (p.156), according to the position of the head of Levi in the twenty-four elders. The Law-Interpreter, if he were the head of Benjamin, has now been promoted to the position of third leader. As will be shown, the Chief Priest and the Warrior may also have received their positions through promotion.

The addition of sons of Zadok in Stage III illustrates a division in the ranks of the superior priests who had remained in the Teacher's party at the schism. At that point, there is reason for suspecting that the military faction had remained on the Teacher's side, from the title "House of Truth" and the facts of the Teacher's arrest, together with his retention of the eastern Diaspora and proselytes (pp.159, 163). The writer of 1QpHab has a viewpoint identical with that of the Teacher, expecting a victory through eschatological fulfilment, but three sons of Aaron had joined the Law-Interpreter's military party in Stage II. With increasing pressures to make war on the Romans, more superior priests have now come over. 1QpHab shows the existence of a priestly party, opposed to the schismatics, but holding spiritual warfare, even after the renewed Roman threat. There are, then, three parties, each representing one of the original three issues:

(a) priestly supremacy, spiritual warfare, continuing the policy of the Teacher, represented by 1QpHab;

(b) priestly-lay equality, spiritual warfare, anti-asceticism; the schismatics in Jerusalem;

(c) priestly-lay co-operation, physical warfare, asceticism; the Community, Stages II and III.

The superior priests have been divided between (a) and (c); there are none in (b). The Chief Priest is one of these, promoted from being one of the sons of Zadok to be the future Messiah of Aaron.

The Warrior, according to his title, Messiah of Israel, and the reproduction of the hymn concerning the Teacher's Messiah of Israel (p.172), is both a Star and Sceptre, both levitical and davidic. As davidic, he is a member of Judah, part of which had remained at the schism (pp.175-6). Their tribal head had gone over in 1QS 5:1-20. He is either the tribal head who has returned, or the *sar* of Judah, one of the twelve *sarîm* (second rank of laymen) who have remained and become the "perfectly holy men". The subsequent writings show the further history of the portion of Judah still in the Law-Interpreter's group, calling them the *sarîm* of Judah (below pp. 185-6). This indicates that their leader was the *sar*, under whom are the subordinate *sarîm* (of hundreds, fifties, tens), and that the head of Judah has not returned. With the increased pressure to war, the first of the "perfectly holy men" (Judah was the first tribe, p.120) has been promoted to be leader of the laity. He is a Star because the lay ministers have now been given the duties of levitical priests, baptizing, and also give the Spirit of holiness as symbolic superior priests.

The similarity, yet difference, between Stage III and the Teacher's Stage I, accounts for 1QS 9:10: "they shall be judged by the first laws by which the men of the Community began to be disciplined". In common were: the threefold leadership; the two holy Houses, one lower than the other; and the superiority of priests to laymen. But the new lay ministry takes the Teacher's view of symbolic priesthood much further. The co-operation of priests and laymen in a single structure, and the war policy, represent the Teacher's Stage 1B. On the other hand, the sole control of the sons of Aaron over the property breaks down the Teacher's distinction of flesh and spirit, as does the use of the same ministers to give both baptism and the Spirit of holiness. The changes account for "began". The Teacher, from the later point of view, had begun to give the true doctrine and organisation, but it was corrected in the next stage (Cf. the parallel in CD 1:5-11, on the "blindness" of the stage preceding the Teacher).

* **Synthesis**

The stages following the Teacher are consistent with the historical hypothesis. The signs that the militarist faction had stayed in the Teacher's party after the schism are supported by the evidences of a new lay ministry appearing at least two years afer his death. The leader was a levitical priest, a supporter of lay equality; he was "zealous" for the military form of the future expectation. The rival party in Jerusalem, although also lay supporters, and having a military background, were still considered as opponents; this is consistent with their anti-ascetic views, unsuited to physical warfare. The Teacher's original point of view — spiritual warfare with eschatology; priestly supremacy; asceticism — is represented in a third group, including the writer of 1QpHab. The various elements in the previous history — priestly versus lay domination; spiritual versus physical warfare; asceticism versus a hellenizing view of the Law — are still apparent, but are found in new combinations.

The cause of the developments is, again, the central factor in the whole history, a Roman threat. As 1QpHab shows, the Romans had now made a new intrusion, "marching across the land" with a display of military strength. This led to the merger of two of the three parties which held themselves to continue the Teacher's tradition, their common ground being asceticism. The priestly group, as at the time of the formation of the Plant-root, sacrificed their preference for priestly supremacy and avoidance of aggressive war, and joined wih the militarist faction. The merger was facilitated by the action of some levitical priests, returning from the hellenizing party at the threat of war. There returned also one of the tribes, Benjamin, whose head may have been the leader of the lay militarist faction; they had come back during the Teacher's lifetime. Some of Judah had never gone over. A leading Zadokite, and a davidic member of Judah, joined the Law-Interpreter as future Messiahs of Aaron and Israel.

TABLE 4
Stages of the Schism

STAGE I(A). Before the schism

NORTH		SOUTH
Priestly-lay equality		Priestly supremacy
Physical warfare/spiritual warfare		Spiritual warfare
Messiah of Israel		Priestly Messiah (Teacher)
12 sons of Levi		12 sons of Zadok
12 heads of tribes	spiritual warfare	Sons of Aaron
12 śarîm	physical warfare	

STAGE I(B). After the schism

MESSIAH OF ISRAEL		TEACHER
Priestly-lay equality		Priestly-lay co-operation
Spiritual warfare		Physical warfare/ spiritual warfare
Anti-asceticism		Asceticism
12 sons of Levi		12 sons of Zadok
12 heads of tribes		Sons of Aaron
		12 śarîm
All tribes except part of Judah		Part of Judah

STAGE II

SCHISMATICS	LAW-INTERPETER	PRIESTLY PARTY
Priestly-lay equality	Priestly-lay co-operation	Priestly supremacy
Spiritual warfare	Physical warfare	Spiritual warfare
Anti-asceticism	Asceticism	Asceticism
12 sons of Levi	3 sons of Aaron	12 sons of Zadok
11 heads of tribes	12 former śarîm (lay ministers)	Sons of Aaron
All tribes except part of Judah, and Benjamin	Part of Judah Benjamin (Returnees)	

STAGE III

SCHISMATICS	COMMUNITY STAGE III	PRIESTLY PARTY
Priestly-lay equality	Priestly-lay co-operation	Priestly supremacy
Spiritual warfare	Physical warfare	Spiritual warfare
Anti-asceticism	Asceticism	Asceticism
	Chief Priest, son of Zadok, Messiah of Aaron	
	Warrior, śar of Judah, Messiah of Israel	
	Law-Interpreter, Prophet	
Remaining sons of Levi	Some sons of Zadok, Holy of Holies	Some sons of Zadok
11 heads of tribes	Some sons of Aaron, Holy House	Some sons of Aaron
	Some sons of Levi, former śarîm (lay ministers, perfectly holy men)	} House of yaḥad
All tribes except part of Judah, and Benjamin	Part of Judah Benjamin (Returnees)	

THE NEW COVENANT IN THE LAND OF DAMASCUS
The Sources

The sources used for the study of this period are: CD; 4Q*174* (4QFlor) with 4Q*177*, which are both parts of the same work;[55] and 4QpNah. Reasons will be given why they are to be grouped as follows:

PHASE I. The Law-Interpreter and the Warrior
4Q*174-7*
CD 7:10b *('ăšer katûb)* - 21a

PHASE II. The Law-Interpreter
CD 2:14 - 7:10a with 7:21b - 8-21 and ff. (missing in MS A)
20:1 - 13a
20:17b - 27a
10:10b - 12:22a

PHASE III. The Messiah of Aaron and Israel
4QpNah
CD 1:1 - 2:13
19:7b *(bèyad)* - 15a
19:32b (=8:18b) - 20:1
20:13b - 17a
20:27b - 34
15:1-15ff (completed in 4QD^a)
16:1-18
9:1 - 10:10a
12:22b - 14:22
4Q*266*[56]

The original order of columns of CD has been given by Milik,[57] on the basis of 4Q manuscripts (some not yet published). See pp.190, 196 below on the compilation of the above into the medieval MSS A and B, our main source of the text at present.

Phase 1, the Law-Interpreter and the Warrior, and
Phase II, the Law-Interpreter

4Q*174-7* is to be closely linked with CD, especially CD 7:10-21a. With this passage, it has in common: the restoration of the fallen tabernacle of David (4Q*174* 1:12-13, CD 7:16); the Law-Interpreter and the davidic leader as the only two leaders (4Q*174* 1:11,, 4Q*177* fr.10 - 11:5, CD

7:18-21); an exile (4Q*177* frs. 5-6:7-9 "will flee . . . like a sparrow from his place", cf. 1QH 4:8-9, the Teacher's exile drives him "like a bird from its nest"), and CD 7:10-14, Judah, the community, has been driven to the land of the north, parallel to the exile of 587 B.C. The Returnees of CD 4:2, 6:5, 8:16 are found in 4Q*174* fr.9-10:5. Both works rely heavily on the prophet Ezekiel.

According to CD 4:2-3 and 6:5, the members went out of the land of Judah into the land of Damascus. There is not the slightest indication that Damascus is symbolical.[58] The argument of CD 7:10-14 draws a parallel between three separate events of the OT period (the secession of Ephraim at the death of Solomon; the destruction of Ephraim in 721 B.C.; and the fall of Jerusalem in 587 B.C.) in order to "prove" that the southern party, Judah, are parallel to the OT Judah, and the secessionist party, Ephraim, are parallel to the OT Ephraim; in consequence, the present Ephraim are doomed to destruction. The present Judah are said to have gone to Damascus (15); in this they are like the OT Judah, who went to the land of the north (Babylon). As the argument is forced to conflate three events artificially, and draw a parallel between two different places, Babylon and Damascus, it loses all point if there was not a literal exile to the north by the present Judah.

Many of the regulations of CD are for members living in a Gentile environment, e.g., 12:6-11, including a law on selling animals and birds to Gentiles. This is a further sign that they were living in a literal Damascus.

The archaeological evidence does not preclude an exile of the leaders to Damascus and their permanent residence there from this point. Qumran was equipped as a scribal centre, and copies of CD and the other works from this period were found in the caves there. If it were retained as a publishing house, for the copying and distribution of the works sent from Damascus, the signs of occupation of the site by a large number, until its destruction in 68 A.D., would be the same as if the leaders were there.

Damascus was outside Palestinian territory. The Chief Priest, the first in rank of the three leaders in Stage III, is not present in 4Q*174-7*, although the sons of Zadok appear there (4Q*174* 1:17). The previous stage of the Community has been seen to be marked by intense political activity, with a plan for war against the Romans. This gives a sufficient reason for the exile to Damascus. The Chief Priest has suffered for his leadership of the army in the wilderness, and the remaining members have been driven into political exile. The new phase in Damascus is said to be connected with the rise of the schismatics in CD 5:20 - 6:3, but the statement that the "land was ravaged" as a result of their false teaching (5:21) gives a political reason indirectly. The phrase parallels 3:10, "their land was ravaged" ('*arṣam . . . šĕmamâ*), referring to the events of 587 B.C. Cf. the parallel drawn between Nebuchadnezzar and the ruler of Rome in CD 1:6 (p.55). There has been an attack by Rome, and the subsequent exile of the leaders gives an opportunity for the parallel with the events of 587.

The argument from the past exile of Judah implies that they will again return to Jerusalem and recover the temple. The hope that has inspired the movement since before the formation of the Plant-root has not yet been abandoned. 4Q*174* 1:1-7 describes the temple that will be built in the Future Time, referring, very probably, to 11QT: "the house which [. . .] in the Future Time, as it is written in the book of [. . .] the sanctuary, O Lord, which thy hands have established". Cf.11QT 29:9: "I myself will create my sanctuary". It will not suffer the same fate as the temple of 587 B.C. ("strangers shall not again make it desolate as they desolated formerly the sanctuary of Israel", 5-6). It is emphasized that it is "a human sanctuary *(miqdaš 'adam)* in which offerings *(maqtîrîm)* will be made". The emphasis may imply an opposite point of view of a spiritual temple only, consistent with the outlook of Diaspora Jews.

4Q*174-7* and the parts of CD listed under Phases I and II above, contain organisational similarities, yet differences. Their common features are:
(a) There are two leaders only, the Law-Interpreter and the davidic Warrior. CD 7:18-21 presents the Star and Sceptre prophecy in such a way as to make it clear that the Star, placed before the quotation, is different from the Sceptre, placed after it. The Law-Interpreter is the priestly Star, as he is a levitical priest. 4Q*177* frs.10-11:5 reads: "the Law-Interpreter, for there is no [. . .]". It may mean that in the absence of the Chief Priest, the Law-Interpreter has been forced to adopt the role of supreme priestly leader. The Warrior becomes the Sceptre only, as the lay leader. This supports the suggestion of p.177 that he was the *śar* of Judah, not the head of Judah. The tribal head was also a levitical priest, and could not so easily give up his priesthood, whereas the *śarîm* had simply been given priestly functions.

(b) The Elect of Israel as ministers of the Future Time. CD 4:3-4: "the Elect Ones of Israel . . . who will stand up in the Future Time"; 4Q*174* 1:19, "the Elect Ones of Israel in the Future Time". In Stage II, the Law-Interpreter had appointed the twelve lay ministers (former *śarîm*) as Elect

Ones, together with the three sons of Aaron (p.168). In Stage III, they had been separated from the sons of Aaron and put into the House of *yaḥad*, probably with the sons of Levi (pp.174-5). They were called the "perfectly holy men"; there are rules for perfectly holy men in CD 20: 1-8; cf. also 7:4-5. The lay ministers have come to Damascus.

The differences are:

(a) The presence of literal sons of Zadok in 4Q*174* 1:17, their absence in CD. In CD 4:3 the Elect Ones of Israel are called "sons of Zadok", using the term symbolically, as is shown by the fact that all the elements in Ezek 44:15, interpreted in this passage, are understood symbolically (below p.184). The symbolic use of the term, for the same Elect Ones, is also found in 1QS 9:14 (p.168).

(b) The use of *yaḥad*, "Community", and Council of the Community, in 4Q*174* (1:17) and 4Q*177* fr.3-6:16; and its complete absence from CD.

(c) The use of "sons of Light" in 4Q*174* 1:8-9, 4Q*177* fr.10-11:7, its complete absence from CD.

These are significant omissions. 4Q*174-7* clearly represents a continuation from Stage III, except for the loss of the Chief Priest, but between its writing and that of CD something has occurred to cause the series of omissions.

The term *yaḥad,* and the name "sons of Light" are both bound up with the presence of literal priests. The *yaḥad* consisted in the commonality of priests and laymen, each in their own *yaḥad* (pp.139-41). If the loss of the sons of Zadok noted above (a) meant also the loss of all literal priests, there could be no *yaḥad*. Nor could there be any "sons of Light", as this name was given to the laity when a symbolic priesthood was bestowed on them by those possessing literal priesthood (p.129). The differences between 4Q*174-7* and CD all indicate a complete exodus of priests after the arrival at Damascus.

This is confirmed by the information concerning the First Ones, *hari'šônîm).* CD 3:20 - 4:10 reads:

> As God determined for them through the prophet Ezekiel, saying: "The priests, the levites and the sons of Zadok, who kept the charge of my sanctuary when the sons of Israel went astray from me, they shall offer me fat and blood" (Ezek 44:15). The "priests" are the Returnees of Israel, who went out of the land of Judah. And "those who joined" *(hannilwîm,* play on *lĕwîyîm;* proselytes, p.99) are with them as "levites". The "sons of Zadok" are the Elect Ones of Israel, men called by a name, who will stand up in the Future Time. Here

is a list of their names, their genealogies, the period of their holding office, and the number of their sufferings; the years of their sojournings and the list of their works. (The list is omitted by the medieval copyist). . . . the holy one (last word in the list). They are the First Ones[59] for whom God atoned, and they justified the righteous and condemned the wicked. All who come after them are to do according to the exact interpretation of the Law by which the First Ones were disciplined, until the completion of the Period of these years.

8:14-18 also contains the doctrine of the First Ones:

As Moses said, "It is not because of your righteousness and the uprightness of your heart that you come to inherit these Gentiles *(haggoyîm),* but because of his (God's) love to your fathers, and his keeping the oath" (Deut 9:5, 7:8). This is the law for the Returnees of Israel, who departed from the way of the people. Because of the love of God for the First Ones who testified after him, so he loves those who come after them, for theirs is the Covenant of the fathers.

The first passage argues that Ezekiel meant symbolic priests only. He spoke of two grades: sons of Zadok, and ordinary supreme priests, sons of Aaron (also levites, see below). These two grades are represented by the two ranks of lay leaders now present in the community. The higher rank are the Elect Ones of Israel, the perfectly holy men, the lay ministers, who now give the Spirit of holiness and baptize (p.173). In 9:14 the Law-Interpreter had called them symbolic sons of Zadok/righteousness (p.168). They do not include the sons of Levi, who may have been grouped with them in the House of the *yaḥad* in Stage III. If sons of Levi were present, the name *yaḥad* could still be used.

The lower rank are the Returnees of Israel, the leaders of the tribe of Benjamin. According to 6:6, God called all the Returnees *śarîm.* They are distinguished in that passage from the "nobles of the people" *(nĕdîbê ha'am,* from Num 21:18), who are grouped with the Law-Interpreter as the higher rank. This means that the second rank of laymen, the leaders of Benjamin (see below on the tribe of Judah) have been promoted to *śarîm,* to take the place of the perfectly holy men, former *śarîm. (Śarîm* always means the second rank of lay leaders). As subordinates to the perfectly holy men or Elect Ones, they are the equivalent of Ezekiel's "priests". They have the symbolic priesthood of all laymen.

All of these symbolic priests are First Ones (3:20 -4:10). CD 8:14-18 deals with the Returnees as First Ones; they correspond to the OT fathers.

This argument would be made necessary by the loss of all literal priests. As the first rank in the community, they held the authority. The messianic doctrine implies a theory of succession, at least before the Future Time:

the heavenly spirit entered into each successive high priest, and similarly into other priests. The lay ministers are now given the succession because they are First Ones. They had been present in the Community from the time of the Teacher, the perfectly holy men as the *śarîm,* and the leaders of Benjamin as members of the laity. They have now received the Covenant of the OT fathers, having retained the succession from them.

At the end of 8:14-18, the succession is denied to the schismatics: "God hates the Wall-builders" (8:18b). They were in a position to make a similar claim, as their lay-levitical leaders had also been among the first members.

Both passages speak of "those who come after (the First Ones)" to show that they form a continuing succession. See below pp.188-9 on "those who come after". This doctrine fully supports the evidence of the loss of all priests.

The loss of the priests is a further reason why the Star and Sceptre can no longer be combined in a single person (p.182). The combination had been an expression of the theory of the *yaḥad.*

The presence of all the leaders of Benjamin in Damascus ("God called them all *śarîm,* 6:6), together with their original *śar,* one of the perfectly holy men, meant that anyone born in the tribe of Benjamin who wished to be baptized into the whole community (still not finally separated from the schismatic party (p.175), must enter into the Damascus party.

Further evidence shows the next event in the history. After the argument for the First Ones in 3:20-4:10, the passage continues: "During *(bẽ)* the completion of the Period, according to the number of these years, there is no more joining the House of Judah, but everyone stands upon his watchtower. 'The wall is built, the decree/bound is far' ". 8:3-13 declares that "the *śarîm* of Judah have become *(hayû)* those upon whom fury is poured out . . . All are rebels, who have not departed from the way of the Traitors". Their actions are compared, point by point, with the list of virtues expected of the members of the Damascus community, set out in 6:11 - 7:9 (see ch. IX, note 14). They are Wall-builders (8:12). In 6:7 the Law-Interpreter is declared to be the Staff *(mĕḥôqeq),* a name for the davidic leader in 4QPB (p.136). In the descriptions of the ministry of 3:20 - 4:10 and 6:3-10 there is no place for the leaders of Judah: the second rank are only Returnees, Benjamin. These are indications that the remainder of the tribe of Judah has now gone over to the schismatic party, to be reunited with their separated brethren who had joined it at the time of the schism. With them has gone their leader, the Warrior, the *sar* of Judah, and his subordinate *sarîm*, leaving the Law-Interpreter to act as the Staff, the davidic leader. It is consequently no longer possible for anyone to be baptized into the tribe of Judah ("there is no more joining the House of Judah"); it is forbidden by the Damascus party. Its membership list is complete: "the wall is built" (cf. p.151 on "wall-building" as proselytisation).

The pressure upon the remainder of Judah to go over may be the subject of 4Q*174* fr. 4:4: "Belial shall open [. . .] to the House of Judah hard things, to have enmity against them [. . .] and shall seek with all his strength to scatter them".

The Simple of Judah, eastern Diaspora Jews and proselytes, were attached to Judah (pp.159-60), the Simple of Ephraim, other proselytes, would have exerted pressure upon them.

4QpNah 2:8-9 reads: "(The schismatics) will lead many astray; kings, *sarîm*, priests and people together with the proselytes *(ger nilweh)"*. The list accounts for the loss of the literal priests, the Warrior (a future king), the *sarîm* of Judah and their tribal members, and the Simple of Judah. Both the literal priests and all connected with Judah had changed their allegiance after the arrival in Damascus. The priests went first; cf. the presence of the Warrior in one passage of CD (7:10-21a).

4QpNah also shows that the rival party are still established in Jerusalem, which they have made "the city of Ephraim" (2:2).

What was the reason for the change of sides of the priests and the remainder of Judah? The motive of the priests is readily understood. They had traditionally been opposed to aggressive war, and had allied themselves with an army only when an invasion of the Romans had forced them into it, as at the formation of the Plant-root and of Stage III of the Community. With the exile to Damascus and the new frustration of military hopes, they had reason to return to the anti-military party in Jerusalem. The pro-Gentile outlook of this group, reflected in their hellenizing view of the Law, removed any enthusiasm for physical warfare against the Romans, while giving them a motive for continuing the Teacher's policy of proselytisation. Their lay outlook was not rigorous, as the leader had adopted the high priestly role. The priests differed from them only on the question of asceticism, and some compromise may have been reached on this point.

It is more difficult to account for the change of allegiance of the remainder of Judah, led by the Warrior. They had not left at the same time as the priests, but later. They were militarists, and were presumably the "men of war *('anšê hammilḥamâ)* who returned *(šabû,* changed allegiance) with the Man of a Lie" of CD 20:14-15. Apart from the failure of the war plan, there are no indications in the texts of the reason for their change from a military to a non-military point of view.

4QpNah 1-9 - 2:1, describing the followers of the rival leader (who is taken to be the subject of Nah 2:14) speaks of his "warrior bands" "w[ho are in Jerusal]em" (1.10) and also his "messengers", whose "voice is heard among the Gentiles" (2:1). The latter sentence is consistent with a proselytising programme. The former would be consistent with the Teacher's view of spiritual warfare; he had given a symbolic or spiritual meaning to other military expressions, e.g., "volunteers". The "warrior bands" may be understood as "soldiers" of the truth, missionaries.

Following the loss of the remainder of Judah, the Law-Interpreter had now only the tribe of Benjamin with which to make war, and no Warrior to lead. This accounts for the emphasis on teaching in the passages reflecting the loss of Judah. In 6:3-11, "he who teaches righteousness" *(yôreh haṣṣedeq)* will stand up in the Future Time. He is the Law-Interpreter, named as the only leader in 6:9 (now called the Staff, p.185). The Well of Living Waters, "dug" in Damascus (3:16, 8:34) by the baptizing ministry, is "the Law" (6:4). The leaders of Benjamin are all promoted because they "sought" (root *daraš); cf.* the role of their leader, the Law-Interpreter *(dôreš hattôrâ).* In Stage II, he had established the Way both as a community for the study of the Law, and as an ascetic discipline for warfare (p.169). The former purpose is now given new emphasis. The name "the Way" was used in Stage II to reflect both purposes (p.169), and was still used in the Damascus era, cf. CD 1:13, "those who depart from the way/Way".

The remaining evidence for Phase II of the Damascus sojourn shows a new development, consistent with the Law-giver's introduction of a lay ministry in Stage II of the Community. In 5: 16-20, following a history of the Remnant, showing its progressive narrowing from the beginning of OT history (2:14 - 3:12), and the establishment of the present Remnant on the basis of the true calendar (3:12b-16a), the text continues:

They dug a Well of many waters, and those who despise it (the schismatics, cf. 7:9) shall not live. They wallowed in human sin *(hem hitgôlĕlû bĕpeša' 'ĕnôš),* in the ways of uncleanness, and they said: 'It is ours' *(lanû hî).* God, in his marvellous mysteries, atoned for their sin and forgave their wrongdoing, and built for them a sure house *(bayit ne'ĕman)* in Israel, such as there has not been from the Former Times *(millepanîm,* OT times, p.28) and up till now. Those who cleave to it will have eternal life, and all the glory of Adam/ a man will be theirs.

There is grammatical continuity between "they dug" in the first sentence and "they wallowed" in the second. The second sentence, however, hardly seems to refer to the leaders who dug the Well, and for this reason it has been taken as an interpolation, inserted at the expense of the meaning.[60] The expression "It is ours" is from Ezek 11:15, the words of the Jews in Palestine who claimed that they had the rights over the land that had been lost by the exiled Jews in Babylon. The sentence contrasts a Palestinian point of view with that of the leaders in Damascus, whose situation is likened to the Babylonian exile in many parts of CD. The structure of the paragraph makes it possible to see its meaning as follows: "The true community was established in Damascus (cf. 6:3-5, "they dug the Well . . . in Damascus"). It contained, however, a Palestinian point of view, denying privileges to the Damascus membership. God corrected their error and established for them a new kind of "temple" ("sure house", 1 Sam 2:35), of a different kind from that in the OT period, and also from that held in the community up to now". It refers to a radical change in the ministerial structure. The intensity of the expression "they wallowed in human sin" is designed to support the innovation.

The paragraph is then constructed to form a parallel with the history of the original Community, as set out in 1:5-11: the Plant-root was founded; there was a period of error; then the error was corrected by the Teacher. Cf. also 1QS 9:10 (pp.177-8).

In 3:20 - 4:4, in the list of leaders who correspond to Ezekiel's faithful "priests, levites and sons of Zadok" (p.184) the "levites" are "those who joined", that is, the proselytes (p.99). They are grouped with the two kinds of lay ministers as their third rank (levites). In both passages on the First Ones (p.184), "those who come after" are named as inheriting the succession from them. The First Ones are the two ranks of lay ministers of 3:20 - 4:4. 20:8-9 gives rules for the First Ones and the Last Ones ("Every Despiser *(kol hammo'es,* used absolutely for the schismatics in 7:9) among the First Ones and Last Ones *(bari'šônîm ûba'-aḥărônîm)* who sets idols on his heart . . ."). It is a warning to members of this group not to go over to the rival party. They belong to the House of the Law, from which they will be expelled if they show sympathy with the other party. The name "House of the Law" reflects the Law-Interpreter's interests.

The Last Ones may be suggested to be Diaspora Jews and proselytes, "those who joined", who are now admitted to the ministerial ranks. They had previously formed the class of the Simple, who had been denied such privileges, while the centre was in Palestine. The Palestinians had said "It is ours". But as the community, the Well, was now established in the Diaspora, it was no longer possible to maintain this exclusive attitude. New members were coming in from these sources, and, as the ministers were fully lay, there was no reason why the new members should not be admitted to the ministry. This arrangement was different from the rules of membership of both the OT period and the previous Community. The Law-Interpreter, however, who had already made innovations with his lay ministry, held that it was a true "temple", a "sure house in Israel". The First Ones formed the equivalent of the upper House, the Holy of Holies, while the Last Ones formed the equivalent of the Holy House. As there was no longer a *yaḥad,* these terms could not be used, but the structure was maintained. The expression "Last Ones" reflects the "last priests" of the Teacher's Community, the levitical Holy House.

In order to support the development, the Law-Interpreter had available to him the Teacher's theory of the New Covenant, which denied the privilege given by Jewish birth. The name "New Covenant in the Land of Damascus" is the most frequent one for the community (6:19, 8:21, 20:12).

In consequence of the change, it was hoped that Peleg, western Diaspora Jews who had gone over to the rivals because of their hellenizing viewpoint (pp.156-60) would come back. CD 20:22-25 sets out the conditions for their return. They will be admitted back into the Holy Council, that is, have the status of fully initiated members, as there is no bar now to their full initiation and progress towards promotion.

A distinction is made between those born Jews, and proselytes, on the ritual law. Members now included Palestinians: the Law-Interpreter himself, the perfectly holy men, and the *śarîm* of Benjamin . Members of the tribe of Benjamin may still have been living in Palestine, receiving their direction from Damascus. CD 10:10b - 12:22a contains directions on ritual law which include a reference to the *maśkîl* (12:21), using an almost identical phrase to that which introduces him in 1QS 9:12. *Maśkîl* is another name for the Law-Interpreter (p.169). All members must observe water purifications and the sabbath (10:10b - 12:6a), but other laws of uncleanness (12:6-18) are to be kept only by those born Jews, "the seed of Israel", including the *maśkîl* himself (12:20-22). They are also to be kept by those in the cities of Israel (12:19).

The Law-Interpreter's "temple" of laymen, Diaspora Jews and proselytes would have little chance of being accepted as the priesthood of a recovered Jerusalem temple. Its development would be encouraged by the worsening political situation, illustrated in 4QpNah. It was believed that Jerusalem was going to be destroyed (2:4-6) and the whole land devastated (4:3-6, Manasseh also will fall to the Gentiles). There was little hope of the survival of the temple, and every reason for developing a permanent symbolic temple outside Palestine. The image of "Israel in the wilderness", found in connection with the Well in CD 6:3-4, is consistent with the loss of hope of the restoration to the homeland. In consequence, there was no reason for support of the literal temple. The rules which formerly enjoined limited attendance only at the temple, without participation in the sacrifices, are now repeated for the New Covenant in Damascus. The first rule in the new code (6:11 - 7:9) forbids members to enter the temple and participate in the sacrifices ("light his altar"). 11:17-21 allows Palestinian members to make a sabbath offering only, and also allows the sending of offerings to the altar, provided that the messenger is clean. If no messenger is available, prayers will be a sufficient alternative offering.[61] Those in Palestine were no better off than those in Damascus, who offered prayers as a full substitute for temple attendance. The passage includes rules for attendance at the local houses of worship *(bêt hiśtaḥăwôt,* 11:21-22), where God may be worshipped by prayer alone.

.It would appear that the Law-Interpreter now compiled a document with the following contents:

(i) History. 2:14 - 6:11a. It contained (a) 2:14 - 4:12a, an account of the history, from OT times to the removal to Damascus, written to deal with the loss of the priests and the House of Judah; (b) 4:12b - 5:19, an independent document on the sins of the schismatics; (c) 5:20 - 6:11a, an account of the history of the move to Damascus, written to deal with the loss of the Warrior.

(ii) Laws of the New Covenant in Damascus: (a) 6:11b - 7:9a, rules of the New Covenant; (b) condemnation of those breaking the rules and going over to the rival party: 7:9b *(wĕkol hammo'ăsîm)* - 8:21ff, missing in MS A, and 20:1-13a, 17b-27a. Into the first of these was inserted 7:10b *('ăśer katûb)* - 21a, written while the Warrior was still present.

190

The Reconstruction

(iii) Additional laws: 10:10b - 12:22a.
This document is not extant. See further p.196.

* Synthesis

An exile in Damascus, the subject of CD, is readily linked with the military activity of the previous stage, and with the central factor in the history, the Roman threat. The plans for war had again been frustrated by the greater power of Rome. The loss of the priests to the rival party in Jerusalem, occurring shortly after the exile, is also consistent with their previous history: they now reverted to their traditional avoidance of war. The development in Damascus of a new theory of succession of the lay ministry was necessitated by the loss of the priests, who held the succession from the Teacher. A new ministry including Diaspora Jews and proselytes was also developed as an extension of the existing lay ministry, to attract back the followers of the rival party, and in response to the conviction that the temple was about to be destroyed. After the loss of the priests and the remaining part of Judah (the change of allegiance of the latter being unaccounted for), the Damascus group was led by the Law-Interpreter alone. It was still called "the Way".

Phase III. The Messiah of Aaron and Israel

In CD 19:7-15, 19:32 - 20:1, 20:14-17 and 12:22 - 14:22, the leader of the community is called "the Messiah of Aaron and Israel". That there is continuity with the previous phase is shown by the use of "Well of Living Waters" in 19:33-34. The Law-Interpreter was not a Messiah, and was not of Aaron.

In 12:22-14:22, 15:1-15ff, 16:1-17, 9:1-10:10a, the ministry includes priests (sons of Aaron, 13:2, cf. p.98), levites (14: 4, 5) and *mĕbaqqĕrîm*. Judges are from Levi and Aaron (10:4).

20:13b-17 gives the clue to these changes.

"From the day of the gathering in of the Teacher of the Community (*hayyaḥid*, see below pp.195-6) until the destruction of all the men of war who returned (changed allegiance) with the Man of a Lie, there are forty years. In that Period the wrath of God shall be kindled against Israel, as he said: 'There is no king, no *śar*, no judge, and none who rebukes in righteousness' ".

In the documents of the Law-Interpreter, there is little reference to the Teacher of Righteousness. The Law-Interpreter will himself be "he who teaches righteousness" (6:11). The ministry listed above is identical

191

with that of the Teacher, including the characteristic *mĕbaqqĕrîm*. *There has been a return to the organisational features of the Teacher,* from which the Law-Interpreter's lay ministry marked a considerable departure.

It is announced that in the period since the death of the Teacher there has been no lay leader of any kind. The absence of a king and a *śar* is attributable to the change of allegiance of the Warrior and the *śarîm* of Judah, referred to in the first sentence. But the statement that there has been no judge, and none to rebuke in righteousness, means that there has been no lay leader of any kind since the Teacher's death. Yet these documents are certainly from the Damascus period: cf. "the New Covenant in the land of Damascus" (19:34). The statement denies the existence of the lay leaders of Phases I and II in order to expunge them from the record. A new leadership and policy has taken over, quite different from the previous one, and has expelled the Law-Interpreter.

A full priesthood has now been restored, under a Messiah who includes Aaron. He is a supreme priest, who will reign over the whole community, including laymen. At the time of Stages II and III, there was reason for seeing three parties in the community (p.177): one standing for priestly supremacy and eschatology, continuing the outlook of the Teacher; and two others standing for priestly-lay equality or co-operation, divided by their views on asceticism (the schismatics, and the Law-Interpreter's party). It appears that the first has now taken control in Damascus. The reason may again be connected with the political situation. An increasing fear of war would lead to the flight from Palestine of the priestly party, and to the return there of the Law-Interpreter, who had always held a military policy. The anti-war stance of the priestly party would lead to a rejection of the authority of the previous lay leadership, both the Law-Interpreter, and the "men of war" who had gone over to the Jerusalem group.

The identity of the Messiah of Aaron and Israel may be discussed in connection with his future expectation. In 19:7b-15a a new passage appears in the Rules for the New Covenant, in place of 7:10b-21a, which deals with the Warrior and the Law-Interpreter (in MS B, see further below p.196).[62] The context is the same: it concerns the punishment of the Despisers, the schismatics, "when God visits the land" (7:9, 19:6). In the new passage, "Visitation" *(pequddâ)* appears as a noun, and refers to the future, as in the Teacher's usage (1QS 4:18-19), whereas in the first version, the noun referred to the fall of Jerusalem in 587 B.C. It now refers to a future fall of Jerusalem:

192

"These (the faithful) will escape in the Period of Visitation, but those who remain (play on 'Remnant') will be given up to the sword, when the Messiah of Aaron and Israel comes. (It will be) as it was in the Period of the first Visitation, of which he said through Ezekiel: 'They shall put a Taw (X in the archaic script) on the foreheads of those who sigh and groan', but those who remained (in the city) were given up to the avenging sword of the Covenant (19:10-13).

The Teacher's Visitation is now identified with the coming fall of Jerusalem. The schismatics, former members of the Remnant, will remain in Jerusalem, their headquarters, and, like those who remained in 587 B.C., will be given up to the sword. The faithful members of the community, who have escaped from the city, are under God's protection. The destruction of the rival party is dwelt on in 4QpNah 2:4-6: "There shall not depart from the midst of their congregation the Gentile sword . . . and a multitude of guilty corpses shall fall in their days".

The Teacher's eschatology, the expectation of a divine intervention at the Visitation, has been adjusted to a Visitation in the form of a catastrophic fall of the city. Its supernatural dimension has been lost: there will be no meeting of heaven and earth. It is a compromise between the plan for victory by human warfare of the Law-Interpreter's party, and the Teacher's view of a catastrophe brought about by divine initiative.

4QpNah 3:4-5 predicts that "when the glory of Judah is revealed" the Simple of Ephraim will flee from the *qahal* of the rival party and join themselves to Israel, the true party. CD 20:14 speaks of the destruction of all the men of war who went over to the rivals (the remainder of Judah, above pp.185-7). These passages show that the Messiah of Aaron and Israel regards the Visitation as the means of destroying all false teachers, not as a destruction of all wicked men, such as the Romans. With the loss of the supernatural dimension, he has reduced the scale of the Teacher's expectation, but retains the element of victory over falsehood, contained in the Teacher's view of spiritual warfare.

The Messiah of Aaron and Israel is, then, much closer to the Teacher than was the Law-Interpreter. As a priestly leader, he is a member of the third, priestly party. This group was first discerned in 1QpHab (pp.170-1); it was struggling then to uphold the Teacher's eschatology, in the face of a chronological disappointment. A further adjustment in the Teacher's eschatology has now been made, while his views on priestly supremacy and spiritual warfare are upheld. The Messiah of Aaron and Israel may perhaps be the same as the writer of 1QpHab, who has now made a further adaptation, or he may be another member of his school. He is responsible for 4QpNah, from this period, and there may therefore be one indication that he is different: these two writings have different views on the legality of the crucifixion of the rival leader, as noted pp.164-5. As he is a potential priestly Messiah, he is one of the sons of Zadok, one of those who did not go over to Stage III of the Community with the Chief Priest.

The prophecy of the 390 years now finds its place. It is in CD 1:5-11, in one of the two sections of the Admonition of CD which give importance to the historical Teacher, and may therefore be attributed to the Messiah of Aaron and Israel (1:1-2:1, 2:2-13). It has been suggested pp.55-6 that this prophecy comes from a time when the Teacher's eschatology had been given up, but there was an expectation of coming great suffering from the Romans. The new priestly leader expects that Jerusalem will be destroyed by the Romans at a modified Visitation, but that they will then dominate Palestine (or the world) for 390 years, the figure supplied by Ezek 4:5. The starting-point had been the foundation of the Plant-root, a coalition formed for military purposes, against the customary viewpoint of the priestly party. The implication is probably that the false military doctrine had been a cause of the imposition of the Roman power.

The other problem raised by our interpretation of CD 1:5-11, that it supposes the use of the conventions of the *pesharim*, as against the usages of most of CD (p.55), is met by the link between the Messiah of Aaron and Israel and the writer of 1QpHab. Most of the Admonition of CD (2: 14 - 8:21) comes from the Law-Interpreter (see p.190-1), whose use of a more allegorical approach (for example, "the Well is the Law," 6:4) is another point of difference from the priestly party of the Teacher. The *pesher* method is attributed to the Teacher in 1QpHab 7:1-4.

The forty years of CD 20:14, between the death of the Teacher and the fall of Jerusalem, is clearly part of a chronological scheme, and to be linked in some way with the forty years' plan of 1QM 2:6-16. Did the priestly party plan for a forty years' campaign of proselytisation, as a spiritual substitute for the war plan? If so, a new forty years must have commenced in the time of the Teacher, twenty years or more after the original one. In any case, the Messiah of Aaron and Israel holds that he is living in a certain pre-determined forty years, and that at its end the Visitation, in the form of the destruction of the city and of the rival party, will occur. It is dated from the death of the Teacher of Righteousness. If it is also the date of the beginning of a campaign of spiritual warfare, then the Teacher died at the beginning of the campaign. There is unfortunately not sufficient evidence to clarify these problems. The likelihood of constant adjustments to the scheme following disappointments, together with the reticence of the texts as a consequence of these manoeuvres, mean that care must be exercised in forming a hypothesis concerning the chronology. It may be remarked, however, that some connection with the end of the 490 years of 11QMelch 7 should be considered, as this piece contains the Teacher's high priestly doctrine.

The loyalty of the new leader to the Teacher is shown in 20:27b-34. Members are to be "disciplined by the first laws by which the men of the Community were judged" (20:31-32). The leaders of Stage III had also claimed continuity with the Teacher, in 1QS 9:10, but with the addition of "began", allowing for their innovations (pp.177-8). But members are now to "obey the voice of the Teacher" (20:28, 32), following his policy alone. In these lines and 20:15, the writer seems to speak as if both the Teacher and the Man of a Lie were still present; this may be compared with 1QpHab 12:5, predicting the destruction of the rival leader after he is already dead; their present influence is equated with their presence.

The new leader does not re-introduce the term *yaḥad,* which is not found as a present name in his documents. It had stood for the union of priests and laity in a commonality of authority and property, and had ceased to be used when all the priests left (p.183). He now has priests and *mĕbaqqĕrîm* to form a bridging class, but does not re-introduce the term. Consequently, he can rule as Messiah of both Aaron and Israel, as the two Messiahs do not need to be kept apart, each over his own *yaḥad.* As Aaron is superior to Israel, and all higher ranks incorporate lower ranks, Israel is included in his domain.

The reason, apart from the need for a single leader only, is that he has retained in his organisation the lay ministry of First Ones and Last Ones, as is shown by the retention of the rules concerning them in the columns containing his laws (19-20). The conditions of Damascus make it appropriate to continue the lay "temple", with the addition of the priests and levites who have come with him from Palestine. They are to rule (13:3) and perform ritual duties (13:5). The lay ministers may perhaps be the judges who are prominent in his legislation (9:9-10, 9:23-10:1, 10:4).

The name "the Community" is found for the Teacher's stage in 20:1, 14, 32. The spelling in the medieval MS is *yaḥîd,* usually meaning "Only One". It may be original, and be an attempt to revise the original doctrine, in order to support a single Messiahship: the Teacher also had been an Only One. The Messiah of Israel is excised from the history, like the lay leadership of Phases I and II.

According to the evidence of MSS A and B and what is known of the Cave 4 fragments of CD, and in the light of the above, the Messiah of Aaron and Israel now revised the document of the Law-Interpreter (pp.190-1) by inserting 19:7b-15a in the Rules for the New Covenant in place of 7:10b-21a (to remove all references to the Warrior), revising also the passage beginning 8:18b and substituting 19:32b - 20:1, inserting 20:13b-17a and completing the Rules of the New Covenant with 20:27b-34. At the beginning of the History he added the history of the Teacher, neglected by the Law-Interpreter: 1:1 - 2:13 (also, possibly, columns preceding 1:1, found in Cave 4 copies). A large number of additional rules were added to the third section. His version is represented by MS B. Subsequently, his version was revised to include the earliest piece, on the Warrior, 7:10b-21a, and the passage beginning 8:18b, so as to give MS A, a complete record of the Damascus period.

* Synthesis

The final phase of the Damascus sojourn reflects an intensification of the threat from Rome, leading to an expectation of the imminent destruction of Jerusalem and devastation of Palestine. The third, priestly party, who repudiated warfare, now gained control in Damascus, expelling the lay militaristic group. They brought with them priests and levites, who had probably fled Palestine because of the coming war. The new leadership was by those priests who had never renounced asceticism and a rigorous view of the Law; they held almost the whole of the Teacher's doctrine, except that the cosmic element in his eschatology was removed. The Jerusalem party was still opposed by them on account of its hellenizing views, and it was expected and hoped in Damascus that the destruction of Jerusalem would bring about their total extermination. The Teacher's organisation was restored, except for the priestly-lay *yaḥad*. The new lay ministry was retained. There was only one priestly-lay leader, who used the title "Messiah of Aaron and Israel".

SUBSEQUENT HISTORY

Whatever the date in the Roman period of the history derived from the analysis of organisational terms (see next chapter), there can be little doubt that the final episode, for some of the members, took place on the plateau of Masada in 73 A.D. Fragments of Qumran writings were found there,[63] showing the presence of members of the community among the 960 Zealots who committed suicide when it was known that their long campaign against the Romans had failed. The presence of a military faction in the community, aiming at the overthrow of the Romans by physical war, has been traced from the foundation of the Plant-root to the final expulsion of the Law-Interpreter. The Law-Interpreter had declared himself to be a man "zealous *(mèqanne')* for the decree, and his time is for the Day of Vengeance" (1QS 9:10). Either he or his successors were present on that final day, to bring to an end the history of one of the three parties in the community that had for so long planned to recover the temple and the Jewish state.

NOTES

1. On levites in this and later sources, see further my forthcoming study *"Mĕbaqqer* and *Episkopos* in the Light of the Temple Scroll".

2. See *Mĕgillat-hammiqdaš*, I, p.195.

3. The word *hallĕwiyim,* the last word in the line, was in the original phrase, not *lewi,* as the article has not been added later.

4. R. Abba, "Priests and Levites in Deuteronomy", *VT* 27 (1977), 257-267; "Priests and Levites in Ezekiel", *VT* 28 (1978), 1-9. On Deut. 18:1-8, Abba concludes that there are "no adequate grounds for denying the possibility of *kol-šebet lewi* designating a larger group including *hakkohǎnim hallĕwiyim* in 18:1, and some evidence to support this interpretation". ("Priests and Levites in Deuteronomy", 263-4.)

5. Like 11QT, it is in the form of a biblical book (a divine revelation to Moses), and sets out rules for the true cult, drawing on the calendar and chronology depending on the number seven (3:1, 10). Like 11QT and 1QM 2-9, it is lacking in the distinctive doctrines of the period of the Teacher of Righteousness.

6. Despite the cogency of his demonstration of the divisions and order of 1QM, P. R. Davies (*1QM, The War Scroll . . .,* 25-26) misunderstands the significance of 2:1-6, on the temple arrangements. He believes that it describes the temple service during the sabbatical years of the war, reading in this sense 2:6: "all these things shall be arranged in the season of the year of release (the seventh year)". He is then forced to speculate on the programme for the first six years, as the extant columns describe

only the last thirty-three years. The meaning is that the first six years of the war will be devoted to the recovery of the temple (Davies agrees p. 28 that "the occupation of the Temple is one of the objectives of this phase of the war; at the outset of hostilities the Temple is perhaps in improper hands"). In the seventh year of that phase, the first sabbatical year only, the temple service will be restored according to the views of the writers, and will operate continuously from that point.

7. S. Talmon ("The Calendar Reckoning of the Sect from the Judaean Desert", *Scripta Hierosolymitana* IV, Jerusalem), followed by Leaney (*The Rule of Qumran* . . ., 91-107) holds that the twenty-six heads of *mišmerot* here are the sect's version of the twenty-four heads of divisions of 1 Chr 24:7-18, found also in the sectarian *Book of the Priestly Courses;* the number is altered from that of 1 Chr to conform to the solar calendar of fifty-two weeks.

Milik, howevei, has now supported his view (*Ten Years* . . ., 107-9) that the sectarian temple roster contained only twenty-four with further fragments from the calendars of 4Q (*The Books of Enoch. Aramaic Fragments of Qumran Cave 4*, Oxford: Clarendon, 1976). The twenty-four were used in a six-year cycle, not a one-year cycle, as Talmon assumes (52 × 6 = 312 weeks, 24 × 13 = 312). The 4QS^b piece dealing with the Signs of the fourth jubilee establishes that the temple roster was divided into a series of triennia, i.e. that a six-year cycle was maintained.

The difference between the term *mišmerot* used here, and *maḥlĕqot* in 1 Chr 24:1, may perhaps be seen to suggest that the twenty-six had a different function. 1QM 2:4 lists the various feasts and sabbaths on which they are to "stand" (*hityaṣṣeb*), followed by "every day of the year". This may mean that they formed a yearly roster for purposes of prayer at all hours of the day as well as at the feasts, while there was also a roster of twenty-four for weekly temple service.

8. Davies (*1QM, The War Scroll* . . ., 26) reads the passage as giving three sets of twenty-six, priests, levites, and laymen, because of the three uses of the term. But each of the three uses shows that the tweny-six are priests: 1.2 places them after the chief priests and before the levites; 1.3 places them before the heads of tribes and levites (fathers); 1.4 gives them the duties of priests. There is one group, whose different aspects are described.

9. After *'anšê haššem* the scribe has written *yiktobu*, which has been deleted as an error. In 2:6-7, the *'anšê haššem* are distinguished from the *ra'šê 'ăbot ha'edâ*. The sense in 3:4 requires "and" after *'anšê haššem*.

10. In the lacuna at the beginning of 1:29 Lohse, following *DJD* I, inserts [*śare haššeba*]*tim*. On the evidence assembled in the present work, it should be [*ra'se haššeba*]*ṭim*, as the *śarim* are the second rank of lay leaders and the "heads of tribes" are the first rank.

11. K. G. Kuhn, "The Two Messiahs . . .", 55.

12. R. Leivestad ("Enthalten die Segenssprüche 1QSb eine Segnung des Hohen-priesters der messianischen Zeit?", *ST* 31 (1977), 137-145) denies that

1QSb contained a separate blessing on the high priest, but holds that 3:22 - 5:19 includes a blessing on him: "nur er kann 'ein Diadem fur das Allerheiligste' sein (iv, 28), nur zu ihm kann man von der 'Krone deines Hauptes' sprechen (iv, 3)" (p. 140).

13. Milik holds *(DJD* III, 181) that 1QS 1:1 - 3:12 could come from a separate liturgical document. Cf. also "Milkî-ṣedeq . . .", 135.

14. See H. Muszynski, *Fundament. Bild und Metapher in den Handschriften aus Qumran. Studie zur Vorgeschichte des ntl. Begriffs THEMELIOS.* AnBib 61. Rome: Biblical Institute, 1975.

15. *DJD* I, 117. The editors state that the reading is certain. Milik suggests a scribal error for *yolik.*

16. See p.98.

17. Milik, "Milkî-ṣedeq . . .", 127-30.

18. J. M. Baumgarten, "The Duodecimal Courts of Qumran, Revelation and the Sanhedrin", *JBL* 95 (1976), 59-78, p.63.

19. *DJD* V (Allegro). Baumgarten ("The Duodecimal Courts . . .", 61) accepts this reading.

20. J. Strugnell, "Notes en marge . . .", 196. Y. Yadin, "Some Notes on the Newly Published *Pesharim* of Isaiah", *IEJ* 9 (1959), 39-42.

21. Davies *(1QM, The War Scroll . . .*, 91): "There are no good grounds for connecting X-XIV as a unit to either II-IX or XV-XIX". He considers the possibility that 10-12 is a unit. On p.95 he demonstraꞈ that there are close links in form and vocabulary between 1QM 10:8b-16 and 1QH 1:1-37. His view that 10-12 contains a series of hymns is not inconsistent with our treatment: 10:1-8a is here treated as redactional.

22. See Jeremias, *Der Lehrer . . .*, ch.6.

23. Cf. Jeremias, *Der Lehrer . . .*, 88.

24. The pesharist has added to the biblical phrase "city of blood" an additional word *š-w-w* (=*š-w-'*), "vanity", giving "city of vanity in blood". K. Elliger (*Studien zum Habakuk-Kommentar . . .*, 210), Carmignac (*Textes de Qumrân*, II, p.112, n. 11) and Jeremias (*Der Lehrer . . .*, 88) agree that the bloodshed here is not to be taken literally; it is in the biblical text, and the pesharist has not taken up the point but dealt only with false doctrine.

25. The symbolic meaning for "bloodshed" appears to have been extended as far as using "put to death" for "expel from the community". This sense would be more appropriate in CD 12:2-4, in view of the fact that the laws are for Jews living under Gentile rule. "Every man who is in the power of the spirits of Belial so as to speak rebellion, shall be judged according to the law for a medium or a wizard (i.e., put to death, Lev 20:27). But everyone who errs so as to profane the sabbath and the feasts shall not be put to death (against Ex 35-2, Num 15-32-36), for it is for the sons of men to keep it" (see ch. VI, note 43). Cf. also CD 9:16-17: some community offences are *děbar mawet,* "a matter of death", and CD 10:1.

26. Murphy-O'Connor, "The Essenes . . ., 228.

27. Jeremias, *Der Lehrer* . . ., ch. 3.

28. Jeremias (*Der Lehrer* . . ., 89) includes also Men of War, *'anŝe hammilḥamâ*) of CD 20:14, but see p.192.

29. Murphy-O'Connor ("Genèse Littéraire . . .", 536) treats 5:13b-15a as an interpolation. Pouilly, however (*La Règle* . . ., 45-46) defends the unity of 13-20. See also J. Becker, *Das Heil Gottes* (Göttingen, 1964), p.42.

30. See ch. I, note 7.

31. Milik points out ("Milki-ṣedeq . . .", 110) that 4Q*180* and 4Q*181*, belonging together, were entitled *peŝer 'al haqqeṣim, "Peŝer* on the Periods" (*180* 1:1). 4Q*181* fr.2:3 speaks of "seventy weeks" (Allegro, incorrectly, "he has sated with plenty"), and 11QMelch is to be linked with them as part of the same work, not only on the grounds of its jubilees chronology, but because of its theological vocabulary, exegetical procedures, and essential themes — the intervention of angels in human affairs and the importance of the priesthood. He regards all as parts or copies of a single work.

32. See ch. IX, note 14, on Murphy-O'Connor's view on the "Wall-builders".

33. *Ant.* 18§21; Philo, *Quod Omnis* §75.

34. For a close study of the double meanings and biblical allusions, see S. Holm-Nielsen, *Hodayot: Psalms from Qumran* (Copenhagen, Universitetsforlaget, 1960), 52-64.

35. K. G. Kuhn ("The Epistle to the Ephesians in the Light of the Qumran Texts", in J. Murphy-O'Connor, *Paul and Qumran* (London: Chapman, 1968) refers to *Test Levi* 14:5-8 as a possible source (p. 121).

36. Rabin, *The Zadokite Documents* (OUP, 1958, p.17, n.21).

37. Jeremias (*Der Lehrer* . . ., 102 n. 1, and 105) suggests that it was omitted because the writer had reason to introduce a third sin, "defiling their holy spirit," not found in the "nets". But this sin is shown by the correspondence of *miqdaŝ* (4:18) and *qodŝehem* (5:11) to be the third example of the sin of defilement.

38. Jeremias, *Der Lehrer* . . ., 97-104.

39. Jeremias (*Der Lehrer* . . ., 102), following Rabin (*Zadokite Documents* . . ., 19) takes *dam zôbah* (5:7) to mean the irregular flux of Lev 15:25, and connects the accusation with rabbinic disputes concerning the appearance of a flux in the eleven days following the seven days of Lev 15:19. But *zabâ* is used of the regular flux in Lev 15:19, and the introduction of *harô'â* ("who (fem.) sees") adds the element of a conscious breaking of the Law (cf. *kattôrâ*, 5:7) more appropriate to a breaking of the primary law.

40. B. E. Thiering, "The Biblical Source of Qumran Asceticism", *JBL* 93 (1974), 429-444.

41. *De Somniis* 2§271.

42. *Quod Omnis* §82. Cf. E. Bréhier, *Les idées philosophiques et religieuses de Philon d'Alexandrie* (Paris, 1925).

43. H. G. M. Williamson ("The Translation of 1QpHab 5:10", *RevQ* 9 (1977), 263-265) argues that the passage means "who were reduced to silence by the reprimand of the Teacher of Righteousness and (so) did not help him". This, however, disregards the Habakkuk lemma; "why do you . . . stay silent?".

44. The Roman domination, under Pompey, had divided the country into Judea (with Gazara and eastern Idumea), the southern districts of Samaria, most of Galilee, and a strip of Transjordan. Judea alone retained its boundaries from the Hasmonean period. (*Ant.* 14§§ 74-76, *J.W.* 1§§ 155-7.)

45. See p.51 for a more detailed discussion of 1QpHab 8:16 - 9:2.

46. See p.30 on the continuity of this phrase with "it reads".

47. *The Dead Sea Scrolls of St. Mark's Monastery*, Vol. II, Fascicle 2: Plates and Transcription of the Manual of Discipline. M. Burrows, J. C. Trever, W. H. Brownlee. (American Schools of Oriental Research, New Haven, 1951.)

48. Milik, RB 67 (1960), 413: "Dans S^e, sur la ligne correspondante, *byd mšh* est suivi immédiatement par ix 12ss".

49. See Vermes, *DSSE*, 23-24.

50. Yadin ("Some Notes on the Newly Published *Pesharim* of Isaiah") shows that "not lacking" in l.6 is based on Zeph 3:5. "It may therefore be suggested that this refers to the precious stones of the Urim and Thummim whose number is full, and thus their light is not inferior to the sun in its full light".

51. Davies (*1QM, The War Scroll* . . ., 113-121) holds that col. 1 is editorial, binding together 2-9 and 15-19. In note 54 a possible reason is given why 1 is from the early part of the Damascus sojourn. The information of 1:2 is, however, consistent with that of 15-19, the period of the Chief Priest and the Warrior.

52. Davies, *1QM, The War Scroll* . . ., 114-115.

53. Murphy-O'Connor ("An Essene Missionary Document?", 210-213) holds that *šabê yiśra'el* means "Returnees of Israel" in a physical sense: they were the Jews who had returned from Babylon to Palestine in the Maccabean period. Elsewhere in CD *šub* is used metaphorically, meaning "to repent" (2:5, 20:17). He argues that the meaning in CD 2:14-6:1 is different from elsewhere. In a later article ("A Literary Analysis of Damascus Document XIX, 33-XX,34") he points to *šabu* in 19:33-34 as having a literal meaning: "All the men who entered the New Covenant in the land of Damascus, and returned (*šabu*) and betrayed and departed from the Well of Living Waters". But it is here parallel with "betrayed", and has a metaphorical meaning. Cf. also 20:14-15, the schismatics "returned" after the Man of a Lie. All uses are accounted for by the meaning "change allegiance" (sometimes leading to a physical return).

54. "Desert of the Peoples" appears in 1QM 1:3 as the place from which the sons of light attack. It is also found in the medieval Karaite literature

(p.77). P. R. Davies (1QM, The War Scroll . . ., 115) holds that it means Babylon, on the basis of Ezek 20:35; this is in accordance with his Hasmonean hypothesis. If, according to the typology of Babylon in CD 7:10-14, it means Damascus, then col. 1 of 1QM comes from shortly after the beginning of the Damascus phase (see further p.183). This meaning is supported by the Karaite use: Damascus is the last known place of residence of the community, according to the present reconstruction. If this is the case, then "Desert of the Peo[ples]" should not be restored in 4QpIsaᵃ frs. 5-6: 2.

55. J. Strugnell ("Notes en marge . . .", 304, 237), following a suggestion of P. W. Skehan.

56. 4QDᵃ, see pp.45-6. (It includes a reference to the sons of Aaron. See further p.191).

57. Ten Years . . ., 151-2.

58. Cross supports the symbolical interpretation, with some hesitation, in Ancient Library . . ., 59, note 46. As Murphy-O'Connor points out ("An Essene Missionary Document . . .", 212-13), the evidence is entirely circumstantial: the fact that copies of CD were found in the caves. He himself holds that it is a symbol for Babylon; but his view is made untenable by CD 7:18-21: the priestly leader will come to Damascus, the place where the community now reside; in Murphy-O'Connor's view, they had left Babylon and were at Qumran.

59. Text: š-w-n-y-m. A resh is missing, as Lohse sees. Cf. also Klinzing, Umdeutung . . ., 77.

60. Murphy-O'Connor ("An Essene Missionary Document . . .", 208) holds that the sentence is an interpolation introduced at a later stage when it had become clear that the appeal to join the sect which he finds in 3:17 had failed.

61. Josephus 18§19 says that the Essenes continued to send offerings to the Jerusalem temple. Klinzing (Umdeutung . . ., 24) disputes this. Cross shows (Ancient Library . . ., 100) that offerings could still be sent without involvement in the cultus or accepting the legitimacy of the priesthood.

62. Carmignac ("Comparaison entre les manuscrits 'A' et 'B' du Document de Damas", RevQ 2 (1959-60), 53-67) holds that the 'B' text of this passage of CD is the earlier. Murphy-O'Connor, however ("Critique of the Princes of Judah", 200-205) establishes that the 'A'-text is earlier.

63. Y. Yadin, Masada (London: Weidenfeld & Nicholson, 1966), 168-179.

CHAPTER ELEVEN

The Historical Setting

The analysis of the organisational terms has been able to give a reconstruction into which a very large number of details from the sectarian writings has been fitted so as to give a self-consistent history. If an analogy may be permitted — one appropriate to the work of scrolls research — it is as if a sizable jig-saw puzzle has been completed, using very many pieces of data. The result is a unified picture which it would be hard to say was assembled by arbitrary procedures. On an assumption of consistency and specificity of terms, each piece has been found to fit a history whose different phases flow out of one another. No interpolations have been supposed.

The differences from previous reconstructions are due to the use of a different basis, resulting from the process of re-examination of the accepted basis, the conclusions giving a Hasmonean date for the Teacher. The new evidence of the Temple Scroll has also supplied the missing starting-point of the history.

At all stages of the history, as reconstructed in chapter X, the inspiring motive has been found to be the recovery of the religious leadership of the Jewish state. Following the expulsion of the Zadokite high priesthood by the Hasmoneans, an opportunity was seen to restore the high priestly dynasty to power and to bring the religious and political life of the people under the Essene viewpoint. This motive was pursued in the face of a series of threats arising from the Roman occupation of Palestine. Each phase, except the first, has been seen as a response to the presence of the Romans.

The history of the community was, then, played out on the public stage. It was no small isolated minority in retreat at Qumran, dealing in religious fantasies with little relation to reality. Despite the fantastic element in the plans for war of 1QM and the rigorous ethical-hierarchical structure, there was a real intention of political action on a large scale. In this case, we may look for some sign of the community in the histories of the fairly well documented period of the occupation of Qumran, 150 B.C. - 68 A.D.

The earliest phase, that of 11QT, has been seen to represent the formation of a hope that the temple would be recovered, with the help of God, but without catastrophic action, and with no sign of a plan for war. The next stage, that of 1QM 2-9, reflects an intrusion of the Romans, so as to make military action against them a necessary means of recovering control of the state. Twenty years later, the plan for war was transformed into a plan for proselytisation. During the next forty or more years, however, the history is marked by a series of reactions to a threat of the destruction of Jerusalem and the devastation of Palestine by the Romans. A plan for war against them was again formed. In the last phase, it was held to be certain that the city was about to fall.

In the period in question there were two main stages of Roman intrusion. The first was in 63 B.C., when Pompey arrived in Jerusalem and made the state a tributary of the Romans.[1] Despite his initial discourtesy in entering the Holy of Holies, the religious life of the state was left untouched.[2] A series of high priests, under Roman control, gave religious independence. From 37 B.C. to 6 A.D. the Herodian house gave even greater independence, leaving the people with no strong sense of Roman domination. In 6 A.D., following the removal of Archelaus, direct rule of the Roman procurators was imposed. The census of Quirinius was seen as a symbol of Roman domination, and excited a fierce reaction and an attempt at restoration of national independence by war. The motive of the Zealot party, which appeared at this point, was both religious and political. "They urged that in the case of success the Jews would have laid the foundation of prosperity, while if they failed to obtain any such boon, they would win honour and renown for their lofty aims, and that Heaven would be their zealous helper . . .".[3] According to Acts 5:37, the movement was scattered after it first appeared. Josephus, however, traces the war of 66-73 A.D. to their activity. "And so these men sowed the seed of every kind of misery, which so afflicted the nation that words are inadequate . . . Some were slain in civil strife . . . others were slain by the enemy in war."[4]

From about 30 A.D. there was a fear that the city of Jerusalem was going to be destroyed. According to rabbinic tradition,[5] Rabbi Zadok began fasting at this time in order to prevent its destruction. It fell forty years later.

The theme of war and fear of destruction of the city running through the Qumran history is sufficient to direct attention to the second stage of Roman intrusion, from 6 A.D. onwards, as its historical setting. There was no real reason, in the first stage, for such intense reactions to the Roman power to have occurred.

Prior to 6 A.D., and especially in the reign of Herod, the Jews had little reason to plan war against Rome. One of Herod's actions was the rebuilding of the temple according to a new plan. The date is given in *J.W.* 1§401 as his fifteenth year, 23-22 B.C., in *Ant.* 15§380 as his eighteenth year, 20-19 B.C. The event, and the date, were remembered as significant: cf. John 2:20: "The Jews . . . said: 'It has taken forty-six years to build this temple' ". Preceding the account of the rebuilding in *Ant.* 15, Josephus records that Herod favoured the Essenes, one of whom, Menahem, supported his kingship. "From that time on he continued to hold all Essenes in honour".[6]

Archaeological research at Qumran has shown that the water system was dislocated and remained in disrepair for some time, following a fire. The site was, apparently, abandoned during this period. De Vaux[7] holds that the fire is connected with the earthquake of 31 B.C., which also left its mark, and dates the abandonment during most of the reign of Herod, occupation being resumed at the beginning of the Christian era. E.-M. Laperrousaz[8] holds that the abandonment took place between 67 and 20 B.C., and a re-occupation was shortly followed by another abandonment.

De Vaux's dating gives support to a placing of the phase of 11QT in the reign of Herod the Great. In the early part of Herod's reign it was known that he favoured the Essenes and that he planned to rebuild the temple. Partly as a consequence of the earthquake and partly because they were now accepted at court, the Essenes left their retreat. They formed the hope of persuading Herod to re-establish the Zakodite high priesthood in power. Supporting his intention of rebuilding the temple, they produced their own plans, in the form of a "lost" biblical book, to ensure that it would be built in an acceptable way. Herod, however, recognized that a Zadokite high priest would have popular support and be a rival to his power, so accepted neither their plans nor their high priest. They returned to Qumran in disappointment.

1QM 2-9 has been seen to represent the next stage in the history, when the Essenes formed an alliance with a group of northern laymen with whom they developed a plan for conquest by military means on a world scale. The community was called "the Plant-root". Their willingness to forego priestly supremacy and throw themselves into a project of war is accounted for by a sudden intensification of the Roman threat to the independence of national religious life.

The Zealot movement originated in the north, under the leadership of Judas, called a Galilean in *J.W.* 2§18 and Acts 5:37, a Gaulanite (from the east of the Sea of Galilee) in *Ant.* 18§3. Its religious aspect, noted above (pp.204-5) was suited to appeal to the Essene desire for a pure religious state. The finding of portions of the scrolls at Masada is evidence of a link between the Zealots and the Essenes of that time (73 A.D.). If the Plant-root were formed in the second Roman phase, as is suggested by the correspondence of 11QT with the events under Herod the Great, and the recurring theme of war, there is a correspondence with the Zealot uprising. The subsequent alliance between Essenes and Zealots is to be traced back to about 6 A.D., the first appearance of Zealotry. The loss of the native kingship and the direct imposition of Roman rule were felt to be such an acute threat to the Jewish religion and state that normally peaceable groups joined with the Galileans to plan war. Believing themselves to have God's support, they aimed to exterminate the Romans from their domains throughout the world, thereby conquering the world for Judaism.

In 1QpHab, after the time of the Teacher, who came twenty years after the Plant-root, the Roman armies are "marching across the plain . . . inspiring . . . fear and dread" (3:1, 4). "They sacrifice to their standards and worship their weapons of war" (6:3-5). This event corresponds very well to that in 37 A.D., when Vitellius, the Roman governor of Syria, marched through Palestine on his way to make war against Aretas, the king of Arabia. "Since he had started to lead his army through the land of Judaea, the Jews of the highest standing went to meet him and entreated him not to march through their land. For, they said, it was contrary to their tradition to allow images, of which there were many attached to the military standards, to be brought upon their soil".[9] The charge of "worshipping" their standards gives a reason for the fear of defilement of the holy land.

There appears to be good reason, literary and historical, for linking the phase of 11QT with Herod's rebuilding of the temple, the phase of 1QM 2-9 with the formation of the Zealot party, and the background of 1QpHab with the appearance of the armies of Vitellius. There is an exact fit in both content and order of the three stages. The fear of the destruction of Jerusalem, illustrated in writings after 1QpHab, would then be seen as a well-justified one, accounting for the final flight to Damascus of the priestly party; the city fell in 70 A.D.

The sole objective evidence against this conclusion is the palaeographical dating that has been given to some of the scrolls. As shown ch. IV, it is far from certain that those writings which have been thought to give a Hasmonean date for the Teacher do so in fact; they are not in the clearcut formal and semiformal series, but all belong to obscure classes of script. There remains, however, the problem of the earliest piece of the Temple Scroll, Rock. 43.366, which is middle Hasmonean and, as Yadin remarks,[10] is very like the script of 1QIsa[a] and 4QDeut[a]. According to our hypothesis, this work was composed about 20 B.C. (a date compatible with the early Herodian script of the main scroll).

Our hypothesis also requires an adjustment in Cross's dating of 1QM, which he holds to be early Herodian (30-1 B.C.), but which the present view would place some time after 37 A.D., when the work was completed. On p.47 a caution has been entered about the growing habit of regarding palaeographical dates as a fixed starting-point for historical study. The leading palaeographers themselves take historical evidence into account in conjunction with the datings.   They would accept that the dates of scripts must be extended by another two generations to allow for the possibility of a scribe trained in youth retaining the same hand into old age. This commonsense observation supplies a solution to the problem of 1QM, other early Herodian scripts, and also of Rock. 43.366, the anomalous script among the Herodian hands that copied the Temple Scroll. It cannot be said that its Hasmonean style precludes entirely the present hypothesis; such a hand may still have been used in 20 B.C.

The Teacher of Righteousness

It is our aim in this chapter simply to find a historical setting for the Qumran community under the Teacher of Righteousness, without developing

207

the consequences of placing it in its period. It will be apparent that further questions of very great interest are now emerging. The Teacher of Righteousness appeared twenty years after the formation of the Plant-root, to which a date has now been given: about 6 A.D. Moreover, the writer of CD 20:14, who held the destruction of the city to be imminent (pp.192-3), says that the date will be forty years after the death of the Teacher of Righteousness. Assuming that his expectation was correct, these indications place the Teacher between 26 and 30 A.D., in one of the most sensitive of all historical periods, that of the founder of Christianity. These few years are among the most thoroughly researched of all eras of history. Even at the level of simple identification to which we are confining ourselves here, it is not possible to give a figure like the Teacher these dates, without asking the further question: can he be identified with a known religious leader at that time?

The following facts may be selected from all that has been said in the foregoing concerning the Teacher of Righteousness. He was a preacher of an eschatological judgement by fire (p.69), and foresaw also the pouring out of the Spirit of holiness (pp.67-9). The wicked would be destroyed, and the davidic Messiah would be used as God's "axe" (p.143). He baptized (p.156) in the Wilderness of Judea (the area containing Qumran), teaching that Jewish identity did not give salvation (p.98). He was an ascetic (p.158), upholding a rigorous view of the Law (p.159). With the date supplied by the above conclusion, this selection of facts points in the direction of John the Baptist, who according to both the Synoptics and the Fourth Gospel appeared in A.D. 27-28.[11]

John has been the subject of a number of recent researches,[12] as it has been apparent from the time of the first discovery of the scrolls that they provided a general background to his mission. In order to ask the question concerning correspondence, it will be necessary to confine ourselves, in the first instance, to the unequivocal statements of the NT and of Josephus. It is agreed that the NT accounts of John are influenced by the motive of comparing him with Jesus, and considerable allowance has to be made for both omissions and additions, for the sake of drawing parallels and making judgement concerning superiority and inferiority. For example, W. Wink holds that the statement appearing only in Matt 3:2, that John preached the kingdom of heaven in the same words as Jesus, is "clearly editorial".[13] Matthew's motive, he holds, is to assimilate the preaching of John to that of Jesus: he "therefore redefines the central thrust of John's message: not baptism, but the kingdom of heaven".[14]

On the external matters that concern us here, the brief account of Josephus, whose genuineness is usually accepted,[15] is a better starting-point.

It is not necessary to press its details to gain some strong points of correspondence. The Teacher was engaged in religious and political activity aimed at recovering control of the religious life of the state. He was concerned to admit as many people as possible to his community before the shortly coming Future Time, and this included Diaspora Jews and proselytes. 4QpPs^a 4:27 notes that he had an "eloquent tongue". His arrest and death have been found to be connected with the presence of the militarist faction in his party (pp.163, 170), and there was some indication that it was at the hands of a northern government (p.163). John is presented by Josephus as a political influence, attracting large numbers by his preaching. "When others too joined the crowds about him, because they were aroused to the highest degree by his sermons, Herod became alarmed. Eloquence that had so great an effect on mankind might lead to some form of sedition."[16] His arrest and death at the hands of Herod (tetrarch of Galilee and Perea) are connected entirely with the political motive.

Josephus' account of John's baptism is that "they must not employ it to gain pardon for whatever sins they committed, but as a consecration of the body implying that the soul was already thoroughly cleansed by right behaviour".[17] This has been found (p.65) to correspond exactly to the Teacher's view of inward and outward purification.

The Q account of the preaching of John (Matt 3:7-12, Luke 3:7-9, 16-17) contains the themes of eschatological judgement, the loss of Jewish privilege ("God is able from these stones to raise up children to Abraham"); and God's "axe", that have been listed above among the doctrines of the Teacher. It is noteworthy that a disproportionate amount of the Q collection concerns John the Baptist, showing a special interest in him in this source.

The Teacher was of Zadokite descent. Luke notes that John the Baptist was of Zadokite descent on his father's side. Zechariah was "of the division of Abijah" (1:5), the eighth division of the Zadokite courses (1 Chr 24:10). John's mother was a daughter of Aaron, giving him pure priestly ancestry.

The statement in John 1:8 that John was "not the Light" shows, as W. Wink agrees,[18] that some followers of John thought that he was the Light. "The Light" was one of the central images of the Teacher's high priesthood (p.128).

The Teacher's name, *moreh hassedeq*, is, as Jeremias agrees,[19] a play on the two senses of *yarâ*. It means both "he who teaches righteousness" and "he who rains down righteousness". In the latter sense, it refers to the imagery of entry into the community: members were given bestowed righteousness at initiation, when they saw the "light of life" and were made symbolic priests (p.129). As high priest, the Teacher gave righteousness with the gift of the Spirit at full membership. His name meant "he who gives a spiritual baptism". The baptism with water was a levitical task (p.97), appropriate to the levitical Messiah of Israel, but after the schism the Teacher had, apparently, been forced to adopt all three leadership roles himself (p.156), and so was "he who baptizes" in both senses. There is, then, a possible correspondence in the names of the leader. Cf. the form *ho baptizōn* (Mark 6:14).

The lack of real names throughout the scrolls, and the use of pseudonyms — one of the main reasons for the difficulties in historical identification — may perhaps be due to a custom of changing names at initiation, reflected in the phrase "named men" for initiates (p.130); but there is no clear evidence of this.

It would appear that at the level of external detail and clearcut statements, a good case may be made out for an identification between the Teacher of Righteousness and John the Baptist.

But, on closer scrutiny of the NT text, the view meets serious resistances. Where is the evidence that John expected to be the priestly Messiah, the supreme leader of a highly structured community? Although according to Luke 3:18 he was a *mēbaśśer (euangelizōn)*, and according to Mark 1:6 and Matt 3:4 an Elijah, both images used for the priestly Messiah p.78), the Teacher's sequences *mēbaśśer-Elôhîm*, and Elijah-priestly Messiah, are not found for him

Signs of a priestly Messiahship role for John are not entirely absent. W. Wink,[20] on Luke 1-2, has taken up a suggestion first made by H. Schonfield,[21] and has developed the textual analyses of R. Laurentin[22] to consider the possibility that there existed a Christian Ebionite exegesis of Malachi, using a Qumran two-Messiahs doctrine, in which Jesus represents the Messiah of Israel and John the Messiah of Aaron. Luke in chs. 1-2 has used the material but included a polemic against it, in the interests of a higher Christology.

Wink follows Laurentin's[23] suggestion that the exegesis of Malachi in these chapters is making John the restorer of the covenant of Levi (Mal 2:6, 3:1, 3:23-24) and Jesus the Lord, who "comes suddenly to his temple" (Mal 3:1). Wink affirms[24] that "in Christian circles 'the Lord' when used of Jesus is equivalent to 'the messiah', that is, the davidic or kingly messiah".

He finds some strong points in favour of a presentation of John and Jesus as priestly and davidic counterparts. Jesus' role as davidic Messiah and king are, as he says, "nowhere more pronounced than in Lk 1-2". Cf. 1:27, "of the house of David", 1:32, "the throne of his father David", 2:4, "the city of David", 2:11, "city of David". He "helps Israel" (1:54), is "the consolation of Israel" (2:25), "the glory of Israel" (2:32), "set for the fall and rise of many in Israel" (2:34); cf. "Messiah of Israel". By contrast, John's priestliness is heavily emphasized; descended from priests on both sides, and a son of Zadok. John will be "in the spirit and power of Elijah" (1:17), "the great prophet-priest of old, who had kindled the fire of God on a water-soaked sacrifice and restored true offerings to Israel".[25]

But even more strikingly, there is a series of parallels drawn between John and Jesus which have the effect of presenting the two as "co-redeemers, co-deliverers, the dual instruments of God's salvation".[26] The annunciation of the birth of both is made to one parent by the angel Gabriel; the parent in each case is troubled, told not to fear, asks for a proof, and is given a sign. A song of blessing is uttered; the child will be "great". The birth, rejoicing, circumcision and naming of the child, accompanied by remarkable events; the further greeting and song of blessing; the child's growth, are all matched. Wink concludes that "a two-messiahs theory . . . provides an explanation for the remarkable parallelism between the accounts of Jesus and John".[27]

But Wink's view that it came from a Christian Ebionite tradition scarcely takes into account the fact that a two-Messiah theory would make the priestly Messiah the superior one, the davidic his subordinate. It is necessary to look beyond a Christian source for a tradition that John was a priestly Messiah. These two chapters do, however, supply evidence of the role for John.

Nor is the evidence entirely lacking that John led a structured community. In Acts 19:1-7 Paul in Ephesus meets a group of men, called "disciples", and asks them: "Did you receive the Holy Spirit when you believed?" They reply: "We have never even heard that there is a Holy Spirit" (in some papyri and D: "that certain people receive the Holy Spirit"). Paul asks them: "Into what then were you baptized?" Their reply is: "Into John's baptism". Paul then gives them baptism in the name of the Lord Jesus. "Into the baptism" of John *(eis to . . . baptisma)* implies more than

211

"with the baptism": they had entered *into* something. Käsemann[28] has made a thorough study of the passage, concluding that it shows the existence of a community of followers of John. Luke, for reasons of his own, has taken the account of their conversion and made them out to be originally "an odd species of Christian".[29]

It may be pointed out that the statement "we have never even heard that there is a Holy Spirit" or "that certain people receive the Holy Spirit" is consistent with the initiation doctrine of the Teacher of Righteousness, as applied to Diaspora Jews and proselytes. As they lived at too great a distance from the temple to attend it in the Future Time, they were given provisional membership, baptism, only, but not admitted to the higher grade and reception of the Spirit of holiness (pp.99-100). There are signs that the giving of the Spirit was one of the secrets of the community, not divulged until the higher grade was reached. It is not mentioned in the initiation document (1QS 1:1-3:12), although the water-washing is there dealt with. Josephus states[30] that at full initiation the Essenes were made to swear tremendous oaths to keep the community secrets.

To be able to point to some evidence for John's high priestly leadership of a community is not, however, to remove the resistances to an identification. There would still remain a very great deal to be done, to explain why the New Testament does not contain strong positive evidence on these central matters, but gives the impression that John was a solitary in the wilderness, pointing the way to another Messiah.

This means that it will not be possible to draw a conclusion on the question of the identification of the Teacher of Righteousness. It appears that there is a strong initial case for seeing him as John the Baptist, but, until the work of closer examination of the NT sources is done, the question must be left open.

The Schism

It has been found that shortly after the appearance of the Teacher a large number of his followers separated from him. They represented the northern, lay interests in his community, and broke away on the grounds of his re-introduction of priestly supremacy. The seceding party, led by the Teacher's second-in-command, a man of both davidic and levitical descent who was expected to become the Messiah of Israel, maintained the Teacher's levitical-lay organisation under the body of twenty-four elders, *mĕbaqqĕrim* (NT *episkopoi),* who included twelve tribal leaders (pp.126-7). They used the organisational terms *qahal* (NT *ekklēsia)* (p. 149) and *yaḥad* (NT *koinonia)* (p.149).[31] Their outlook was anti-ascetic, and they did not observe the ritual laws (pp.156-9). Although the northern sector had originally had a militarist policy, they maintained the Teacher's doctrine of spiritual warfare by proselytisation among Gentiles (p.159). Their leader, in order to regain the southern party and fulfil the original purpose of the community of winning the world for Judaism, came south and established his centre in Jerusalem, knowing that his action would lead to conflict with the Jerusalem high priesthood. As a result, he was crucified by a Roman ruler of Jerusalem who was given the pseudonym "the Young Lion of Wrath" (p.164). His followers remained in Jerusalem and it was later believed that they were in danger of destruction from the fall of the city (p.193). They were joined by priests, and by former community members from Damascus who had changed their point of view (pp.185-7). But the tribe of Benjamin, with its leader, after going over to the rival party at the schism, returned to the original community (p.176). Either the members of Benjamin or their successors were present at the mass suicide at Masada (pp.196-7).

If the identity of the Teacher of Righteousness with John the Baptist were established, these details would be sufficient to make a case for identifying the seceding party with the early Christian Church, which, as the NT acknowledges in all four Gospels and Acts, emerged in some way out of the movement of John the Baptist.

The question of the Teacher's identity has been left open, although there is a *prima facie* case. A conclusion cannot, therefore, be built on it. There are, moreover, even greater difficulties at first sight for the present question than in the case of John. Those that are immediately apparent are: there is no sign that Jesus inherited a structured community from John, or that there was any dispute on the question of priestly supremacy; and the combination of religious and political motives in the Qumran movement is not evident in the community of Jesus. Although the legitimacy of Jesus' high-priesthood is a NT issue (Heb 3:1, 7:1-19, it is not known that the question of Zadokite descent was crucial to it. There is no sign that Jesus was ever a secondary Messiah.

Yet the conclusions that have been drawn in this work make it necessary to put forward at least a provisional solution to the problems. So constant are the correspondences between the Teacher and John on the one hand, and the rival leader and Jesus on the other, that the possibility must be entertained that we have in the Qumran literature and the New Testament the two halves of the one history. Each has omitted a great deal, in the interests of its own doctrinal position. The movement of John the Baptist

213

had split into two parties, the greater majority accepting the leadership of Jesus. The disappointed minority group had understood the purposes of John in terms of a restoration of pure Judaism, and believed that the interpretation of Jesus, which took it well beyond Judaism, was a betrayal of John's intentions. Their writings express only the bitterness of defeat, through distortions and exaggerations. The New Testament, conscious of the originality of Jesus, and with reason to attribute to him the absolute authority that had been held by the high priestly leader, omitted all overt evidence that would show him to have derived his organisation and authority from another. As the early stages receded into the past, more of the facts could be admitted, accounting for the presence in Luke-Acts of the clues discusssed above. But at the same time the schism had ceased to be of importance or interest; the losing minority was too small, and the creative power of the Christian version so great, that to set out the full history of the stages of growth would have been to do an injustice to the genuinely new event that the Christian Church had become. Its origin in the preaching of John the Baptist was fully admitted in all the Gospels, and this was felt to be sufficient acknowledgement.

Such a possibility must surely be considered, on the evidence assembled here. But there are still major objections to be met, concerning the silence of the NT sources. Research into these problems must be conducted through a study of the nature and motives of the NT accounts, using all the tools that NT scholarship has made available. This is clearly a second project of far greater size than the present one. It will be necessary to leave this question open also, and to be content, for the moment, with the conclusion that has been drawn here, that the Teacher of Righteousness finds his proper setting in the intense political and religious movements of the second phase of the Roman occupation of Palestine.

NOTES

1. *Ant.* 14§73, *J.W.* 1§153.

2. Tacitus, *Hist.* 5§9.

3. *Ant.* 18§5. M. Hengel, *Die Zeloten, Untersuchungen zur jüdischen Freiheits-bewegung in der Zeit von Herodes I bis 70 N.Chr.* (Arbeiten zur Geschichte des Spätjudentums und Urchristentums, Leiden, 1961.)

4. *Ant.* 18§6,8.

5. TalBab *Gittin*, 56a; Midrash Rabbah on Lam 1:5§31. Cited in R. E. Brown, *The Gospel According to John* (London: Chapman, 1971), I, p.122.

6. *Ant.* 15§, 373-379, 378.

7. De Vaux, *Archaeology* . . ., 20-24.

8. E-M. Laperrousaz, *Qoumran*: *l'établissement es sénien des bords de la Mer Morte. Histoire et archéologie du site* (Paris: Picard, 1976); Remarques sur les circonstances qui ont entouré la destruction des bâtiments de Qumrân à la fin de la période 1B de leur occupation", *VT* 7 (1957), 337-49.

9. *Ant.* 18§§121-122.

10. *Měgillat-hammiqdaš*, I, 16-18.

11. Luke 3:1, the fifteenth year of Tiberius, October 27-28. See G. B. Caird, *Saint Luke* (London: Pelican, 1963), p. 71. R. E. Brown *(The Gospel* . . . I, 116) points out that John 2:20 gives the same date for the year of Jesus' appearance, if the date given in *Ant.* 15§380 for Herod's building of the temple is accepted.

12. H. Braun, *Qumran und das Neue Testament*, II, 1-10; D. Flusser, "The Baptism of John and the Dead Sea Sect"; R. Schütz, *Johannes der Täufer* (1967); J. A. T. Robinson, "The Baptism of John and the Qumran Community"; C. H. H. Scobie, *John the Baptist*, and "John the Baptist" in M. Black (ed.) *The Scrolls and Christianity;* O. Cullmann, "Secte de Qumran, Hellénistes des Actes . . .; M. Black, *The Gospel and the Scrolls*, 565-579, and *The Scrolls and Christian Origins*, 98-101; O. Betz, "Die Proselytentaufe der Qumransekte und die Taufe im Neuen Testament", *RevQ* 1 (1958), 212-234; J. Schmitt, "Le milieu baptiste de Jean le Pré- curseur", *RevScRel* 47 (1973), 391-407; C. Spicq, "L'Epître aux Hébreux: Apollos, Jean-Baptiste, les Hellénistes et Qumran", *RevQ* 1 (1958) 365-390; W. H. Brownlee, "John the Baptist in the New Light of the Ancient Scrolls", in K. Stendahl, *The Scrolls and the New Testament;* H. H. Rowley, "The Baptism of John and the Qumran Sect", in *New Testament Essays* (Manchester, 1959), 218-229.
   On John, without comparison with the scrolls: W. Wink, *John the Baptist in the Gospel Tradition* (C.U.P., 1968); E. Bammel, "The Baptist in Early Christian Tradition", *NTS* 18 (1971), 95-128. (See Wink for a bibliography.)

13. Wink, *John the Baptist* . . ., 53.

14. In this Wink follows W. Trilling, "Die Täufertradition bei Matthäus", *BZ* 3 (1959), 271-89.

15. *Ant.* 18§§116-119. See Loeb edition, p.81, note b.

16. *Ant.* 18§118. See Loeb edition, note f, on *stasis*

17. *Ant.* 18§117.

18. Wink, *John the Baptist* . . ., 88.

19. Jeremias, *Der Lehrer* . . ., 313.

20. Wink, *John the Baptist* . . ., 60-81.

21. H. J. Schonfield, *The Lost Book of the Nativity of John* (Edinburgh, 1930).

22. R. Laurentin, *Structure et Théologie de Luc I-II* (Paris Gabalda, 1964).

23. Laurentin, *Structure* . . ., 56-60.

24. Wink, *John the Baptist* . . . 76.

25. Wink, *John the Baptist* . . ., 74; see also 74, note 1.

26. Wink, *John the Baptist* . . ., 74.

27. Wink, *John the Baptist* . . ., 77.

28. E. Käsemann, "The Disciples of John the Baptist in Ephesus", in *Essays on New Testament Themes* (London: SCM, 1964).

29. Käsemann, "The Disciples . . ., 142-143.

30. J.W. 2§§139-142.

31. For a discussion of the use of these terms in the Jerusalem Christian Church, see J. A. Fitzmyer, "Jewish Christianity in Acts in the Light of the Qumran Scrolls", in *Essays on the Semitic Background of the New Testament*.

ABBREVIATIONS

QUMRAN LITERATURE

1QS	The Manual of Discipline
1QSa	The Messianic Rule
1QSb	The Blessings
1QH	Hymns of Thanksgiving, Hodayot
1QM	The War Scroll
CD	The Damascus Document
11QT	The Temple Scroll
1QpHab	The *pesher* (commentary) on Habakkuk from Cave 1
4QpNah	The *pesher* on Nahum from Cave 4
4QpPsª	The *pesher* on Psalm 37
4QTestim	Testimonia
4QPB	Patriarchal Blessings
4QFlor	Florilegium (= 4Q*174*)
11QMelch	Writing on Melchizedek
Rock. 43.3666	Rockefeller fragment of Temple Scroll
4QSᵉ	Fragment of the Manual of Discipline
4QDª	Fragment of the Damascus Document

JOURNALS, PUBLICATIONS

BASOR	*Bulletin of the American Schools of Oriental Research*
Bib	*Biblica*
CBQ	*Catholic Biblical Quarterly*
DJD I-V	*Discoveries in the Judaean Desert of Jordan*, vols. I-V, (Oxford: Clarendon Press, 1955-68)
DSSE	G. Vermes, *The Dead Sea Scrolls in English* (London: Pelican, 1962)
ETL	*Ephemerides Theologicae Lovanienses*
HR	*History of Religions*
IEJ	*Israel Exploration Journal*
JBL	*Journal of Biblical Literature*
JJS	*Journal of Jewish Studies*
JSS	*Journal of Semitic Studies*
NorTT	*Norsk Teologisk Tidsskrift*
NTS	*New Testament Studies*
OTS	*Oudtestamentische Studien*
PEQ	*Palestine Exploration Quarterly*
RB	*Revue Biblique*
RechBib	Recherches bibliques
RevQ	*Revue de Qumran*
RevScRel	*Revue des Sciences Religieuses*
ST	*Studia Theologica*
VT	*Vetus Testamentum*
WMANT	*Wissenschaftliche Monographien zum Alten und Neuen Testament*
ZAW	*Zeitschrift für die alttestamentliche Wissenschaft*

(References to the note containing the full bibliographical details of each author)

	P.	n.		P.	n.
Abba, R.	197	4		72	27
	197	4		89	56
Allegro, J. M.	31	8		202	62
	31	8	Cross, F. M.	20	4
Baillet, M.	103	29		32	19
Bammel, E.	215	12		48	1
Barthélemy, D.	71	1		48	3
Baumgarten, J. M.	32	32	Cothenet, E.	102	15
	199	18	Cullmann, O.	103	28
Becker, J.	200	29	Dagut, M. B.	20	9
Betz, O.	215	12	Davies, P. R.	72	14
Birnbaum, S. A.	48	25		72	14
Black, M.	73	38		72	19
	103	28	Davies, W. D.	74	46
Braun, H.	103	28	Delcor, M.	21	10
Bréhier, E.	201	42		102	15
Brekelmans, C. H. W.	71	1	Dequeker, L.	71	1
Brown, R. E.	71	1	Dupont-Sommer, A.	21	10
	89	58		31	8
	215	5	Elliger, K.	21	10
Brownlee, W. H.	57	2	Fitzmyer, J. A.	72	22
	73	32		88	17
	73	41		216	31
	215	12	Flusser, D.	73	37
Bruce, F. F.	74	51		103	27
Buchanan, G. W.	74	54	Frey, J-B.	48	22
Burgmann, H.	20	9	Gärtner, B.	72	17
Burrows, M.	7	5	Gnilka, J.	88	12
	201	47	Guilbert, P.	71	3
Caird, G. B.	215	11	Hanhart, R.	71	1
Cantineau, J.	48	8	Hanson, P. D.	74	45
Carmignac, J.	7	9	Hengel, M.	214	3
	20	9	Hoenig, S. B.	32	12
	20	9	Holm-Nielsen, S.	200	35
	57	1	Hübner, H.	71	8
	57	1	Huppenbauer, H. W.	103	36
			Jeremias, G.	7	7

	P.	n.
de Jonge, M.	72	20
Käsemann, E.	216	28
Klinzing, G.	72	18
Kuhn, H. W.	71	1
Kuhn, K. G.	73	38
	74	46
	88	11
	200	35
Lagrange, M. J.	88	31
Lamberigts, S.	71	1
Lapperrousaz, E-M.	215	8
Laurentin, R.	216	22
Laurin, R. B.	87	10
Leaney, A. R. C.	71	2
Leivestad, R.	198	12
Liebermann, S.	102	18
Lohmeyer, E.	89	49
Lohse, E.	21	29
	73	32
Maier, J.	71	1
Mansoor, M.	71	1
Milik, J. T.	48	17
	48	21
	48	28
	198	7
	73	32
Miller, M. P.	88	22
Muilenburg, J.	48	23
Murphy-O'Connor, J.	7	11
	111	14
	111	14
	111	14
	111	14
	111	14
	72	31
Muszynski, H.	199	14
Noth, M.	71	1
Nötscher, F.	71	1
von der Osten-Sacken, P.	72	14
van der Ploeg, J.	101	9
	57	2
	111	2

	P.	n.
Pouilly, J.	111	14
Priest, J. F.	102	15
Pryke, J.	74	49
Rabin, C.	101	10
	73	37
Rabinowitz, I.	58	74
	89	44
Ringgren, H.	89	58
Robinson, J. A. T.	73	38
Rowley, H. H.	32	21
	102	15
	215	12
Sabugal, S.	88	25
Schechter, S.	87	1
Schmitt, J.	215	12
Schonfield, H. J.	215	21
Schütz, R.	215	12
Scobie, C. H. H.	73	39
	73	39
Segal, M. H.	57	2
Spicq, C.	215	12
Starcky, J.	21	13
	48	7
	48	15
Stegemann, H.	20	3
Stendahl, K.	73	38
Strugnell, J.	48	6
	72	11
Sutcliffe, E. F.	102	22
	111	14
Talmon, S.	198	7
Thiering, B. E.	200	40
	21	14
	8	
	72	30
Trever, J. C.	38	fig. 1
Trilling, W.	215	14
de Vaux, R.	7	4
Vermes, G.	73	32
Wieder, N.	87	3
Wilcox, M.	32	36
Wildberger, H.	74	49

	P.	n.		P.	n.
Williamson, H. G. M.	201	43	Yadin, Y.	32	30
Wink, W.	215	12		72	15
Winston, D.	74	50		88	27
van der Woude, A. S.	72	20		111	1
	72	20		199	20
	87	8		202	63
				73	42
Wright, G. E.	48	1	Zeitlin, S.	88	35

INDEX OF REFERENCES TO QUMRAN LITERATURE

1QS
1:1-3:12   90, 109, 126, 129, 132, 199n., 212
1:1-7:25   166
1:7   130
1:11-12   140
1:11   73n., 130
1:13-15   129
1:14-15   173
1:16-3:12   72n., 90
2:4-10   138
2:12   19, 76
2:14   68
2:17   19
2:19-20   130
2:19-21   139
2:19   76, 90
2:19   76, 90
2:24   130
2:25   132
2:35   19
3:4-5   103n.
3:4-12   90
3:4   66, 93
3:6-8   128
3:6-9   65, 66, 67, 68, 72n.
3:7   73n., 83, 93, 95, 98, 129
3:13-4:14   109, 125, 126
3:17   84, 85
3:18-22   16
3:19   16
3:20   158
3:22   158
3:24   73n.
4:2   158
4:5   16, 130
4:6   130
4:7   86
4:11-14   69
4:13   73n.
4:15-26   125, 126
4:17   130
4:18-19   170, 192

4:18-22   65, 66
4:20   73n., 85
4:21   16, 69, 93
4:23,   82, 84
5:1-20   126, 153, 166, 167, 168, 169, 173, 174, 177
5:1-2   100, 149
5:2   149
5:2-3   5, 108
5:3-6   129
5:4-7   63
5:5   98
5:6   6, 99, 141, 144
5:10   73n., 149
5:11-14   149
5:13-14   149
5:13-15   200n.
5:13-20   200n.
5:13   93, 95, 101, 171
5:17   83
5:20-7:25   109, 126
5:20   125
5:21-22   127, 133, 140
5:21   127, 130
5:22   130, 133
5:23-24   133
6:2-3   134, 138
6:2-7   93
6:3-4   134
6:3   134
6:4-6   94
6:4   72n., 102n.
6:5-6   102n., 134, 136
6:6   94, 134
6:7   134
6:8-13   134
6:8   127, 134, 139
6:12   91, 137
6:13-23   91, 94, 96, 99
6:13   98, 130
6:14   135
6:16   93, 94, 171
6:18-19   132

221

6:20   94, 137, 141
6:22-23   94, 97, 132, 140
6:22   17, 62, 94, 130
6:25   92, 94, 171
7:2-3   128
7:3   92, 94, 171
7:16   92, 94, 171
7:18-20   134
7:18-25   102n.
7:18   68
7:19,171
7:20   93
7:23   68
7:25   93, 166
8:1-15   70, 109, 111n., 126, 166, 167, 173
8:1-2   167
8:1   111n., 166, 167, 169, 172
8:2-4   129
8:2   168
8:4-6   63
8-4   86
8:5-6   93, 141
8:5   55, 167, 168, 169
8:6-7   129
8:6   167, 168
8:9   167, 168, 172
8:10-11   167
8:10   172
8:11-12   169, 170
8:13-16   167
8:13   149, 166, 168, 169
8:14-15   169
8:15   94, 170
8:16-9:11   109, 126, 166, 171, 173
8:17   93, 94, 171
8:18   72n.
8:20-9:2   171, 172
8:24   93
9:2   166
9:3-6   63
9:3-11   166
9:3   172

9:5-11   173
9:6   141
9:7   5, 17, 108, 171, 173, 175
9:8-9   101n., 175
9:10   171, 174, 177, 195, 197
9:11   87n., 94, 135, 171, 174
9:12-26   109, 126, 149, 166, 167, 169
9:12   169, 189, 201n.
9:13   170
9:14   68, 158, 168, 170, 183, 184
9:16   68
9:17-18   16, 168
9:17-20   167
9:17   149
9:19-20   167, 168, 169
9:19   172
9:21   169
9:23   170
10:2   19
10:18   68, 85
10:19   68
11:2-3   129
11:6   82, 84
11:7-8   61
11:8   132, 139
11:9   82
11:10   82, 84
11:15   82, 84
11:16   82
11:17   72n
11:20-21   85
11:22   72n.
4QS^d
9:17-18   168
4QS^e
8:13   16, 168
8:15   166
9:14   168

1QSa
1:1   64, 125
1:2   126, 134
1:4-6   131

1:4   131
1:6-9   132
1:6   91, 98
1:8-9   135
1:8   64, 129
1:9-10   64
1:11   131
1:12-15   132
1:13   129
1:14-15   127, 132
1:15-16   133
1:15   129
1:19-20   64
1:19-22   97
1:21   62, 131
1:22-23   127
1:22-24   133
1:22-25   126
1:22   133, 135
1:23-24   126, 127
1:24   126, 127, 132
1:25   97, 126
1:27-2:3   132, 140
1:29-2:1   125, 127, 141
1:29   127, 129, 198n.
2:2   17
2:4-11   97, 131
2:4   82, 125
2:5-7   64
2:5   132
2:8   17
2:9-10   97
2:9   100, 125, 131
2:11-12   136
2:11-22   87n., 93, 127, 135, 152
2:11   17, 125, 130, 134
2:12   94, 128, 135
2:13   17, 127
2:14-17   152
2:14   93
2:15-16   137
2:15   125, 132
2:16   156

2:17-22   102n.
2:17   64
2:19-21   93, 127
2:19   94
2:20-21   93
2:22   135
2:25   125

1QSb
3:1-21   87n.
3:22-5:19   199n.
3:25   126
3:25-26   70
4:20-28   81, 141
4:23-26   70, 128
4:27   128
5:20-29   87n., 136
5:21   136

CD
1:1-2:1   194
1:1-2:13   109, 180, 196
1:1   196
1:5-11   2, 3, 4, 6, 54, 188, 194
1:8-10   146
1:10   146
1:13   16, 187
1:16   159
1:18-19   159
2:2-13   194
2:5-6   73n.
2:5   201n.
2:11-12   79
2:11   17
2:12   73n., 79, 99
2:14-3:12   187
2:14-4:12   190
2:14-6:1   16, 112n., 201n.
2:14-6:11   190
2:14-7:10, 109, 180
2:14-8:21   194
3:6   158
3:12-16   187

3:16   82, 187
3:17   84
3:19   63
3:20-4:4   188
3:20-4:10   183, 184
3:20   82
3:21-4:3   99
4:2-3   181
4:2   176, 181
4:3-4   182
4:3   183
4:5   62
4:11   13, 21n., 112n.
4:11   13, 21n., 112n.
4:12-5:19   112n., 157, 190
4:19   14, 112n., 151, 162
5:12   159
5:17   28
5:20-6:3   182
5:20-6:11   190
5:20   159
5:21-6:1   80
5:21   182
6:3-4   159, 190
6:3-5   188
6:3-10   185
6:3-11   187
6:4   56, 187
6:5   176, 181
6:6   14, 184, 185
6:7   185
6:9   187
6:11-7:6   112n.
6:11-7:9   185, 190
6:18   89n.
6:19   189
7:4-5   183
7:9-8:21   190
7:9   188, 192
7:10-14   149, 151, 181
7:10-21   109, 180, 186, 190, 192, 196
7:13   14
7:16   180

7:18-21   87n., 136, 180, 182, 202n.
7:21-8:21   109, 180
8:3-13   113n., 185
8:3-18   112n.
8:5-8   113n.
8:5   113n., 158
8:7   113n., 158
8:11   54, 56
8:12   112n., 151, 185
8:14-18   184
8:16   176, 181
8:18   185, 196
8:21   189
9:1-10:10   109, 180, 191
9:1   82, 89n.
9:9-10   195
9:16-17   199n.
9:16-23   137, 138
9:21   92, 94
9:22   138
9:23-10:1   195
9:23   92, 94
10:1   199n.
10:4   195
10:8   82
10:10-12:6   190
10:10-12:22   109, 180, 189, 191
11:16   82
11:17-21   190
11:21-22   190
12:2-4   89n.
12:4   82
12:6-11   181
12:6-18   190
12:15-16   141
12:16   82
12:20-22   190
12:21   189
12:22-14:22   109, 137, 180, 191
12:23   79
13:1-7   138
13:5-7   98
13:7-22   98

13:11-12   138
13:12   62
14:4-5   18, 94, 99, 191
14:4   139, 151
14:6-7   133
14:6   102n.
14:9   102n., 138
14:11-12   138
14:11   82
14:12-15   141
14:19   79, 80
15:1-15   109, 180, 191
15:15   97
15:7-15   91, 137, 138
16:1-18   109, 180, 191
19:6   192
19:7-15   109, 180, 191, 192, 196
19:10   79
19:12   162
19:25   82, 162
19:32-20:1   109, 180, 191, 196
19:33-34   191, 201n.
19:34   192
19:35   62
20:1-8   183
20:1-13   109, 180, 190
20:1   195
20:3   19
20:6   19
20:8-9   188
20:12   189
20:13-17   109, 180, 191, 196
20:14-15   14, 187, 201n.
20:14-17   191
20:14   193, 194, 195, 200n., 208
20:17-27   109, 180, 190
20:17   201n.
20-22-23   157
20:22-25   189
20:22   100, 149
20:23   158
20:24-25   100
20:26   19

20:27-34   109, 180, 195
20:27   21n.
20:28   195
20:31-32   195
20:32   195
4QD^a
101n.
4QD^e
101n.
6Q15
80

1QH
1:1-37   199n.
1:15   82
1:22   68
1:25   84
1:27   82
1:32   84
1:34   84
2:1-19   71n., 86
2:11   145
2:13   130, 158
2:17   85
2:21   145
2:25   82
2:31-39   71n.
3:1-18   71n.
3:7-18   153, 155, 176
3:9   85, 137
3:10   85
3:21-23   61
3:21   68
3:25-36   64, 69, 73n.
3:25   143
4:5-5:4   71n.
4:6   19
4:6-9   160
4:8-9   18, 181
4:8   86
4:9   89n.
4:15-16   19
4:15-18   159

4:22   89n.
4:23   86
4:27-32   68, 83
4:28   132
4:30   82, 84, 85
4:32   82
4:36   89n.
4:38   82

5:5-19   71n.
5:7   89n.
5:10   89n.
5:11   82
5:15   82
5:16   143
5:18   143
5:20-7:5   71n.
5:22   143
5:31   86, 89n.
5:32   19
5:36   68
6:4-5   145
6:5   149
6:11   82
6:13   61
6:18   73n.

6:24-35   70, 142
6:25   70
6:26   132
6:36   132
7:1   89n.
7:6-7   99
7:6-25   71n.
7:7   89n.
7:9   132
7:10   86
7:20-21   16
7:20   99

7:24-25   99, 128
7:24   19
7:32   86
7:34   149
8:4-40   71n.
8:10-11   86

8:16-25   89n.
8:16-27   99
8:16   21n., 99
8:36   19, 86
9:15   84, 85
9:25   19
9:26   19
10:3   82
11:6   82
11:10   84
11:11-12   61
11:12   68
11:20   84, 85
11:26-27   19
14:18   132
14:21   132
15:13   84
15:21   68, 84
17:13-14   69
17:15   83
17:27   82
18:14   81

1QM
1:2   54, 174, 175, 176, 201n.
1:3   77, 201n.
1:16   19
2:1-3   107, 126
2:1-6   77, 122, 124, 129, 197n.
2:1   77, 107, 124, 128
2:3   123, 124, 127, 131
2:4-6   128
2:5   107, 124
2:6-7   123, 198n.
2:6-14   116
2:6-16   194
2:6   197n.
2:7   126
2:9   124
2:11   100
3:2   124
3:3-4   123
3:4   116, 132, 198n.

3:5   116, 124
3:13-4:5   107, 117, 124
3:14   124
3:16   107, 124
4:1   107, 121
4:6   124
4:9   116
4:10   124
5:1   123, 128, 136
6:6   116, 124
7:3   107, 116, 124
7:5   170
7:9-9:9   144
9:7-9   144
10:1-8   199n.
10:7-18   172
10:8-16   199n.
10:8-13:16   110, 143
10:14   82
11:1-2   143
11:6-7   136
11:7-8   143
11:8   79
11:9   143
11:11-12   53, 83
11:13   143, 156
11:16   143
12:1-5   62, 130, 143
12:1   130
12:6-18   143
12:9   137
12:13   19
12:14-15   144
13:14   143
15:4   77, 172, 174
15:6   172
15:9   149
16:13   77, 172
17:1   86
18:5   172
18:10   19
19:1-8   172

11QT
15:17-18   119
15:18   103n.
16:15   121
16:16   121
16:18   121
19:11-25:10   107
21:4   119, 141
21:5   107, 120
22:02   121
22:4   118, 119
22:11-13   116
23:10   120
24:11   119
24:10-11   120
26:7   121
26:9   121
29:8-10   106
29:9   182
31:4   107, 121
39:6   121
39:7   107, 116, 124
39:12   116, 120
40:6   116
42:7-17   116
42:13-15   120, 121
42:14   121
42:15   121
43:12-13   99
44:13   118
44:14   107, 117, 118, 119
45:01-04   118
53:1-7   134
55:3   107
56:13   120
57:4-5   121
57:6-8   124
57:6   121
57:7   120
57:8   121, 131
57:9-10   121
57:11-13   107, 116, 121

227

57:11   120
57:12   119
57:14-15   120
58:1-15   107, 121
58:16   121
58:18-19   126
59:13-21   136
61:8   116, 118, 119
63:3   118, 119
64:6-7   28
64:6-13   28, 29, 164

4QpPs^a

1:19   18
2:3   14
2:6-8   14
2:12-14   13, 144
2:13-14   175
2:13   21n.
2:14   13
2:16-18   15
2:17-18   52, 145, 151, 163
2:17   4, 5, 31, 128
2:18   70, 163
2:19   53
2:22-23   14
3:1   86, 176
3:2   83
3:3-4   14
3:7-8   51
3:7   14, 15
3:11-12   14, 15
3:14-15   85
3:14   128, 137, 156
3:15   70
4:1-2   14, 145
4:7-8   13
4:7-9   163
4:7-10   52
4:8   15, 80, 145, 162, 163
4:10   53
4:11   14
4:13-14   13, 144

4:13   13
4:21   14
4:27   101, 209

1QpPs
frs.9-10:1-3   144
frs.9-10:4   53
4QpIsa^a
frs.5-6:2   202n.
frs.8-10   53, 143
frs.8-10:17   87n.
4QpIsa^b
2:6-7   160
4QpIsa^c
2:10-11   160
4QpIsa^d
17, 126, 127, 139, 141, 170
1   151
2   140
4   126
4QpHos^b
4, 22, 31
fr.2:2-3   150
fr.2:3   141, 151, 152
1QpMic
frs.8-10   11
frs.8-10:   5-6, 160

4QpNah

1:1-2:1   22
1:1   27, 53
1:3   26, 53, 54, 148
1:5-6   4
1:6-7   164
1:7   29, 30
1:8-9   28, 164
1:8-2:1   29
1:9-2:1   187
1:10-2:1   30
1:11-12   150, 164
1:11   160
2:2   53, 149, 151, 159, 160, 164, 186
2:4-5   26

2:4-6   190, 193
2:4   18, 53, 160
2:5   54, 149
2:8-9   186
2:8   151
2:9   99, 157
3:4-5   193
3:5   99, 149, 157, 158
3:7   152, 158
3:9   149
3:10   53
4:1   100, 149, 157
4:3-6   190
frs.1-2:3   53

1QpHab
2:3   98
2:5   170
2:6   145
2:11-13   73n.
3:1   171, 206
3:12   55
4:5   17
4:10   17
5:3   53
5:9-12   160, 162
5:9   11, 12
5:10   201n.
5:11   12
6:3-5   206
7:1-2   170
7:1-4   194
7:4-5   159
7:7   170
7:10   16
7:12   16, 170
7:17-8:3   175
8:1   13
8:2-12   9
8:2   86
8:3   85
8:7-9:12   12
8:8   12

8:9-10   8, 17
8:9-11   21n.
8:9   8, 16
8:11-12   150
8:11   9, 145
8:13-9:12   51, 164
8:16-9:2   201n.
9:1-2   9, 165
9:1   51, 53
9:4   5, 141, 160
9:5   150, 151, 152
9:6   170
9:7   52
9:8-9   9, 10, 15
9:9-12   9
9:10-11   51
9:10   165, 170
9:12-10:1   10
9:12-10:5   12
9:16-10:1   15
10:3-5   51
10:3   51
10:5-11:1   12
10:6-9   15
10:6-13   145
10:9-10   15
10:10   17, 151, 156
11:2-12:10   12
11:4-8   4, 8, 10, 18, 160
11:5-6   160, 161
11:8-14   158
11:12-15   10
11:12   162
11:16-12:5   144
12:1-2   10
12:2-6   51
12:4-5   99
12:4   97, 98, 132, 175
12:5   51, 165, 195
12:7-8   10
12:8-9   158
12:9-10   150
13:2-3   51

13:3-4   69

4QTestim
1-20   87n., 172
12-13   136
14   126, 174
21-30   9, 150, 152
25-26   10
25   10
29-30   10

4QPB
126, 136
3   87n.
6   137, 152

4Q180-181
149

4Q181
fr.1:2   150
fr.1:3-6   61
fr.2:3   200n.

11QMelch
4   64, 81
5   64
6   78
8   64
9-10   78, 80
10   64
15-24   78
16   80
18   79

1QDM (1Q22)
1:3   121
3:1   197n.
3:10   197n.

4QŠirŠabb
62, 72n.

4Q174 (4QFlor)
1:1-7   106, 182
1:6   82
1:8-9   183
1:11   87n., 180
1:12-13   180
1:17   181, 183
1:19   182
fr.4:4   186
frs.9-10:5   181

4Q177
frs.3-6:16   183
frs.5-6:7-9   181
frs.10-11:5   180, 182
frs. 10-11:7   183

4Q266
109, 180

4Q275
fr.3:3   138

4Q247
54

1Q34^bis
2:6   90

5Q13
fr.2:7   137

1QarGen
20:21-22   103n.

4QarP
89n.

2Q24ar
fr.4:16   121, 136

Absalom, House of 11, 160, 162-3, 174

Adam 81 ff.

Alcimus 25, 159.

Alexander Jannaeus 4, 7n., 20n., 23, 25, 27, 29.

Angels 61f., 87, 142.

Antiochus 23, 24, 25, 26, 29.

Archaeology of Qumran 1, 205.

Arrogant Man 12, 15.

Asceticism 158, 169.

Babylon 2, 181.

Baptism 65, 95, 97, 131, 167, 210, 211.

Benjamin, Tribe of 174, 175-6, 185, 187, 189.

Blood, eating 134, 158.

Calendar 124, 169-70.

Camps 116, 124, 125, 132, 138.

Chief Priest 122, 123, 128, 172, 174, 181.

Chronology 194-5.

Church, Christian 7.

Community (see *yaḥad*).

Council of the Community 97, 131f., 140f., 169.

Council, Holy 124, 125, 131.

Covenant, New 2, 13, 98, 180ff.

Crucifixion 23, 27, 28, 164, 194.

Damascus 7n., 152, 180ff.

Damascus Document 75
   Date 45ff.
   Compilation 190-1, 196.

Day of Atonement 8, 10, 18, 19, 78, 81, 162.

Day of Vengeance 170.

Death, Second 51-2, 165
   Attitude to 51, 86.

Demetrius I 24, 25, 26, 29.

Demetrius III 23, 24.

Diaspora Jews 99f., 158f., 189f.

Distribution of Terms 108-9.

'edâ 110, 121, 124, 125, 149, 154.

ekklēsia 121.

Elect Ones 168ff., 182-3.

Elijah 76ff., 89n.

'Elôhîm 62, 64, 80ff.

Ephesus 211.

Ephraim 4-5, 14, 17, 31, 53, 99, 149, 151f., 163, 181, 186, 193.

Eschatology 2, 60ff., 142ff., 209.

Essenes 1-2, 99, 147, 151, 159.

Fathers 121, 123-4, 125, 126, 127, 139.

Fifteen, The 168ff.

First Laws 174, 177-8, 195.

First Ones 110, 183ff., 195.

Flesh 65ff., 83, 95, 140, 178.

Forty Years 14, 194.

Future Time 60, 64, 67, 81, 86, 99, 101, 107, 132, 135, 170.

geber 73n., 85, 137, 156.

Gentiles 9, 26, 27, 99, 144, 164, 181.

Glory 83, 162.

Hasidim 8, 17, 63.

Hasmoneans 8, 20, 63, 163.

Hasmonean semiformal script 3, 35ff.

Heaven 62, 68.

Heavenly temple (*see* Temple).

Hellenization 156ff., 169.

Herod the Great 148, 204, 205.

Herodian formal script 3, 44.

Herodian semiformal script 39, 44, 45.

High priest 9, 17, 19, 50, 76ff., 121, 127-8, 142.

Holy House 141, 142, 154, 167, 173, 189.

Holy of Holies 141, 142, 148, 154, 167, 173-4, 189.

Holy Men 173.

House of Judah 13, 21n., 174, 175-6, 181, 185ff.

Hymns of the Teacher 61, 71n., 83, 107.

Initiation 83, 90ff.

Israel 17, 18, 29.

Jericho 9, 10, 151.

Jerusalem 10, 11, 18, 25, 26, 29, 54, 55, 77, 99, 160ff., 186, 192-3, 204.

   New Jerusalem 20, 70, 142, 149.

Jesus 77, 78, 213.
Jewish Birth 98, 209.
John the Baptist 65, 208ff.
Jonathan 1, 8, 10, 21n.
Judas the Essene 1.
Judas the Galilean 206.
Judas Maccabeus 9, 25.
Judges 132, 192.
Karaites 75ff.
Kĕneset 137, 152.
King 26, 79, 120, 123, 137, 142.
Kittim 3, 6, 10, 12, 26, 53f., 107, 144, 164.
Last Ones 188f., 195.
Last Period 170.
Last Priests 4-5, 31, 141, 150, 152, 189.
Law-interpreters 134-5.
Law-Interpreter, The 169, 176, 182, 187, 192, 197.
Lay equality 125, 146, 147, 155, 172.
Lay ministry 155, 168.
Leper 98, 138.
Levites, levitical priests 97, 116, 117ff., 123, 126, 133ff., 141, 142, 167, 174.
Lie, Man of a 10ff., 144, 149.
Lies, He Who Drips 10, 149.
Light 19, 126, 128, 129, 146, 209.
    Sons of Light 107, 129, 183.
Literary Evidence 5-6.
Living Waters 187, 191.
Manasseh 4-5, 14, 31, 53, 149, 151f., 163.
Manhood 83, 98.
Manual of Discipline
    Date 47
    Divisions 126, 166
    Marginal Marks 166.
Many, The 134, 138.
Masada 197.
Maśkîl 168, 169, 189-90.
Meal, communal 2, 92ff., 134, 135, 149, 153-4.
mĕbaqqer 91f., 137ff., 140-1.
mĕbaśśer 78ff., 210.

Melchizedek 64, 72n., 78ff., 88n.
Men of Scoffing 149.
Men of Iniquity 149, 153, 166.
Menahem 205.
Menelaus 8.
Menorah 19, 128.
Methodology 107ff., 111n.
Messiah
    of Aaron and Israel 191ff.
    of Israel 128, 135ff., 142, 152f, 156.
    Priestly 75ff., 177.
    of Righteousness 137, 140.
Name 16, 209, 210.
Named Men 17, 21n., 123-4, 125, 135.
Naśî' of the Congregation 123, 128.
nĕśî'îm 121, 124.
New Covenant, *see* Covenant
New Jerusalem, *see* Jerusalem
Nineveh 10, 25, 29, 53, 54.
Palaeography 3, 33ff., 207.
Palmyra 48n.
Palmyrene script 35ff.
paqîd 91, 102n., 131, 135, 138.
Parallelism 21n.
Peleg, House of 100, 149, 157, 189.
Pentecost 90, 92, 131.
Perfectly holy men 172f.
Pesharim 28
    Methods 10ff., 23, 27, 30, 194.
    Tenses 50ff.
Plant-root 2, 55, 146, 147, 153, 168, 182, 194, 206.
Pompey 26, 163, 204.
Poor ('ebyônîm) 110, 143.
Pregnant Woman 155-6.
Priesthood bestowed 162.
Priests 110, 116, 130, 133ff., 134, 186f.
    Aaronite 118, 122, 127, 151, 154, 175, 198n.
    Last, *see* Last
    Qumran 63, 87
    Symbolic 128f.
    Three 167.

Property 101n., 140, 150f., 159, 175, 178.
Prophet 79, 85, 172, 176.
Proselytes 98ff., 144, 156ff., 188, 189f.
Purity 92ff., 131.
qahal 110, 121, 124, 125, 131, 149, 158, 193.
Qumran (place) 1, 208, 160.
Remnant 187f.
Returnees 176, 184.
Righteousness, bestowed 129, 158.
Romans 3, 26, 27, 52, 55, 147f., 194.
Sacrifices 66, 97, 190.
Saints 124.
śarîm 121, 124, 125, 132, 154, 158, 168, 173, 177, 182, 184, 186, 192, 198n.
Ṣaw 10, 14, 149, 157, 162.
Schism 20, 148ff.
Schismatic party 101, 111.
Scoffing, Man(Men)of 10, 149
Second Priest 121, 122, 137.
Seekers-after-smooth-things 18, 24, 25, 29, 159, 164.
Semicursive script 46.
Serek 130, 133.
Servant, Suffering 86.
Simon Maccabeus 9, 10.
Simple 97, 99f., 131-2, 144, 156ff., 186, 189f., 193.
Sin 65, 67
sôd 132, 139, 167.
Son of Man 85f.
Sons of Light *see* Light.
šôtĕrîm 132.
Spirit of holiness 66f., 83, 90, 129, 131, 161, 167, 173, 211.
Star and Sceptre 136, 172, 177, 182, 185.
Syrian scribes 37, 45.
Taw 193.
Teacher of Righteousness 2, 3, 11, 12, 17, 21n., 31, 47, 50, 52, 70, 86, 89n., 99, 107, 125, 146, 147, 192, 194, 195
    Absence from records 2-3, 56

Arrest 163
Eloquence 101
Exile 18, 160f.
High priest 4, 8
Identity 207ff.
Temple 63, 99, 141, 142, 190
    Courts 116-7
    Future 70, 182
    Heavenly 60ff., 129-30.
Temple Scroll 1, 28, 60, 105f., 205-6.
Tenses *see Pesharim*
Testimonia (4QTestim) 171-2.
Third Leader 137.
Three hundred and ninety years 2, 54f., 194.
Torn flesh 30.
Truth 9, 16, 121, 130, 154, 168.
Twelve men 172.
Twenty-four elders 126, 134, 137, 139, 141, 152, 162.
Usage of hierarchical terms 93-4.
Violence 9, 13, 144f., 199n.
Visitation 60, 65, 66ff., 83, 107, 170, 192, 193.
Vitellius 206-7.
Volunteers 110, 130, 168.
Wall-builders 14, 148, 151, 157-8, 185.
Warfare 107, 116, 120, 124, 205
    Literal 146
    Spiritual 129f., 142ff., 146, 159, 187.
Warrior 137, 143, 172, 177, 182, 186.
War Scroll: Divisions 106f., 198n.
Water-washing 66ff., 90, 95.
Way, The 16, 169, 187.
Well, The 187, 188, 191, 194.
Wicked Priest 4, 8ff., 152ff., 163
    Death 8-9, 51
    Drunkenness 18, 158
    High priest 4.
Wilderness 77, 169.
Woes in Habakkuk 12.
Women 131, 158.
Wrath 148.

yahad 73n., 110, 125, 134, 139ff., 142, 149, 174, 175, 183, 195.

Yawan 26, 54.

yĕsôd 132, 133, 167, 173.

Young Lion of Wrath 4-5, 22ff., 164.

Zadok, Sons of 110, 126, 127, 146, 154, 168, 174, 183.

Zadokite high priest 4, 17, 60, 63, 141, 146, 151, 162, 163, 205-6.

zakar 137, 156, 176.

Zealots 197, 204ff.